SECURITY AND DEVELOPMENT
The Political Economy of Insurgency in Manipur

Security and Development

The Political Economy of Insurgency in Manipur

K. Gyanendra Singh

AKANSHA PUBLISHING HOUSE
NEW DELHI • GUWAHATI • VISAKHAPATNAM

AKANSHA PUBLISHING HOUSE
4649-B/21, Ansari Road
Darya Ganj, New Delhi - 110 002
Ph.: 23263193 / 9811582579 / 09435116718
Fax: 011-23263193
Email: ektabooks@yahoo.com
www.akanshapublishinghouse.com

Security and Development: The Political Economy of Insurgency in Manipur

First Published 2011
ISBN 978-81-8370-248-5

PRINTED IN INDIA

Published by Akansha Publishing House, New Delhi and Printed at Harmain Offset Press, Delhi.

Contents

Preface

The relationship between insurgency and economic development is the most debated issue today. There exists a two-way interlinkage between insurgency and economic development. But it is often alleged that economic underdevelopment is the outcome of insurgency. However, one needs to keep in mind that a weak material base often provides the base for the growth of insurgency.

The state of Manipur has been undergoing a serious turmoil since Independence. The initial democratic movement for statehood turned into militancy movement in the later years due to various factors like failure of the Indian state to accommodate the nationalist inspirations of Manipur in general and Meiteis in particular, economic under-development, losing credibility of the state power elites, corruption, etc. These militant movements have, over the years, degenerated and are now involved in various unwanted activities, sometimes in connivance with the state power elites. This has further robbed the state of her peaceful existence and development.

The ethnic composition of the state is another source of tension in Manipur. As these different ethnic groups often come into conflicting claims, accommodating the interest one group is possible only at the cost of other groups. This has resulted in a serious wave of ethnic explosion in the state.

The economy of Manipur is also undergoing a low growth syndrome. Agriculture is the mainstay of the economy of Manipur. However, the strategy of development which focused on social sectors has left the real sectors of the economy virtually handicapped. The peripheral location, non-availability of core natural resources, lack of infrastructural facilities leading to high transport cost, etc. have contributed to her industrial backwardness and left the state far behind her counterparts in the country. The low growth syndrome has resulted in high unemployment, which in turn has escalated the problem of militancy in the state

The present book, which is the outcome of my research work carried out in the Department of Humanities and Social Sciences, National Institute of Technology, Silchar for the award of the degree of Doctor of Philosophy in Arts (Economics), is a humble attempt to address the issues of development and insurgency in Manipur. As such the book is divided into six broad categories. The first chapter deals with the research problem, review of literature and methodology of the study. The second chapter deals with the growth of identity and nationalism among the major ethnic groups in the state, viz., Meitei, Naga and Kuki. In the third chapter, an attempt has been made to trace the dynamics of growth of economy of the state since feudal era upto the present period. In the fourth chapter, the dynamics of growth of militancy in Manipur has been studied. In the fifth chapter, an attempt has been made to analyze the economic and social costs of insurgency. The last chapter is the conclusion where an attempt has been made to put forward some policy implications to come out of the present crisis.

I am extremely indebted to my guide Dr. Gurudas Das, Associate Professor, Department of Humanities and Social Sciences, National Institute of Technology, Silchar, for his guidance and active supervision throughout the period of this research work. The present work would never have been completed without his guidance and support, both morally and financially. His comments, criticisms and words of encouragement helped me immensely in completing the present study. No words or phrase can ever describe his help and support throughout my career as a student since my higher secondary days.

I am also thankful to all the faculty members in the Department of Humanities and Social Sciences, Dr. N. Bhupendro Singh, Dr. Ashim Kumar Das and Dr. Reena Sanasam, for their valuable advice and comments. I am also thankful to my fellow research scholars in the Department for their support and help.

My special thanks are also due to Dr. S. Kiran Singh, Dr. A. Koireng Singh, Dr. A. Shyamkishore Singh, Th. Amumacha Singh, H. Okendro Singh and N. Sony Devi of Manipur University for their help in carrying out my field survey and providing other logistics during my research work.

I am also thankful to all the persons whom I have interviewed and interacted during the course of my research work. Their views and comments have made this work more insightful.

I am also thankful to Jawaharlal Nehru Memorial Fund, Teen Murti House, New Delhi, for granting Doctoral Fellowship which has immensely helped me in completing the research work.

My sincere thanks also go to my beloved parents, sisters and brothers who have been all along supporting and encouraging, throughout my career. The pain and sacrifices they have undertaken while fulfilling my academic pursuits can never be repaid throughout my whole life. I am, forever, indebted to them.

Last, but not the least, I would like to thank the Almighty, under whose spiritual guidance I have existed till today.

K. Gyanendra Singh

Abbreviations

ADCC	=	Assembly Demand Co-ordination Committee
AFSPA	=	Armed Forces Special Powers Act, 1958
AMRTDMWU	=	All Manipur Road Transport Drivers and Motor Workers' Union
AMSU	=	All Manipur Students' Union
AMUCO	=	All Manipur United Clubs' Organisation
AMWJU	=	All Manipur Working Journalists' Union
ANSAM	=	All Naga Students' Association, Manipur
AR	=	Assam Rifles
ATSUM	=	All Tribal Students Union of Manipur
CHS	=	Commission on Human Security
CM	=	Chief Minister
DLP	=	Democratic Legislature Party
FGN	=	Federal Government of Nagaland

FPM	=	Federal Party of Manipur
GOI	=	Government of India
GPRN	=	Government of People's Republic of Nagaland
IBRF	=	Indo-Burma Revolutionary Front
IFP	=	Imphal Free Press
INA	=	Indian National Army
INC	=	Indian National Congress
ISI	=	Inter-Services Intelligence
KCP	=	Kangleipak Communist Party
KIA	=	Kachin Independence Army
KLA	=	Kuki Liberation Army
KNA	=	Kuki National Assembly
KNA*	=	Kuki National Army
KNF	=	Kuki National Front
KNO	=	Kuki National Organisation
KNU	=	Khulmi National Union
KRA	=	Kuki Revolutionary Army
KVI	=	Khadi and Village Industry
KYKL	=	Kanglei Yawol Kanna Lup
LR	=	Land Reforms
MAICL	=	Manipur Agro Industries Corporation Ltd.
MANIDCO	=	Manipur Industrial Development Corporation Ltd.

MANITRON	=	Manipur Electronic Development Corporation Ltd.
MCL	=	Manipur Cement Ltd.
MCCL	=	Manipur Cycle Corporation Ltd.
MDU	=	Manipur Dramatic Union
MHHDC	=	Manipur Handloom and Handicrafts Development Corporation Ltd.
MHU	=	Manipur Hills Union
MKS	=	Manipur Krishak Sabha
MLR	=	Manipur Land Revenue
MNF	=	Mizo National Front
MNU	=	Manipur National Union
MPA	=	Manipur People's Army
MPCCI	=	Manipur Plantation Crops Corporation Ltd.
MPLF	=	Manipur People's Liberation Front
MPM	=	Manipur Praja Mandal
MPP	=	Manipur Peoples' Party
MPS	=	Manipur Praja Sangha
MR	=	Manipur Rifles
MSC	=	Manipur State Congress
MSC*	=	Meitei State Committee
MSCP	=	Manipur State Congress Party
MSMCL	=	Manipur Spinning Mills Corporation Ltd.
MSP	=	Manipur Socialist Party

NC	=	Naga Club
NDA	=	National Democratic Alliance
NDP	=	Net Domestic Product
NEFA	=	North Eastern Frontier Agency
NH	=	National Highway
NHD	=	Naga Hills District
NHDTC	=	Naga Hills District Tribal Council
NHMM	=	Nikhil Hindu Manipuri Mahasabha
NHTA	=	Naga Hills Tuensang Area
NMM	=	Nikhil Manipuri Mahasabha
NNC	=	Naga National Council
NNO	=	Naga National Organisation
NPC	=	Naga People's Convention
NSCN	=	National Socialist Council of Nagaland
NSDP	=	Net State Domestic Product
NWUM	=	Naga Women's Union, Manipur
ONK	=	Operation New Kangleipak
PANMYL	=	Pan Manipuri Youth League
PLA	=	People's Liberation Army (Eastern Region)
PLAC	=	People's Liberation Army of China
PR	=	President Rule
PRC	=	People's Republic of China
PSP	=	Praja Socialist Party
PSS	=	Praja Santi Sabha

PULF	=	People's United Liberation Front
RAW	=	Research and Analysis Wing
RIMS	=	Regional Institute of Medical Sciences
RGM	=	Revolutionary Government of Manipur
RJC	=	Revolutionary Joint Committee
RPF	=	Revolutionary People's Front
SCS	=	Special Category State
SIDO	=	Small Industries Development Organisation
SPF	=	Secular Progressive Front
SRC	=	State Reorganization Commission
TNV	=	Tripura National Volunteers
UCM	=	United Committee Manipur
UK	=	United Kingdom
UKLF	=	United Kuki Liberation Front
ULFA	=	United Liberation Front of Asom
ULP	=	United Legislators' Party
UN	=	United Nations
UNCM	=	United Naga Council, Manipur
UNLF	=	United National Liberation Front
UPA	=	United Progressive Alliance
WTO	=	World Trade Organization
ZRA	=	Zomi Revolutionary Army
ZRO	=	Zomi Revolutionary Organisation

Glossary

Atiya Guru Sidhaba = Sky the immortal guru (*atiya* = sky; *sidaba* = immortal)

Chahi Taret Khuntakpa = Seven Years Devastation (*chahi* = year; *taret* = seven; *khuntakpa* = devastated)

Chandan Senkhai = fee collected for the mark on the forehead (*chandan* = substance used for the mark in the forehead; *senkhai* = fee or contribution)

Chawkidar = watchman

Cheithaba = counting using stick (*chei* = stick; *thaba* = put down)

Kangleipak = old name of Manipur

Kei = granary

Keirakpa = keeper of granary

Khong = canal

Khullakpa = village chief (khul = village; lakpa = chief)

Lakpa = chief official in charge

Lallup = group of male subjects of the kingdom for the service to the country both military and non-military without remuneration for 10 days out of 40 days

Lambu = persons used for communication with the hill tribes during the British administration of the hill areas

Leimaren = homestead goddess

Loukok Eba = keeper of land records

Lourungpurel = official in charge of revenue department

Luplakpa = in charge of a group

Maiba = a person who perform the dual duties of a priest and doctor

Mangba-Sengba = outcast or excommunicate (*mangba*) – purified (*sengba*)

Mantri = minister

Nupi Lan = women's war (*nupi* = women; *lan* = war)

Pana = administrative division

Pangal = muslim

Pari = unit of measuring agricultural land; one pari = 1 hectare or 2.5 acre

Phunan Selungba = an official who looked after all the matters connecting with land

Pothang = an amalgamation of two words, *pot* = things; *thangba* = carry; the village labour had to keep up the roads and schools and they had to carry the things of the Manipuri officials from village to village when on tour

Puya = old Meitei religious books

Sanad = a testimonial or certificate from a high authority

Sanamahi = homestead god

Sangbai = a special basket for measuring paddy, rice, etc.; one *sangbai* is equivalent to 32 seers or (0.933 kg * 32 =) 29.86 kg.

Sel = currency

Senapati = general

Singlup = wood club (*sing* = wood; *lup* = group)

Soraren = god of rain

Takhen = old name of Tripura

Taothabi = a red and tailed paddy

Umang Lais = term used for Meitei gods
(*umang* = forest; *lai* = god)

Yubraj = the heir apparent of the Raja or crown prince

List of Tables

List of Figures

1
Introduction

The security of one person, one community and one nation rests on the decisions of many others – sometimes fortuitously, sometimes precariously [Commission on Human Security (CHS), 2003: 2]. Today's global position of a borderless world spotlights the many interlinkages in the security of all people.

The term 'security' is multi-dimensional. Its meaning, interpretation and scope are too vast, too diffused and diversified to be precisely defined. Security is inextricably linked to defining public and private values, to individual or collective identity and to safeguarding life, property and cultural values of every social group (Mishra, 2000: 1, 9).

The security debate has changed dramatically since the inception of state security in the 17th century. According to that traditional idea the state would monopolize the rights and means to protect its citizens and sustain order and peace. But in the 21st century the challenges to security have become more complex. The state remains the fundamental purveyor of security. Yet it often fails to fulfill its security obligations and at times has even become a source of threat to its own people (CHS, 2003: 2).

Security is facing new challenges. Today it covers international, regional, global and human perspectives. While global security includes a whole range of issues including management of environmental threats, economic threats, human rights, AIDS, narcotics and so on beyond conflictual interaction i.e., coercion, conflict and war to settle issues, international security recognizes that the security of one state is interconnected with others based on cooperative interaction (Reddy, 2001: 822-823). The same premise is also relevant for regional security arrangement.

State security which focused mainly on protecting the state – its boundaries, people, institutions and values and which were assumed to emanate from external forces have become a narrow view with various threats of today's world like environmental pollution, transnational terrorism, massive population movements and infectious diseases like HIV/AIDS. Moreover internal conflicts have overtaken interstate wars as the major threats to international peace and security. With the galloping pace of development, the gaps between rich and poor countries and between wealthy and destitute people have widened. The exclusion and deprivation of people from the benefits of development naturally contribute to the tensions, violence and conflict within countries (CHS, 2003: 5).

State security can be classified into two types, viz., external security and internal security. Whereas external security emanates from competition with other national elites in other state territories, internal security emanates from the competition with other elites within a particular state territory (Hettne, 1988: 91). With the end of cold war and coming of nuclear weapons era the threat to state security from external forces have subsided by degrees though it cannot be ignored totally. Today the threats emanating within the state have become the biggest obstacle towards maintaining the state security and more importantly towards realizing the goals of economic development.

India's security thought largely followed the classical nation-centric theory, which was confined to the issues of territorial inviolability and military preparedness against external threats – mostly physical and defensive in orientation. Its threat perception remained Pak-centric until 1970. It was only during the 1950s that China made the first incursion into Akshai Chin and constructed the strategic road linking mainland Tibet with Xianzang. Today, an eyeball-to-eyeball military confrontation prevails on border. But during the 1990s, India reverted to Pak-centrism. "Sixty-one (originally "fifty-four years" as referred in the book) years war in South Asia" is the current euphemism to describe the eyeball-to-eyeball confrontation with Pakistan (Reddy, 2001: 824-827).

Coupled with the threats from Pakistan and China is the internal threats that India has been facing since Independence. The communal partition at the midnight hour of August 15, 1947 led to bloody violence. It was followed by left extremism in Telangana (1948-51). Then a series of armed rebellions came into being with different aims and objectives. The Naga insurgency, Mizo insurgency, Meitei insurgency, left extremism in Naxalbari, linguistic riots in South, Tripura insurgency, Punjab terrorism, ULFA and Bodo in Assam, Jammu and Kashmir, LTTE, etc. (Reddy, 2001: 868-869).

Internal threats begin only when the armed phase of the struggle begins or violence transcends law and order. Its broader agenda includes a wide variety of politico-socio-economic-technological-security forces concerns besides all forms of governance, administration and psychological warfare. The internal security challenges can be categorized into different heads: secessionist uprisings, religious fanaticism, ideological impoverishment, supra and sub-regionalism out of identity crises and ethnocentrism, terrorism, and societal entropy due to demographic transitions, casteist factionalism, criminalization of politics and moral and physical corruption (Reddy, 2001: 863, 870).

India's approach to counter internal security challenges have been mostly Delhi-centric, episodic, micro-centred and law and order skewed. Such challenges were merely viewed as law and order problem and are dealt with armed forces. Imposition of President's Rule, declaring the affected states as Disturbed Areas and placing them under army control has been the strategic approach. It is this approach that led to the enactment of draconian anti-democratic laws in the Northeast and consequently employing security forces to crush the secessionist movements (Reddy, 2001: 858-859).

Northeastern Region

The Northeastern region, popularly known as the 'seven sisters', comprises the states of Arunachal Pradesh, Assam, Manipur, Meghalaya, Mizoram, Nagaland and Tripura. It is one of the most volatile areas in the Indian subcontinent. Connected tenuously to the rest of India by what is popularly known as 'the chicken-neck' a mere 21 km. wide Siliguri corridor, these states are vital to India's security. Yet, these states have suffered a state of insecurity from the time of independence.

The Northeastern region is surrounded by Bangladesh, Bhutan, China and Myanmar and inhabited by the social groups having close affinities with their counterparts across the border.

The region is hot-bed for violence, conflicts can be traced at different levels: between individual states and the centre, between state and society, between the states themselves and between social groups within the states. Elite group competition, ethnic assertions, and interethnic as well as intra ethnic conflict and competition have resulted in fratricidal wars within each state. While some of the movements seek redressal within the constitutional framework of the country, some others seek to attain their goals through extra-constitutional means. Both types of movements create security threats. While constitutional movements raise internal security, the extra-constitutional movements, often being linked with outside powers, create far more serious threat to countries' sovereignty and integrity. The social insecurity created out of the operation of various militant groups negatively impact upon the local economy. Economic decisions like production, investment, saving and capital formation – all are informed of the existing socio-political milieu. This is far truer when there is a social dichotomy between the enterprising community and the indigenous community, which lays claim over the social space. This dichotomy is omnipresent in all the social spaces across the northeastern region. The efforts towards ethnicizing the economic space, i.e., monopolizing the economic opportunities by a particular (often politically dominant) ethnic group have various forms of manifestations. One such form is the demand for complete secession, which is often presented under the disguise of the right to nations/for self-determination.

However, economic issues, although very important, is not always at the root of all secessionist demands. The issues of livelihood do not only guide the threat perceptions of a community. There are hosts of other issues that can also pose a threat to the life of the community. For example, unrestricted immigration may pose a threat to political power structure of the host community in democratic set up (as happened in case of Tripura). Apart from immigration, cultural invasion, differentiated value system, religion, language, etc., which a community values may also get threatened and community may seek redressal through secessions.

Manipur

Manipur lies in the northeastern frontier of India. It is a charming place encircled by nine hill ranges on all sides with a small and oval valley at the centre. The state splits up naturally into two tracts, viz., the hills and the dales. The state has 352 km. long international border with Burma (Myanmar) to the southeast and 502 km. long border with adjacent states of Nagaland on north, Cachar district of Assam on the west and Mizoram on the south and the southwest.

The genesis of insurgency in the Imphal valley goes back to the days when the ruler of Manipur signed the Standstill Agreement and the Instrument of Accession with India on August 11, 1947. The state was, then, merged with the Indian Union with the signing of Merger Agreement on September 21, 1949 which came into effect on October 15, 1949. Subsequently, Manipur was declared a province of the Chief Commissioner and was put under the category of Part 'C' State. In the initial years, the denial of statehood of Manipur spurred Meitei sub-nationalism and led to the formation of the militant wings committed to the formation of an 'independent socialist republic'. However, in 1956, Manipur became a Union Territory with Territorial Council which was upgraded to Territorial Assembly in 1963. It was in 1972 that Manipur became a full-fledged state.

Although Manipur had a long history of state formation, the denial of statehood had negatively impacted upon the peoples' psyche. People of Manipur felt the sense of deprivation while Nagas were offered statehood before them. The granting of statehood to the Nagas had sent a wrong signal to the other communities in northeast who were clamoring for the same demand. Communities interpreted the incident as without arm power nothing will come on the way. Perhaps this feeling has led to the formation of a number of insurgent groups in the region *a la* Naga National Council (NNC).

In November 24, 1964 some group of people organized the United National Liberation Front (UNLF) on the basis of Pan-Mongoloid concept with the aim to drive out foreigners (Indians) and liberate Manipur and its neighboring states from the Indian dominion. It forged links with Naga and

Mizo insurgents and even sought assistance from Pakistan. The root causes were real as well as psychological: feeling of distrust, relative deprivation, utter negligence by the central government, alienation, unemployment, growing pressure on land and growing community awareness.

The economy of Manipur still remains predominantly agricultural. It has virtually no industrial base. It has very limited scope for industrialization due to inadequate availability of mineral resources, paucity of infrastructural facilities, limited size of the local market, etc. The economy of Manipur has not changed fundamentally as well as positively to tackle the menace of the threatening size of surplus manpower resources.

Lack of economic opportunities of the ever growing 'reserve army' has led to large-scale social frustration. The competition for the limited opportunities has led to inter-ethnic conflicts which further widened social cleavages. The resentments against the outsiders have robbed the region of investments, which could have given fillip to economic development. Out-migration of people from business class and professions has sent a wrong signal to the investors. Development has been a major casualty of such anti-outsider movements.

The large-scale social frustration has strengthened the ideology of secession preached by various insurgent groups. Unemployed youths have joined the rank and file of these groups who often paint rosy picture about their future in independent Manipur. The resource mobilization by these groups for carrying out their operations and fund arms procurement activities has further robbed the local economy which desperately needs investment funds.

As these militant groups are well trained, better organized and have some credibility, the electoral political process often use them for electoral gains. The unholy alliance between the militant groups and parliamentary political parties and their leadership has further aggravated the problems of security and development.

The question of the role of the 'sons of the soil' is always entangled with the goals of development. Economic development as a goal is desired but it should be brought by, and directly beneficial to the sons of the soil. The nexus between politicians, bureaucrats and contractors is responsible for siphoning off the government funds and a part of these funds finds its way to the underground for financing the violent campaigns.

Manipur reflects a combination of high degree of social fragmentation, stagnating economy and insurgency-dominated activities. Even after so many years of independence, political and administrative reforms and efforts towards plan economic transition, political uncertainty has shown no sign of abatement. It is also a known fact that insurgency has come to stay in the state. The region is, thus, caught in a vicious cycle of insecurity and underdevelopment. Lack of security of life, property and business has resulted into the flight of capital, skill and talent from the region and thereby allowing underdevelopment to perpetuate. Again, the perpetuation of underdevelopment is generating outright frustration and a feeling of deprivation among the local youths leading to the growth of militant movements demanding separation and secession, which further worsen the security environment.

Manipur is one of the backward states of India. Its underdevelopment is the outcome of its peripheral location, non-availability of mineral resources, security threats, inadequate market access, high transport cost, etc. The proposed study seeks to investigate as to whether economic underdevelopment is the root cause behind the growth of militancy in the state or it plays a secondary role in exacerbating the problem of militancy. It seeks to find out the paradoxical trade-off between development and security. It will attempt to throw some light on the chicken-egg problem, i.e., whether underdevelopment is the cause of insecurity or insecurity is the cause of underdevelopment? How do the insurgent activities drawing upon the resources of the state? How these activities are impacting upon: a) the investment decisions, b) business confidence, c) economic growth, d) implementation of various development projects, e) utilization of development fund, f) provision of the social and community services like education and health which have both intrinsic and instrumental value for the formation of human capital, g) progress of industrial development, and h) functioning of various agencies and institutions in the state.

The study will also focus on the alternative options available for the reconciliation of various socio-political conflicts in the state by weighing the costs and benefits involved in such conflicts.

Review of Literature

Over the past years many writings have been published on economic development and security environment of the northeastern region. Most of the studies have focused on the region as a whole. Of course, a few writings have also brought the issues in Manipur into the focus. But still there is a dearth of literature on Manipur as far as our problem is concerned. These studies, although, are descriptive in nature, they offer deep insights and contesting perspectives which are, no doubt, of immense value.

Allen (2003, *Gazetteer of Naga Hills and Manipur*), Banerjee (1934, *The Eastern Frontier of British India*), Bhattacharyya (1963, *Gazetteer of Manipur*), Brown (2001, *Statistical Account of Manipur*), Dun (1981, *Gazetteer of Manipur*), Hodson (2007, *The Meitheis*), Hodson (2007, *The Naga Tribes of Manipur*), Johnstone (2002, *Manipur and*

Naga Hills), Mackenzie (1999, *The North East Frontier of India*), McCulloch (1980, *Valley of Manipur*) and Pemberton (1966, *Report on the Eastern Frontier of British India*) give an account of Manipur and people living therein. They give an account of the origin of the people inhabiting the state of Manipur and detail out the customs, traditions, laws, religion and economic conditions of the people.

Kabui (1991, *History of Manipur*, Vol. 1), Parratt (2005, *The Court Chronicle of the Kings of Manipur: The Cheitharon Kumpapa*), Sanajaoba (1988, *Manipur Past and Present*, Vol. 1), Singh (1987, *Introduction to Manipur*), Singh & Singh (1989, *Cheitharon Kumbaba*) and Singh (1992, *A Short History of Manipur*) deal with the ancient history of Manipur. It covers the period from 33 A.D. till the coming of the British in 1891. However, the chronicle records are available up to Maharaja Boddhachandra, the last king of Manipur before the merger in 1949.

Lal Dena (1990, *History of Modern Manipur*) and Singh (2002, *Colonialism to Democracy: A History of Modern Manipur*) deal with the modern history of Manipur from the time Burmese invasion till statehood.

Bhaumik (1996, *Insurgent Crossfire*), Dev (2009, *The Talking Guns: North East India*), Hazarika (1995, *Strangers of the Mist*), Nepram (2002, *South Asia's Fractured Frontier*), Nibedon (1981, *North East India: The Ethnic Explosion*), Pakem (1996 (ed.), *Insurgency in Northeast India*), Tarapot (1996, *Insurgency Movement in North East India*) and Verghese (2004, *India's Northeast Resurgent*) deal with the insurgency movement in northeast India in general.

Constantine (1981, *Manipur: Maid of the Mountains*), Gopalakrishnan & Thomas (2005, *Conflict to Reconstruction: Some Observations on Nagaland and Manipur*), Hemanta (2007, *Khengjoı Chingsangda*), Kshetri (2006, *The Emergence of Meitei Nationalism*), Parratt (J) (2005,

Wounded Land: Politics and Identity in Modern Manipur), Ranjit (2002, *Unrest in Manipur*), Singh (2005, *Revolutionary Movements in Manipur*), Singh (2008, *Ethnicity and Inter-Community Conflicts: A case of Kuki-Naga in Manipur*) and Tarapot (2005, *Bleeding Manipur*) deal with the insurgency and ethnic conflict in Manipur.

Singh (1989, *Hijam Irabot Singh and Political Movements in Manipur*), Singh (1992, *Social Movement in Manipur*), Singh (1998, *The Unquiet Valley*) and Singh (2006, *Nupi Lan*) deal with the social and political movements in Manipur during the colonial period.

Das (1998) has outlined an account of peripheral limits to economic development in the northeastern region which also appears to be true in case of Manipur.

Das (2002) has pointed out various dimensions of the impact of insurgency movement in an economy in qualitative terms, viz., resource drain, demoralized business confidence, flight of capital, unproductive expenditure, etc. In reference to the insurgency movement in Nagaland, he holds that insurgency is not the direct offshoot of underdevelopment but the latter creates a material base which sustains and strengthens the former.

Datta (2004) observed that the backwardness of the region and insurgency are interlinked, the lack of economic development had fostered discontent and violence and thus in turn has impeded development.

Phanjoubam (2001) has observed that insurgency and investment do not go together. Insurgency impacts upon both private and public investment decision. Private investment is shield away because of the sense of fear that insurgents may interfere directly through extortion, intimidation, etc. As the government's preference in an insurgency prone state like Manipur has been more towards buying guns and ammunition, raising counter-insurgency forces and managing the incidents of violence, neither could it focus on economic development nor could it mobilize resources for public investment.

Mahendra (2000) observed that a bandh costs Rs. 2 crore a day which is very costly for the economy of Manipur.

Rammohan (2002) is of the view that there has been a continual siphoning of developmental funds in Manipur. The insurgency has degenerated and proliferated into a number of ragtag groups and is now primarily, a widespread extortion racket, which has spread like a cancer into all facets of politics, administration and social life of the state.

Joshi (2002) identified inhospitable hilly terrain, lack of infrastructural development in the fields of transport and communication and power as serious hindrances to development in Manipur.

Dutta (1994) has observed that economic change requires supporting changes in the social sphere. It cannot be implanted without the social context.

Sachdeva (2001) has pointed out that in order to encourage private investment, the region has to become investor friendly. The policy maker has to focus on infrastructure, land, labour policies and security.

Sahni and George (2001) have pointed out that a thriving economy of extortion, smuggling, gunrunning, narcotic and an oligopolistic control over government contracts have become the essential feature of the terrorist infested economies of the northeastern region.

Sahni (2001) has pointed out that in northeast a wide variety of economic activities that were integral to the lives of this region – including cross border trade, use of variety of forest product, some collective rights over land use, etc. –

have suddenly been 'criminalized' forcing the otherwise law abiding citizens into a collusive relationship with militants.

Sinha (2001) has pointed out that insurgency in northeast flourishes because people have the feeling of separate identity on the basis of ethnicity, culture or history. This is compounded by a sense of neglect, exploitation and discrimination and economic backwardness. The key to the situation is to provide good, corruption-free governance and economic development.

Barpujari (1997) has observed that insurgencies and ethnic conflicts involving killings, kidnappings and extortions had hit-hard the regional economy and have brought the development works to a standstill. Not to speak of new investments, there had been a flight of capital from the region which is adversely affecting her economic growth.

Nepram (2004) has pointed out that the northeastern region is flooded with small arms and light weapons of all types which have made all sorts of war - ranging from secession to autonomy to self-defence - possible. Most of the arms and arms procurement routes originate from Cox's Bazaar in Bangladesh. A Manipuri gunrunner's route is from Myanmar to Sugnu and from Sugnu, the guns are taken to other parts of the state.

Rajmani and Pradan (1998) have listed an account of various social, economic and environmental factors which acts as constraints to the economic development of Manipur.

Stewart put forward three hypotheses regarding the connections between development and security both within developing countries and globally: that human security forms an important part of people's wellbeing and is therefore an objective of development; that lack of human security has adverse consequences on economic growth and poverty and thereby on development and that lack of development, or imbalanced development that involves sharp horizontal inequalities, is an important cause of conflict.

Collier (2004) observed that the relationship between civil war and failures in development is strong and goes in both directions: civil war powerfully retards development; and equally, failures in development substantially increase proneness to civil war. He also observed that the poorest countries are likely to be stuck in a 'conflict trap'—a cycle of war and economic decline.

World Bank (2002, 2003, 2005 and 2006) has put forward a framework for conflict analysis and identified various variables for analyzing the economic and social costs of conflict. It also put forward various policy options to come out of conflict trap.

Research Methodology

In order to enquire the historical dynamics of the growth of militancy in Manipur, political economy approach towards the study of social development has been adopted. While assessing the dynamics of economic development and its implications for the growth of militancy in the state, we have followed empirical approach. Secondary data published by various government departments, both central and the state, and development agencies have been used. Wherever possible data used in the study have been cross-verified. The simple technique of percentage analysis has been used for comparative assessment. While studying the impact of insurgency on the economic development, emphasis has been given on understanding the processes rather than quantifying the relations. An institutional approach has been followed while interpreting the linkages between insurgency and social and economic, and political agencies. A sample survey has been conducted in order to capture the people's perspectives on the various dimensions and linkages between insurgency and development in the state. Primary data generated in the process have been processed and tabulated in convenient manner for presentation.

As far as the conceptual categories are concerned, there exists a difference between militancy and insurgency. A militant movement turns into insurgency while it establishes links with outside foreign powers. The links with foreign powers may or may not continue for long. Looking at the Manipur experiences, while some groups could establish links with power across the border at one point of time, there are no perceptible evidences that those links still hold good. As a result, words like "militant group", "insurgent group", "underground"—all are used in the synonymous sense.

Similarly, social categories like "ethnic group", "ethno-national group", "ethnic community", all though bear a thin line of differences, but one category can assume the place of other with the growth of group solidarity and political consciousness within the group. As a result, we have chosen not to make finer distinctions between them, as social anthropologists would have like to, and have used them in synonymous sense.

2

Growth of Nationalism in Manipur

A study of the growth of nationalism in Manipur is important in understanding the evolution of the complex political situation in the state. Much of the ideology of the secessionist movements in Manipur is rested on the history. Historical accounts of the growth of ethnic identity, formation of the territorial boundary of the state, its incorporation into the Indian state – need to be read for understanding the diverse trends of ideas that have been at the root of socio-political disintegration of the state of Manipur. Unless the features of the ethno-national movements of Manipur are studied and compared to that of mainland Indian nationalism (read as the ideology of the Indian state), the root of the long drawn battle between them will remain beyond our cognition. Superficial diagnosis will then lead us nowhere and the vicious cycle of conflict between the militants and security forces will perpetuate in the foreseeable future. The dilemma that insecurity leads to underdevelopment or under-development leads to insecurity will continue to be debated in vain.

In this chapter we shall largely draw upon the historical materials in order to characterize the features of ethno-national (sub-national) movements in Manipur.

Growth of Meitei Identity

The people inhabiting Manipur can be grouped into four major groups, viz., the Meitei, the Naga, the Kuki and the Meitei Pangal (Meitei Muslim). The Meiteis are the dominant group and occupy the valley areas of the state. The Nagas and Kukis are the tribals who occupy the hill areas. The Meitei Pangals are a minority group who live in the valley.

Manipur has a unique history. According to the state Royal Chronicle '*Cheitharon Kumpapa*'[1] the state has a history of state formation right from 33 A.D. The first maker of Manipur according to the Chronicle is Nongda Lairen Pakhangba[2] (Parratt, 2005: 21; Singh & Singh, 1989: 1).

The history of the origin of the indigenous people of Manipur is, in fact, shrouded in mystery. There is a number of contesting hypotheses (Brown, Grierson, Hodgson, Hodson, McCulloch, Pemberton, Singh)[3] about the origin of the Meiteis. It is widely believed that like the other Mongoloid groups in the North Eastern Region, Meiteis also migrated from South West China. They defeated the earlier settlers like Poireiton and established themselves in the Imphal valley (Parratt, 2005: 2, 12, 22).

Meitei tradition indicates that the Manipur valley was occupied by several tribes, the principal of which were seven in number, viz., (i) the Ningthouja or Meitei, (ii) the Angom, (iii) the Khumal, (iv) the Moirang, (v) the Luwang, (vi) the Sarang-Leishangthem and (vii) the Khaba-Nganba. For a time the Khumal appeared to have been the most powerful and after its decline the Moirang became prominent. And ultimately the Ningthoujas or Meiteis subdued the whole and the name Meitei has become applicable to all the tribes (Allen,

2002: 11-12; Brown, 2001: 57; Dun, 1981: 13; Hodson, 2007: 5-6; Kabui, 1988: 12-15, 1991: 17-18; Kamei, 2008: 5-10; Manikchand, 1988: 145- 158; McCulloch, 1980: 4; Singh, 1992: 22).

The social dynamics of transformation of these clans into a single ethnonym Meitei is not recorded. However, historians attempted to construct the early history of the Meiteis based on scant information available in *Cheitharon Kumpapa* and other clan-based genealogies and manuscripts[4] of the different clans of the Meiteis.

Social Transition: From Clan to Tribe

The evolution of pristine states usually passes through three stages, viz., tribal polity, chiefdom and state (Kamei, 2008: 79). Manipur Valley, known as *Kangleipak*, was believed to be the habitat of innumerable tribes in the historical antiquity. Following the process of social evaluation and working of the process of fusion, these tribes/clans were regrouped into seven major clans as has already been mentioned. These tribes had their own principality and were independent of each other. A continuous struggle among these principalities to overpower one another was a common phenomenon until the emergence of the Ningthoujas or Meiteis as the supreme power. Tribal chiefs of the Ningthoujas, who were called as kings by their subjects, occupied the territory of Kangla, which played the pivotal role in the subsequent history of this country. Being located at the centre of the valley, Kangla had a strategic importance as far as the inter-clan relation is concerned. The early history of Manipur is the history of the inter-clan war centering around the Ningthoujas. Right from Pakhangba (33-153 A.D.), the first Ningthouja chief, to Ningthoukhomba (1432-1467 A.D.), throughout these long one thousand and five hundred years, the Meitei identity emerged following a process of inter-clan war and accommodation. Ningthouja or

Meitei chiefs subdued some clans through repeated expeditions[5] and endeared some others using the institution of marriage. Ningthouja chiefs practiced polygamy. They used to marry girls from other clans like Khuman, Angom, etc.[6] Ningthouja chiefs gradually accommodated the chiefs and powerful people from other clans. They were regularly consulted along with the important people from within the clan. This process eventually gave birth to the institution of nobility.

Although no historical account is available on the nature of land relations at this stage of social evolution, oblique evidences, like the introduction of the system of pana in relation to the division of land by Loiyumba[7] (1074-1121 A.D.), suggest that land was under the control of the chiefs (Kabui, 1991: 111). Commoners had to pay taxes in kind to the chief. This land-relations had matured further in due course of time leading to the firm establishment of feudal land relation. In fact, the right over the land by the chiefs and feudal lords became firmer as they became stronger politically and militarily.

The system of *lallup,* a unique system developed by the Ningthoujas and also perhaps by the other clans as well, a compulsory obligation of the male members of a particular clan to provide free services for the cause of the collective interest, had developed into its embryonic form. This system had been refined overtime and took a definite shape only after the transition of the society from tribalism to feudalism. We shall have occasion to refer to this unique social system later in this chapter.

A system of social division of labour was in the making. The chief had assigned different activities for different lineages.[8] Right from worshipping the gods to weaving of clothes - activities were assigned to different people having different family surnames. Even a particular activity had been subdivided into a number of categories and each category was assigned to a particular family surname.[9] Thus the clan-economy had elements of meticulous planning although embedded in larger socio-political formation. While role reversal is often observed in tribal communities perhaps due to the smaller size of the social space, it is, indeed, remarkable that the clan chiefs had adopted such elaborate functional division of labour in those days. With the evolution of the society, although these functional division of labour was supposed to be institutionalized, as had happened, say for example, among the Hindus, but due to the Vaishnavite revolution, which had completely re-orientated the Meitei society during the 18th century, it had lost its relevance.

The clan-economy was based on agriculture and forest. As the tradition goes, early settlers brought the seeds and art of agriculture while they had migrated to *Kangleipak* from the South West China (Kabui, 1991: 80; Singh, 1992: 15). The fertile valley soil and climate were conducive for agriculture. As plough was introduced in Manipur only after the arrival of the Muslim war captives, it appears that the technique of shifting cultivation was applied even for the wet rice cultivation that had developed in the valley. Besides agriculture, forests used to play a significant role in providing the sustenance. The forests were rich in animal lives and plant lives. Other economic activities mentioned were fishing, weaving, hunting and animal husbandry.

People used to worship the nature. They used to worship natural objects like fire, the sun and rain. *Soraren*, the god of rain and thunder, is regarded as the king of gods. The people also believed in the god of sky known as the *Atiya Guru Sidhaba*. A number of forest gods known as *Umang Lais* were also worshipped. Besides these, they used to worship the god of the homestead. It was widely believed that the god of homestead protected the family from evil spirits, diseases and theft (Singh, 1992: 26-30). *Sanamahi and Leimaren* are the two homestead gods which people worship from time immemorial. The worship of ancestors was also prevalent among the people. Each clan had their own ancestral god.[10] The objects of worship were very close to either the known aspects or unknown aspects of nature. The purpose of worshipping was to propitiate the entities either for favour or for protection.

Although the society was egalitarian to a large extent, a silver lining of social stratification was also in the offing. The chiefs enjoyed the highest social status followed by their kith and kin that formed the nobility. Maibas, the priest and doctor, also hold an important position in the society. Commoners remained at the bottom.

The Tribal-Feudal Continuum

The process of inter-clan war and accommodation reached to its culmination during the reign of Ningthoukhomba (1432-1467 A.D.) when Moirang, the last independent principality, was defeated and subjugated.[11] In the process of integration of the clans into a common tribe, the ethnonym of the Ningthoujas known as the Meiteis (Parratt, 2005: 12-13) was gradually adopted by others. Meitei chiefs extended their sphere of control over both the social and territorial spaces. With the accommodation of the clan chiefs in the court of the Meitei chiefs, who were virtually graduated to the position of king, the size of the nobility had expanded. The Meitei identity was consolidated as the king mobilized the people of different clans to invade the surrounding hills and the Kabaw valley. With the sharpening of the binary perception between 'we' and 'they' among the Meiteis and Non-Meiteis, the identity formation took a definite shape.

In the process of expansion of the territorial boundary of the kingdom of *Kangleipak* and the political supremacy of the kings, different groups of people were brought into the valley as war captives including the Shans, Muslims,

Tangkhul, Maring, Maram, Moyon, Kabui, Koireng and the Purum. Brahmins from the Mughal India particularly from Bengal also started arriving in Manipur. Thus, different identities were being integrated to enlarge the identity boundary of the Meitei.

With the end of inter-clan warfare, the Meitei kings began to expand their kingdom in the surrounding hills and neighbouring countries. Kiyamba (1467-1508 A.D.), the successor of Ningthoukhomba brought the Kabaw valley under the political control of Manipur and extended the eastern boundary of his kingdom to the Chindwin river. This led to the international recognition of the Meitei kingdom in upper Burma (Kabui, 1991: 196; Parratt, 2005: 38-39; Singh, 1992: 90; Singh & Singh, 1989: 19-20). A frequent feud between Burma and Meitei kingdom over the Kabaw valley continued in the years that followed. This struggle continued till the Burmese invasion of the Meitei kingdom for seven years in 1819 which will be referred later in this chapter. The neighbouring kingdom of Tripura was also defeated during the reign of Kabomba in 1533 A.D. and it was marked by digging of the Tripura canal (Takhen *Khong*) (Kabui, 1991: 203-204; Parratt, 2005: 49; Singh, 1992: 101; Singh & Singh, 1989: 24). The invasion of Kachari-Muslims in 1606 A.D. during the reign of Khagemba (1597-1652 A.D.) was resisted successfully and a large number of Muslim were brought to Imphal as war captives who later on integrated into the Meitei community (Kabui, 1991: 213-215; Parratt, 2005: 67; Singh, 1992: 112-113; Singh & Singh, 1989: 33), eventually leading to the formation of the present day Meitei Pangal community. Various expeditions were also carried out in the northern hills, inhabited by various tribal groups like Marams, Tangkhuls, Marings and Moyons, and western hills inhabited by the Kabuis, Koirengs and Purums. In fact the Meitei tribal kings had not brought these hill areas under their direct political control. At best a kind of transient-suzerainty[12] was established over these tribal groups who were otherwise fiercely independent in nature.

The king was the administrative head. He used to rule the kingdom through a number of local level *lakpas* (administrators). Imphal city area was divided into four sectors. One member from the royal family was assigned the job of a *lakpa* for each area (Kabui, 1991: 218). Other parts of the valley were administered through the local clan chiefs. Areas brought under suzerainty through war were administered through the local chiefs who acted as tributary heads. At the centre, various departments had been created to look after different activities and the members of royal family or the nobles of the king's court were entrusted to work to head such departments.[13]

The traditional clan-economy saw a new era with the coming of the Muslim war captives. They introduced the system of transplantation of paddy and the plough drawn by bullock and buffalo. In order to withstand the high water level and floods Khagemba introduced a new paddy *taothabi* (a red and tailed paddy) (Kabui, 1991: 219; Parratt, 2005: 77; Singh, 1992: 120; Singh & Singh, 1989: 39). Agriculture flourished with the annexation of the fertile Kabaw valley. New market sheds were established and the contacts with Ahoms, Tripuris and Burmese further strengthened trade and commerce. The revenue system was systematized with the improvement in agriculture. A currency called *Sel* was introduced. However, the payment of tax in kind by the land owners still continued. Farmers had to pay 60 pots (two baskets known as *sangbai*) per pari (1 hectare or 2.5 acre) to the king. The revenue officials (*Lourungpurel*) used to get their salary in kinds as well.[14] King also used to make land grants to the nobles and other officials in return to their services. A system of centralized storing facilities was developed by establishing *keis* (royal granaries) in different parts of the state to meet the requirements during natural calamities. The village chief was appointed as *keirakpa* (caretaker of the granary) and the villagers had to contribute to the royal granaries a share of their produce amounting to 12 pots per pari (Kabui, 1991: 218-219).

Besides agriculture, non-farm activities like weaving, pottery, blacksmithy, brassmaking, weapon making and gold washing were also developed during this period. Meitei craftsmen also learnt brick making, perhaps, from their Chinese counterparts.[15] Meitei craftsmen also mastered the art of working with copper, silver, wood and bamboo.

Meiteis were good at cultivation. Unlike the Khasis of present day Meghalaya or the Monpas of present day Arunachal Pradesh, they did not show much interest in trading. Nonetheless, some amount of distance trade used to take place between the Meiteis and the people in the neighbouring countries like Burma, Assam, China, Tripura and Cachar. The trade in elephants was controlled by the king himself. Elephants of Manipur appeared to have a good demand across the countries. These were primarily used in wars. Besides elephants, horses were also exported from Manipur. Meiteis had a good trading relation with the tribals in the surrounding hills.

The system of *lallup* was refined and strengthened further. It became a unique mechanism to provide military security of the kingdom. The kingdom of Manipur was neither very big nor very rich. It was considered to be uneconomic to raise a regular army to ensure territorial security of the kingdom. Hence *lallup* came in handy in mobilizing the people as soldiers in case of war. This system also ensured the supply of labour not only for royal works but also for the public activities undertaken for the welfare of the society. Except the women, old and children, it was mandatory to all the able bodied persons to participate in *lallup* (Johnstone, 2002: 110). Even the members of nobility, the influential *maibas* (priest) and the local chiefs were not spared from this system (McCulloch, 1980: 11-12).

The worship of the nature still continued but the period saw the coming of Hinduism. The construction of Vishnu Temple during the reign of Kyamba in Bishnupur marked the coming of Hinduism but no evidence is found about the conversion to Hinduism (Kabui, 1991: 200-202).

The most important development during this period was in the field of chronicle keeping and literature. Kyamba introduced the system of *Cheithaba* (counting of year using stick). This system later developed into Meitei calendar. Khagemba encouraged reading and writing and encouraged the scholars of his court to produce books (Kabui, 1991: 199, 224; Parratt, 2005: 40, 71; Singh & Singh, 1989: 20, 36).

From Tribe to Ethnic Group

The tribal kingdom of Manipur had experienced a qualitative change since the beginning of the 18th century. The wave of the Vaishnavite movement from Bengal swept over the Imphal valley resulting into a sudden transformation of the socio-economic formation in the valley from tribalism to ethnicity. Unlike Assam, where Vaishnavite movement of Sri Sankar Dev took a pretty long time to transform the tribal Ahoms into ethnic Assamese, Meiteis embraced the Vaishnavite faith without much resistance within a pretty short time which had brought a revolutionary social change.

The forty years rule of Pamheiba (1709-1748 A.D.), who is popularly known as Garibniwaz[16], had been the crucial turning point in the evolution of Meitei identity. Although Charairongba, the father of Garibniwaz, embraced Vaishnavism in 1704 (Kabui, 1991: 237; Parratt, 2005: 113; Singh & Singh, 1989: 68), he had not made much effort to convert his subjects. Unlike his father, Garibniwaz, following the assumption of power, made it a point to draw all his subjects within the ambit of this new enlightenment. Garibniwaz realized the importance of a philosophical framework which could explain the life beyond the mere physical existence. He was completely swayed over with the transition from nature worshipping to Vaishnavite variety of Hinduism.

With the arrival of Shanta Das, the religious guru of Garibniwaz, the process of sanskritisation gathered a new momentum. The king forbade the eating of meat and rearing of pigs and poultry was banned in the capital area. The Meitei religious books (*Puya*) were burnt[17] and even the tombs of former kings and queens were opened and cremated again. The king went to the extent of destruction of the temples of the traditional Meitei gods like forests gods (*Umanglais*). Myths were invented about the traditional festivals and religious believes and rituals in order to connect the Meiteis with the Hindu heritage. The Hindu life-world was superimposed on the traditional Meitei believe system. Hindu system of god and goddesses were synchronized with that of the Meiteis.[18] Meitei festivals were rechristened by way of labeling the names of Hindu festivals.[19] To rationalize the social system *a la* Hindus, the system of gotras was also introduced.[20] Even the evil practices of the Hindu society particularly prevalent in Bengal, like the practice of Sati, was also embraced, of course, fortunately only by a few segments like the members of the royal family and the Brahmins (Kabui, 1991: 258; Parratt, 2005: 143; Singh & Singh, 1989: 96). The influence of Vaishnavism became very strong and it was visible in the change of dress, food habit and even in the adoption of Bengali script for Meitei language (Kabui, 1991: 277). Perhaps it was during this period that the kingdom of *Kangleipak* was rechristened as Manipur. However, the cultural influence of Bengal and Vaishnavism could not only be found in the nomenclature of the kingdom, even people, including the members of the royal family, began to use Hinduised names. In fact, commoners of Manipur developed a hybrid culture accommodating some elements of Vaishnavism alongside the elements of traditional Meitei culture.

Garibniwaz practiced both Vaishnavism and militarism. Vaishnavite philosophy of love and worship could not detain him from expansion of his kingdom and waging war against the neighbouring countries. He fought several wars against the Burmese[21] and even penetrated to the Burman capital Ava. The rise of Manipur under Garibniwaz and the weakening of Burma under Toongoo dynasty coincided. His Burma campaign left a trail of severe cruelty and devastation perhaps due to the fact that he wanted to teach a lesson to Ava against the injustice done to the royal Meitei family.[22] It may not be out of place to note that invasion of Manipur by the Burmese forces led by Maha Bandula in early 19th century appeared to be the retaliation against the insult and humiliation inflicted by Garibniwaz during the first half of the 18th century. However, we shall come back to this point later.

In fact feudalism bloomed to its full and reached to the zenith during the rule of Garibniwaz. His constant war efforts had further solidified the Maitei society. In order to face the collective efforts of Burma and Tripura, he fought vehemently in both the fronts. He had developed very cordial relations with the Kabuis, Thangkuls, Marams, Kukis and other hill tribes residing in the surrounding hills and enrolled them in his army (Kabui, 1991: 246). His campaign against different hill tribes surrounding the valley, their political incorporation through the extension of *lallup* and their induction into the royal army had extended the effective boundary of the feudal Manipur beyond the Valley. Indeed, the outline of the present political boundary of Manipur emerged during this period.

The administration of the kingdom was reorganized in the line of Hindu system. The system of ministers known as the Mantris and the offices of Yubraj (crown prince) and Senapati (general) were introduced in the royal court (Kabui, 1991: 280). The administrative divisions in the capital were still headed by the royal family. With regards to the administration of the hill areas, the villages were administered under the control of *Khullakpa* assisted by *Luplakpa*. Earlier the heads of the hill villages were referred to as chiefs. The administration was further improved with the experiences from Bengal and Assam.

The system of *lallup* had further entrenched deep into the society. With the expansion of political influence over 'other' groups of people like the hill tribes, its reach had widened. As the feudal society was increasingly getting stratified, the upper echelon including the nobles, Brahmins, Vaishnavite gurus, chiefs were gradually exempted from *lallup* (Kabui, 1991: 278) and the burden of the beast fell on the ordinary man. Frequent war, expansion of the kingdom, rise in public activities had called for the intensive *lallup* services.

Besides *lallup*, another feudal custom called *pothang*, by which the villagers had to carry the luggages of the officials while they were on tour and pool their labour to maintain the village roads and common properties like schools, granaries, etc., was also getting strengthened. Although there is no reference available in the early historical works on the introduction of this custom, it appears that this system began around the middle of the 15th century with the transformation of the clan chief into country king. With the expansion of the kingdom and frequent wars with the neighbouring hills necessitated such a custom to facilitate the movement of the kings' army and officials.

The king was the ruler, law maker and judge. For administration of justice a two-tier judicial system had been developed, *Singlup* or wood-club at the village level and the Cheirap at the apex level. *Singlup* was like old Panchayats and headed by village headman and it was given powers to dispose of cases within their jurisdiction. A special court for Muslims was also established to try cases relating to Muslims. Besides these, there were two other courts established in the capital viz., Pacha and Military court. Pacha tried cases relating to women and military court was meant for soldiers. The Cheirap was the highest court and it tried both civil and criminal cases. The people can appeal to the Cheirap if they feel justice had not been done at the lower level courts (Bhattacharyya, 1963: 300; McCulloch, 1980: 19-20; Singh, 1987: 106-107; Singh, 1998: 9).

The feudal economy was firmly rooted in agriculture. Besides tax on agricultural production, land management had been greatly improved for mobilization of additional resources. Land records were prepared under the revenue department by *Loukok Eba* (recorder of field plots). The entry fee was 50 *shels* for one pari. Those who claimed fresh land were charged additional premium.[23] Of course, the agricultural tax continued to be the same, i.e., 60 pots per pari. Several coins, although lacked standardization, were issued and the process of monetization of the economy was in the progress. The non-farm activities also gained momentum. Bell metal industry, tannery, boat making and turnery were developed. With the widening of exposure with the neighbouring countries and particularly with Bengal, scope for long distance trade had also increased. The cultural transformation of the people had generated demand for culture-specific goods which were procured from Bengal.

Be that as it may, the power of the feudal system in Manipur began to decline from the beginning of the 19th century. While the rise of feudal power in Burma in the east and the British colonial power in the west were posing new challenges, internal strife among the members of the royal family for power and the immature handling[24] of the neighbouring powers by some of the princes ultimately led to the subjugation of this great Meitei civilization initially by Burma and then by the British colonial power.

The Feudal-Colonial Era

The period after Garibniwaz and Bhagyachandra was marked by the decline of the kingdom of Manipur. The successive rulers were weak and frequent feuds among the princes to dethrone one another were one of the prime reasons for the decline of the kingdom. The Meitei princes went to the extent of seeking help from their old enemy, Burma, to fight their own brothers. Moreover, the Burmese were bent upon avenging the humiliating defeats meted out to them during the reign of Garibniwaz. During this period the Burmese had grown very strong under the great general Maha Bandula and they were advancing to invade Manipur. The end result was the defeat of the kingdom in 1819.[25] Burmese ruled Manipur for seven years (1819-1826) through their puppet rulers. This period is known in the history of Manipur as *Chahi Taret Khuntakpa* (Seven Years Devatation). This was the darkest period in the history of Manipur. The torture and cruelties inflicted upon the inhabitants by the Burmese were unbearable. Many were taken to Burma as war captives and many fled to the nearby Cachar. Even king Marjit, who was instrumental behind the Burmese invasion had to take refuge at Cachar. Seven years of Burmese rule, thus, led to depopulation[26] of the Imphal valley. While majority of the male members of the Meitei society were either carried away or fled away, the women were only left to fend themselves, look after the child and the old. The supply of labour in Manipur's agro-forest based feudal economy severely fell short. Both production and consumption declined to a significant extent. Economic life was completely dislocated.

Like Manipur, internal strife among the Ahom princes had also played the catalytic role in bringing the Burmese in Assam.[27] Burmese also took the opportunity of conflict between the Cachar king and the Meitei princes to invade Cachar.[28] However, the western thrust and empire expansion of the rulers of Burma had been a cause of security concern for the eastern border of British India.[29] This concern had led to the first Anglo-Burmese war which led to the signing of the Treaty of Yandaboo[30] in 1826 and the withdrawal of Burmese forces from Assam, Manipur and Cachar.

Accordingly, Gambhir Singh, son of Bhagyachandra, who fought against the Burmese along with the British, was recognized as the 'Rajah' of Manipur. British had no territorial ambition in Manipur. Rather, the colonial government wanted Manipur to remain as an independent country as a buffer between Burma and British India *a la* Nepal, Bhutan and Sikkim along the Himalayas. A stable and strong Manipur was, thus, viewed to be of British interest.

Following the installation of Gambhir Singh in the throne as per the Treaty of Yandaboo in 1826 series of expeditions were carried out in the surrounding hills in order to subjugate the hill tribes and realize tributes from them for the restoration of the devastated economy. The western thrust of Manipur was extended to Jiribam, a small valley lying between Cachar and Manipur, which was included into the kingdom in the year 1833 and the Jiri river became the boundary line between Assam and Manipur (Aitchison, 1931: 196). While the kingdom expanded on the western front, it could not make any further advancement in the eastern side. In fact this gain was overshadowed by the loss of the Kabaw valley. The Kabaw valley was now in possession of the kingdom of Manipur but the Treaty of Yandaboo was silent on this issue. This has made way for future confusion between Manipur and Burma. In order to end further conflict and maintain a cordial relation with the Burmese, the British handed over the Kabaw valley to Burma by a treaty in 1834 and Manipur was compensated for the loss of the valley by granting 500 sicca rupees monthly or Rs. 6,000 per annum (Aitchison, 1931: 197; Mackenzie, 1999: 152; Sanajaoba, 1993: 18).

Although Manipur regained her independence but her strategic geo-political importance brought her under the surveillance of the British colonial government. Manipur levy[31] under the British officers stationed at Imphal till 1835 and then on its withdrawal the office of the Political Agent[32] had been created to look after the British interest in Manipur and to deal with the security concerns of the eastern frontier of British India.

The office of the Political Agent in Manipur, avowedly as subordinate to the office of the king, had drawn into the palace politics due to internal squabbles among the princes for power leading to the widening of the political space for the British to intervene in the internal affairs of Manipur. The power-centered palace politics had degenerated to such an extent that the stability of the country was threatened due to frequent coup and re-coup.[33] It was, indeed, an irony that while palace politics had been the source of political destabilization, the office of the Political Agent worked for its restoration. In the process, the office of the Political Agent became the real centre of power by early 1840s. Competition among the princes for getting the support of the British in one's favour had led to gradual acceptance of the recognition of the colonial government as the single most important yardstick for the claim of the throne. British took this opportunity to increasingly dictate terms to the rulers of Manipur. British high-handedness was once challenged in 1891[34] only to bring Manipur under direct control of the colonial government. Although Manipur was never formally annexed to British India, since 1891 it was virtually ruled by the British in the name of the king, as he was made completely dependent not only for the territorial security of the country but also for the political security of his office as well, till the lapse of the paramountcy in 1947.

The Anglo-Manipur War of 1891 subjected the office of the king conditional to the recognition by the British government. The king could remain in power as long as British want him. The succession to the throne along the line of primogeniture was made conditional to the recognition by the British. It was made obligatory for the king to obey all the 'orders' of the 'British Government' (Aitchison, 1931: 198; Sanajaoba, 1993: 309). Thus, Manipur had effectively lost its independence in 1891. The sovereignty of the Monarchy was no more in vague after the acceptance of the *Sanad* of 1891.

The *Sanad* was granted to a minor boy, Chura Chand Singh, who was only 5 years old, on September 18, 1891. He was the great grandson of Maharaja Nara Singh and the last of five brothers. This caused some resentment among the people of Manipur, especially among the Rajkumars (sons of Rajas) as he was appointed independently by breaking the traditional line of primogeniture. During his minority period, the whole administration was vested in the hands of the Superintendent of the State and the Political Agent, who of course was only one person with two separate posts and these posts were held by Major H. St. P. Maxwell. The Raja was handed over the administration of the state on May 15, 1907, when he attained the age of fifteen. But the Raja would be assisted by a Durbar in managing the affairs of the state in accordance with a 'Set of Rules' called the 'Rules for the Management of the Manipur State' sanctioned by the Government of India. The Raja would be the President of the Durbar and the post of Vice-president would be held by a gazetted officer of the Eastern Bengal and Assam Government (Singh, 1989: 1-9).

During the period between 1891 and 1907 Manipur was under the direct control of the British. A number of significant changes had been made during this period under the leadership of Maxwell, the Political Agent and the Superintendent of the State.

The land system underwent a major change. Under the feudal era the land belonged to the king and he distributed the land according to his wishes. The British introduced the Rayatwari system of land holding. Accordingly, a new patta system was introduced, according to which, anyone having a claim on land after 1892 was to obtain a patta from the government. These patta holders were given inheritable and transferable rights on their land. A uniform land tax of Rs. 5 per pari was realized.

British had widened the tax base and also extended the tax coverage. Besides land tax, the other sources of revenue were the fisheries, salt, forest, tea seed, law and justice, foreigners' tax and Kabaw valley compensation. A tax of Rs. 5 per annum was realized from every foreigner family settled in the state. Income tax was levied only on government salaried employees. Fishery and salt industry were important sources of revenue. A good sum was also realized from tea seed trade (Allen, 2002: 122-123; Singh, 1989: 4; Singh, 2002: 94-97).

British abolished the age-old tradition of *lallup* in April, 1892. Over the years the system of *lallup* had developed into an oppressive system for the poor. As noted earlier the Brahmins and other influential persons were exempted from this feudal service. The system of *lallup* was not codified and arbitrarily executed by the king. Under such circumstances the favourites of the king never attended to such service. The nobles and the rich people also started escaping by paying fines. As such the system had become an exploitative system for the poor. The system was replaced by a house tax of Rs. 2 per annum in the valley and Rs. 3 in the hills. The house tax in the valley was, however, replaced by a uniform homestead tax of Rs. 5 in 1900 due to irregularities and tax evasion (Singh, 1998: 50).

Besides *lallup*, British had also abolished *pothang* in June, 1913. As the custom was often misused by the nobles and had become a means of exploitation of the people in remote villages by the state official, there were a number of anti-*pothang*[35] revolts. British considered this custom to be derogatory and hence abolished it. Instead the land tax was increased from Rs. 5 to Rs. 5.15 per pari (Singh, 1998: 54).

Although Manipur was not formally annexed to British India, her economy was incorporated into the colonial framework. Forces of the colonial economy were brought in through the practice of free trade. Manipur being extremely underdeveloped compared to British India, the backwash effects of free trade had swayed her in no time. Except the fertile land, Manipur hardly had anything to boast off. In no time, the lucrative rice trade went into the hands of the comprador Marwaris who entered Manipur along with the British. The British commercial interest in rice trade of Manipur had threatened her food security and caused the historic *Nupi Lan* (women's war) in 1939 about which we shall talk later. Not only the idyllic self-sufficiency was broken, the traditional crafts and livelihoods also faced the colonial onslaughts. The traditional weaving, salt making, metal making and pottery were gradually washed out on the face of competition from goods brought by the Marwari businessmen [Parratt (J), 2005: 13].

British followed a dual policy in conducting the administration of Manipur. While the Imphal valley was governed in the name of the king involving the traditional nobles, hills were exclusively administered by the British through the *lambus*.[36] The Vice-president of the Durbar, a British officer, was directly responsible for the administration of the hills. King had virtually no say in the affairs of the hill administration (Devi, 2000: 171-172; Lal Dena, 1990: 80-82). In fact the integration of the people of the neighbouring hills with the people of the valley had been halted due to the British isolationist policy towards the hill tribes of Manipur. As the hill tribes were fiercely freedom loving people, British followed a policy of minimal administration and inculcation of royalty through proselytism. In fact, immediately after British took over the rein in Manipur in 1891, William Pettigrew,[37] a Baptist missionary, was invited to work among the Thangkuls in 1894 [Constantine, 1981: 246-247; Lal Dena, 1990: 105-107; Parratt (J), 2005: 61-62; Singh, 1991: 67]. While the isolationist policy was followed for the hill tribes vis-à-vis the Meiteis, the similar policy was also followed for the Meiteis vis-à-vis the mainland India. To insulate the strategic eastern border, British introduced the Inner Line and prohibited the free movements of the British subjects from the mainland. Indeed, British were largely successful in isolating Manipur from the political awakening that was taking place in the mainland India.

A regular police force was created in order to maintain law and order. At rural level a *Chawkidar* was appointed by the villagers subject to the approval of the Political Agent for every hundred houses. A state police force was stationed at Imphal. A military police was also raised in order to protect the frontier and prevent inter-tribal conflict among the hill tribes (Singh, 1989: 6; Singh, 1998: 41-42; Singh, 2002: 100-102).

A refined judicial system was introduced during the British period. The old age Cheirap and Muslim courts were retained. In villages, the *Singlups* were replaced by Panchayat courts. In the capital, Imphal, one Town Panchayat Court was established. The Durbar was, however, the highest court of appeal. There were also two British courts and it tried cases of the Europeans, British Indian subjects and hill tribes. However, the confirmation of the Chief

Commissioner of Assam was required for severe punishments like death sentence, transportation of life and imprisonment for more than seven years (Singh, 1989: 5-6; Singh, 1998: 40-41; Singh, 2002: 98-100).

British also introduced the formal education system in Manipur. In feudal Manipur, no institutional arrangement had developed for formal education. Education was imparted by the knowledgeable persons to those who desired for it on personal request. The kings and nobles had access to those people who could impart education to their wards. Mostly the Brahmins and Vaishnavite gurus used to impart education based on the religious texts. However, the first school in Manipur opened in 1872 by the acting Political Agent Capt. Nuttal could not stand for a long time (Brown, 2001: 93). In 1885 an English medium school was established at the initiative of Johnstone, the Political Agent. It is still functioning today under the name of Johnstone Higher Secondary School at Imphal. After the Anglo-Manipur War of 1891, the education system took a definite shape. In 1904, the state had one Middle English School, one Upper Primary school and 28 pathsalas. Although the number of attendants started increasing among the males over the years, there was no significant rise among the females (Allen, 2002: 128). Along with the spread of western education came the community consciousness. A section of people emerged as elites in Meitei society who gradually played the crucial role in Meitei national awakening.

At the fag end of the monarchy in Manipur, kings lost much of their authority and independence to the British. The role of the king was virtually restricted to the management of society while British handled the state revenue and other economic and business affairs. As a result, sources of revenue were dried up for the king. In fact, king's expenditure from the state exchequer was controlled by the British. King used to enjoy freedom only in case of the expenditure related to religious activities (Singh, 2006:140). The Maharaja also exercised a great deal of power in religious matters. He was the head of the Brahma Sabha,[38] a congregation of the Manipuri Brahmins. Along with this Sabha, the Maharaja collected unlawful levy from the common people and oppressed the poor and the downtrodden. The Brahmins, under the royal patronage, had a very strong hold in the society. Any religious rites, marriage ceremony, death ceremony, feasts and even laying foundation stone for any construction could not be performed without them. They had to be referred for any socio-religious aspect of life. As such they had exerted a strong influence over the common people and misused their position for earning money and exploiting the poor and the ignorant.

The case of *Mangba-Sengba* (outcast-purified) and *Chandan Senkhai* were two social evils of the society. The members of the Brahma Sabha used to declare people as *Mangba* (outcast) or *Sengba* (purified). Any person who criticizes the Sabha and disobeys their rules and regulations were excommunicated as *Mangba*. These ostracized people can become *Sengba* by paying a redemption fee. Under this system the hill tribes and the Europeans were considered as *Mangba* and they were denied entry into Meitei house. The practice of *Chandan Senkhai* was another evil through which a regular sum of money was collected from the commoners. According to this practice every Vaishnav had to put on a mark on the forehead with *tilak* and a fee of five annas per house was realized for it (Singh, 1989: 38).

The emerging elites had to fight against these practices. The siding of the king with the Brahmins had made him equally unpopular. In fact, the elites often sided with the British against the king in order to introduce social reforms. The political awakening among the Meiteis began against the monarchy. At times, people also sided with the monarchy to protest against the anti-people policies of the British.

However, no mature political leadership emerged by then to use the contradiction between the feudal and colonial interests for the benefit of the people.

Political Awakening and the Rise of Meitei Nationalism

Although the political renaissance in Manipur is supposed to have started with the establishment of the Nikhil Hindu Manipuri Mahasabha (NHMM) in 1934, the political mobilization of the masses actually began about 30 years before with the first *Nupi Lan* in 1904. The first (1904) and second (1939) *Nupi Lan* were directed against the British administration in Manipur. The first *Nupi Lan* might be seen as the feeble effort of the traditional nobles particularly the Rajkumars to mobilize the people against the colonial ruler. The sabotage[39] was believed to have been instigated by the Rajkumars, who were discontented a lot. They were against the decision of the British to nominate young Churachand as the heir. The new land tax introduced by the British was also a burden on them, as they were never required to pay tax before. They found it more and more difficult to pay taxes unless their hands were in cultivation, which compelled them to sublet their holdings at a reasonable rent. On the other hand the villagers no longer cultivated their lands on rack-renting terms as it was easier to take up new lands under the new patta system. They were all along disloyal to the British government which did not permit them to enslave and ill-treat the poorer inhabitants and when in jail they were treated at par with other convicts (Singh, 2006: 41-53; Singh, 1998: 75-81; Singh, 1990: 118-125, 2002: 109-118).

Although the anti-British movement, first of its kind, had to compromise[40] ultimately, it, however, had tremendous social implications. Firstly, the movement was led by the women while the male were the victims. It may be of some interest to digress a bit at this point to introspect as to how did the women have emerged as a store house of power in Meitei society.

The recorded history of the Meiteis is surprisingly silent on this issue. As has been referred earlier, every adult male was bound by the system of *lallup* and they were engaged as soldiers as Manipur was in the constant warfare with neighbouring powers. As a result, women had to shoulder additional responsibility to look after the children and elderly (Devi, 1988: 161). Moreover, Burmese occupation had depopulated Manipur as the male folks were either killed, carried away or ran away. It appears that since then women played the dominant role in family matter. The women took up vending as their profession which had been gradually institutionalized with the establishment of designated markets during the British rule.[41]

Women in marketplace were in regular contact with each other. They not only exchanged their goods but also shared ideas. In fact, their profession had made them the vanguard of the Meitei society (Devi, 2001: 115). The Meitei menfolk had no such institutions where they could mingle with each other and share their ideas. The Vaishnavite *mandaps*, the place of religious congregation, were used for assembly only occasionally. As a result, in a world where ideas were disseminated only through the word-of-mouth, physical meeting played the most crucial role. The marketplaces, thus, had been the germinator of ideas, medium of disseminations and place of action. This postulate, perhaps, explains as to why women played the leading role in political life of Manipur.

Another implication of the first *Nupi Lan* had been the emergence of the sense of unity. This was an incident where the interest of some of the Rajkumars coincided with the interest of the ordinary people. The revolt had tremendous potential to give birth anti-colonial freedom movement but failed to assume that character because of the inherent convergence of interests of the monarchy and the colonial British in Manipur.

Be that as it may, the first half of the 20th century had been the most rewarding for the people of Manipur. Political awakening coupled with cultural renaissance had revolutionized the age-old social thinking as the educated elites became increasingly aware of the happenings around the world and simultaneously started movements to create a niche for themselves. The all round movements of these elites had transformed the Meitei society from tradition to modernity. The king and the Rajkumars initially encouraged and played a crucial role in this socio-political transformation. The king himself was the first president of the NHMM established in 1934. Initially the NHMM acted as a socio-cultural body and wished to work for the betterment of the Manipuri society.[42] But in no time, the organization dropped the Hindu label and began to press for political demands. The Nikhil Manipuri Mahasabha (NMM) demanded for: (i) the creation of a Legislative Body, (ii) release of Rani Gaidinliu, (iii) keeping the hills under State Administration, (iv) dissolving the Brahma Sabha, (v) abolition of various socio-religious impositions (Singh, 1989: 75-77). The process of politicization received a tremendous boost following the second *Nupi Lan* that took place during 1939.

The second *Nupi Lan* may be seen as the revolt of the Meitei women against the colonial commercial interest of the British who allowed unrestricted export of rice from Manipur leading to the gradual building up of unprecedented food crisis for the people of the country. The increase in export[43] over the years had pushed up the domestic price[44] of rice and the Marwari mill owners were being benefited at the cost of ordinary people of Manipur. The increasing demand-supply gap and consequent persistent rise in price of rice had become a major concern of the ordinary people. By the end of 1939, the price of rice had become double the normal price.[45] In spite of growing peoples' concern, the administration failed to stop export of rice. The specter of famine was looming large while the Marwaris continued to export rice from Manipur. The burden of the situation fell directly on the shoulder of the women who had to arrange two square meals for their family. The women in the marketplace took up the cause and demanded immediate ban on rice export. From the State Durbar to rice mills, they rallied everywhere to prevent the impending food crisis. Unlike the first *Nupi Lan*, this time the women became victorious as they could force the administration to stop the export of rice (For details, Singh, 2006; Singh, 1990: 145-149, 1992: 70-92, 2002: 137-144).

The political fall out of the second *Nupi Lan* was very significant. The movement had cemented peoples' unity which had accelerated the formation of political party outside the NMM. Irabot, the social reformer cum politician, who played the pivotal role in the renaissance and political awakening of Manipur, *a la* Netaji Subhas Chandra Bose in India's freedom struggle, stood firmly behind the second *Nupi Lan* and guided it to the victory. He was a founder member of the NHMM and became the President of the NMM in 1937 and played the key role in directing the organization to launch anti-colonial as well as anti–feudal political movements. His quest for political freedom led him to form the Manipur Praja Sanmeloni in 1940 in order to mobilize the masses in support of the second *Nupi Lan* as the majority members of the NMM wanted to avoid confrontation with the administration on this issue. However, before the Manipur Praja Sanmeloni took off, Irabot was arrested and imprisoned for three years. While he was allowed to enter into Manipur in 1946, he established another party, viz., the Manipur Praja Mandal (MPM). Later on the Manipur Praja Sangha (MPS) was established combining the Manipur Praja Sanmeloni and the MPM. While the MPS was an urban based organization, Irabot also became the president of the Manipur Krishi Sanmeloni[46] in 1946 and rechristened it as the Manipur Krishak Sabha (MKS). Both the MPS and MKS played a very important role in the subsequent political development of Manipur (Singh, 1989; Singh, 2002: 147-169). His people oriented politics ultimately drove him to embrace communist ideas while he was in jail in Sylhet. Thus, Irabot introduced the communist political trend in Manipur politics.

In 1946 while it was becoming increasingly clear that British is going to leave India, the anti-communist liberal members of the NMM formed the Manipur State Congress (MSC) and kept Irabot out of this new organization. Although the MSC was independent of the Indian National Congress (INC) initially, but it worked in tandem with the INC and ultimately got itself affiliated to it following the merger of Manipur with India.

Another political party, viz., the Praja Santi Sabha (PSS), was established in 1948 by the King and his close asscciates to protect the interest of the monarchy.

Thus, three diametrically opposite political camps evolved in Manipur. Communists at one extreme who wanted to bring a radical change in the Manipuri society and the PSS on the other who supported orthodoxy and status quo. In between them was the MSC who were liberal and compromising.

Besides political awakening, socio-religious movements also took root in Manipur during the first half of the 20th century. Two different movements, viz., *Sanamahi* movement and sanskritization movement, were resurfaced and fiercely debated. While the *Sanamahi* movement[47] had been the manifestation of religious backlash against the degenerated-Brahmin-dominated-Hinduism and wanted to revert back to traditional belief system, the sanskritisation movement was basically an effort to reform it. The *Sanamahi* movement, propounded by Naorem Phullo, although failed to draw immediate attention of the educated Meitei elites, do provide the cultural alternative to Hinduism and had become instrumental in the policy of cultural disengagement practiced and propagated by the regional political ideologues. On the contrary, the sanskritization movement led by Pandit Atombabu Sharma advocated for socio-religious reform to rectify the evil practices of Hinduism. Atombabu tried to establish that the Meitei society has been a part and parcel of the grand Hindu tradition evolved through centuries right from the age of the Mahabharata. He translated many Hindu scriptures including Bhagabad Gita, Rig Veda, Gita Gobinda and Srimad Bhagavata. Besides these two views, Irabot also put forward his views on cultural traits of the society which would provide social stability. He believed that strict adherence to Vashnavite philosophy could only resolve the *Mangba-Sengba* problem (Singh, 1998: 120-122).

The educated elites also started taking up literary activities to mobilize the masses and disseminate ideas and information to people. As early as 1922, Irabot edited the first Manipuri journal named *Meitei Chanu* (Kabui, 1990: 159). Two newspapers (*Deinik Manipur Patrika* and *Manipur Matam*) and two journals (*Yakairol*, a quarterly journal and *Lalit Manjuri Patrika*, a monthly journal) were brought out during 1930 and 1940. Other literary activities like theatre plays were also encouraged. They also established schools at private initiatives in order to encourage higher education and female education. Churachand High School and Tombisana High School were established in 1932-33 at the initiative of Dr. Lairen Singh, Gopal Singh and K. Amubi Singh. One of the significant achievements was the establishment of Dhana Manjuri College (DMC) in the year 1946 (Singh, 1998: 118-122).

Political Dynamics of Transition to Democracy and Merger

With political awakening started taking the root, competitive politics between the communist and congress parties led to the popularization of the demand for representative democracy based on universal adult franchise. The office of the king would act as the titular head of the country while the elected representative would actually rule. The MSC, MPS and MKS demanded this political transformation *a la* the INC in India. The king was reluctant to give in to this demand initially for obvious reason [Parratt (J), 2005: 97; Singh, 2002: 175-176]. However, he had to finally agree to switch over to democratic political framework as the British also advised him in favour of this change. Accordingly, a constitutional making body[48] was constituted and the draft constitution[49] was adopted in 1947. The members of the MSC played the key role in drafting the constitution as the MPS and MKS had boycotted the election of the constitutional making committee.

Meanwhile, in view of imminent departure of the Raj, two agreements were signed between the Governor of Assam, Sir Akbar Hydari and the Maharaja as well as the Members of the Manipur State Durbar (Annexure-I). It was agreed that an Interim Council[50] be formed without delay in order to adjust with the new political environment arising out of the departure of the Raj. As a result the implementation of newly adopted constitution was delayed by one year.

It may not be out of place to note that these two agreements along with the Standstill Agreement (Annexure-II) and the Instrument of Accession (Annexure-III) signed on August 11, 1947, just before Independence, have allowed the political status of Manipur vis-à-vis British India to continue even after the lapse of the paramountcy. It may be emphasized here that all these agreements, having enormous polemic importance at present, had been signed between the British and the king of Manipur well before the Independence of India.

However, the Independence and the Interim Council could not bring political stability in the state. Widespread agitation for the establishment of a full responsible government had disturbed the peace and tranquility in the state. With no option left, the Chief Minister of the Interim Council, M.K. Priyobrata Singh made an official announcement on November 23, 1947 that a full responsible government would be established by April, 1948 (Singh, 2002: 186).

The much awaited election to the first Manipur State Assembly began on June 11, 1948 and continued upto July 27, 1948. Results were announced in batches with the final list coming on August 20, 1948 (Singh, 1989: 294).

No party could secure an absolute majority. While the MSC emerged as the single largest party securing 14 seats out of 53, MKS won 5, PSS won 12, Manipur Socialist Party (MSP) won 3, and independents from hill areas won 18 (Kabui, 1990: 168). One member was nominated by the king. Through an unexpected post poll alliance between the royalists and communists, the PSS formed the ministry under the leadership of Maharajkumar Priyobrata Singh with the support from the members from the hill areas on October 18, 1948. This apparent unthinkable political chemistry between the PSS and MKS might have been the result of hostility between Irabot and the leaders of the MSC. Being sidelined politically in spite of emerging as a single largest party, the leaders of the MSC tilted towards the INC and demanded the merger of Manipur with India (Singh, 1995: 108-112).

In fact the Meitei polity was sharply divided into two equal camps on the question of merger. The royalists (PSS) and the communists (MKS) were opposed to merger while the liberals (MSC) and socialists (MSP) proposed it. However, the convergence of approach between the royalists and the communists was due to altogether different reasons. The royalists opposed merger because it would dislodge them from power and privilege and hence they would be benefited if status quo was maintained. The communists opposed the merger as they were guided by the Leninist principle of right to self-determination of the nations. People in the hills of Manipur, however, were not politically organized as the political parties concentrated only in the valley could hardly have any influence over them.

However, there was a congruence of opinion across the political spectrum on the issue of the political status of Manipur in Indian Union. All the political parties in Manipur opposed to the idea of forming Purbachal Pradesh combining the territories of Tripura, Cachar and Manipur as suggested by the leaders of the INC. Political elites of Manipur could visualize that the Meiteis would become minority in such an arrangement and the Bengalis of Cachar and Tripura would dominate the political space. The ethno-cultural identity of the Meiteis would be at stake in case Manipur is combined with Cachar and Tripura. This anti-Purbachal movement had led to the articulation of Meitei community interest and even cemented the inter-community bonds across the plains and the hills.[51]

There was a widespread agitation by the political parties against the Purbachal proposal. So far the state authorities had only listened to the claims forwarded and no drastic actions had been taken upon the agitators. But when Irabot, on behalf of the MKS and MPS, had called a meeting on September 21, 1948 at Manipur Dramatic Union (MDU) Hall to protest the Purbachal proposal, matters changed drastically. On the said day of the meeting, an unfortunate incident happened at Pungdombam[52] which led to subversive actions of the police against the members of the sabha. Arrest warrant was issued against Irabot, who was already a member of the Assembly from Utlou constituency, thus preventing him from attending the session of the State Assembly. The MKS and MPS were declared unlawful organizations. Following this declaration, Irabot and his close associates had gone across the border in Burma (Myanmar) and tried to forward the cause of communist goal from there by forming the Red Guards (Singh, 1989: 311-326). Although, Irabot could not do much from underground and died in 1951 in Burma hideout, the legacy that he created had been reinvented later by the Meitei youths in their fight against deprivation and injustice.

After Irabot's departure from Manipur, the anti-Purbachal movement lost its momentum and subsided as the INC perceived it to be an unrealizable goal. Instead of the Purbachal project, the Union Government of India wanted, like the other Indian princely states under the Standstill and Instrument of Accession treaties, Manipur to merge with India. In fact Manipur had two options left: first, completely merge with India and become a part of the Indian federation; second, stay as a sovereign country under the indirect rule of the Indian state *a la* colonial-feudal arrangement which was institutionalized through the Standstill Agreement and the Instrument of Accession. In fact, the Instrument of Accession along with the appointment of the Dewan,[53] in whose hands rested the whole administrative power of the state, had virtually made the second option meaningless. Moreover, as Sardar Vallabhbhai Patel, the then Home Minister and Deputy Prime Minister of India, wanted to integrate all the princely Indian states with the Indian Union, an indirect pressure had been created upon the Maharaja of Manipur to sign the merger agreement. Sri Prakasa, the then Governor of Assam, and his advisor, N. K. Rustomji, translated Patel's wish into reality and finally made Bodhachandra, the Maharaja of Manipur, to sign the Merger Agreement (Annexure-IV) on September 21, 1949.

On October 15, 1949 at 9 am the ceremony of Integration of Manipur state was performed at Assam Rifles ground, Imphal. With this, the rule of the Maharaja ended and the Manipur State Council and the Assembly were later dissolved with effect from October 15, 1949. Manipur, thus, became a province ruled by a Chief Commissioner under the category of Part 'C' State. The Dewan, Major General Rawal Amar Singh, was appointed as the Chief Commissioner.

Demand for Statehood and Growth of Nationalism

Manipur experienced very fast political change during the last fifteen years of the first half of the 20th century. From 1934, the year of the establishment of the NHMM, to 1949, the year of the merger, within these 15 years, sweeping political developments had taken place in Manipur. The pace of political awakening had, indeed, been lightening with the advent of the World War II (1939-45), penetration of the Azad Hind Fauz into the Valley under the leadership of Subhas Chandra Bose,[54] adoption of constitution, introduction of Legislative Assembly, transformation of the office of the king from monarchy to the titular head of the state, ideological polemics among the communists, socialists, royalists and liberals and withdrawal of British from the Indian sub-continent. To be precise, the change was astounding and dumbfounding and all the parameters were not under the control of the people of Manipur. Events occurred even before national consensus was built around them. There was hardly any scope for the people to exercise their choice. In fact, the political choices were extremely limited due to fluid and volatile nature of political environment arising out of the transfer of power.

From Part 'C' State to Union Territory

Following the signing of the Merger Agreement, Manipur State Assembly, formed only in 1948, was dissolved, the state was made a Chief Commissioner's Province, and the power was transferred to the Chief Commissioner, Major General Rawal Amar Singh, who was selected by the Government of India. The Chief Commissioner was empowered to rule without any accountability to the people of the State. Thus, unfortunately, Manipur experienced a negative political change from peoples' government to a bureaucratic government. The appointment of an army Major General as the Dewan and subsequently as the Chief Commissioner was an obvious indication of the security concern of the Indian state to her north-eastern border. Perhaps, the activities of Irabot Singh, the MKS and MPS as well as the emergence of communist China and strengthening of Burmese Communist Party during that time - all these had been factored into while deciding the political fate of post-merger Manipur by the leaders of the Indian state.

The Part 'C' status of Manipur had become the rallying point for the political forces cutting across fences. The political demand for responsible government or statehood has helped in galvanizing the people in the valley in particular into a strong nationality. Parties across the political ideologies have mobilized the masses in support of this demand. The movement provided a common political space where people forged a strong bonding across the social strata, religious hierarchy and economic status. The movement started in 1950 and continued till the statehood is achieved in 1972. The 22 years long political agitation for statehood in Manipur is itself a unique event in the political history of modern India.

The Manipur National Union (MNU) was formed, perhaps, during 1950, to mobilize the people of the state in support of the demand for statehood. It may not be out of place to point out the fact that the word 'national' had been used explicitly for the first time to mean a political organization. Although the Chief Commissioner, under the severe pressure from the political parties, had constituted the Advisory Council on October 9, 1950, under his presidentship, the formation of the toothless body, however, could not satisfy the political ambition of the people of Manipur. The representatives of the MSC had resigned on February 6, 1951, and the party called for non-cooperation with the Chief

Commissioner and observed February 25, 1951 as the Anti-Chief Commissioner's Regime Day. The MSP and PSS joined hands to demand for the establishment of an Advisory Council with executive power. Although the MKS, MPS and all types of activities by the communists were banned in 1948, the influence of the communists could not be eliminated. Members of the communist organizations went underground but were politically very active. Perhaps, the MNU had the back up from the communist activists. The administration of the Chief Commissioner was up against the communists who had swept over the state in early 1950s. They used cyclostyled bulletins and printed leaflets for mobilizing the masses in their fight against the repression of the government and in favour of the establishment of responsible government. They also criticized the government for converting Manipur into a police state. They also threatened the people of dire consequences if they help the police. In the meantime, the police in collaboration with the Assam Rifles (AR) and Manipur Rifles (MR) conducted operations and raided many villages day after day in search of communist activists and captured many ring leaders. They were tried in July, 1951 and many of them were sentenced to rigorous imprisonment varying from 3 to 14 years (Singh, 1989: 377-401). After this trial the communist activities had subsided. Following the death of Irabot in September 1951, the communist inspiration gradually died down only to resurface in other forms to fight against injustice, perceived or real, meted out to Manipur during the post-merger era.

Alongside the communists, the MNU was also very active during the early 1950s. They were mobilizing the people in support of the establishment of a responsible government in Manipur. The idea of territorial secession and political independence of Manipur was rooted in the MNU movement. It preached for a trade off between political independence and establishment of responsible government. The movement was, however, crushed with the arrest of the top leadership of the MNU (Singh, 2002: 200-201).

Besides communists and the MNU, both the MSC and MSP were also demanding for the establishment of representative government. When the communists and the MNU became weak, the baton of the movement passed over to them. On the face of political opposition against the Part 'C' state, political parties participated in the 1952 general election. Out of 30 seats, Congress won 10, Socialists 1, Communists 2 and Independents won 17 (Singh, 1997: 8). Based on the election results, the Advisory Council was reconstituted in 1952 with 4 members from Congress and 1 independent.

The MSP which won only one seat could not find a place in the Council. However, the MSP took up the cudgel of the popular demand for responsible government to strengthen its support base and began to mobilize the masses. Intense political agitations had been organized throughout 1953-55 to rally the people of Manipur by way of blocking roads, organizing strikes, gheraoing the members of the Advisory Council, organizing mass meeting, forcing the closure of markets, asking people not to pay taxes, calling upon people not to cooperate with the administration, asking the hill people to boycott taxes and registering the students, women, youths, farmers and professionals to join the movements. Unprecedented political mobilization across the hills and plains united the people and strengthened the intercommunity bonds. At times and places, the administration applied force to suppress the movement which had led the police to open fire on the unarmed agitators. Many people became the victims of state repression.[55] Many leaders of the movement were arrested under the Preventive Detention Act.[56] This political mobilization against the Indian state for the perceived social justice had made way to the growth of Meitei nationalism.

It was this intense political movement which perhaps made Jawaharlal Nehru, the then Prime Minister of India, to disagree with the recommendation of the first State Reorganization Commission, 1953 (SRC), submitted in 1955, for merger of Manipur along with Tripura into Assam (Chaube, 1999: 204). In spite of strong plea from all the political parties, the recommendation of the SRC deeply hurt the sentiments of the people of Manipur. Even the MSC sent SOS to the Prime Minister to take measures to protect the political and cultural identity of Manipur. While the SRC report was placed in the parliament in 1956, Jawaharlal Nehru firmly advocated in favour of maintaining separate identity of both Manipur and Tripura. As a result, Part 'C' states were converted into Union Territory. Manipur also graduated from a Part 'C' State to a Union Territory with a provision for elected Territorial Council in 1956 (Singh, 2000: 34-35; Singh, 2002: 208-213).

From Union Territory to Statehood

The election to the 30 member Territorial Council was held in 1957 along with the general parliament election. The result exhibited a fast politicization of the people of Manipur cutting across the plains and the hills. Out of 30 seats, Congress won 12, Socialists 6, Communists 4 and Independents won 8 (Singh, 1997: 9). Political parties could reap the dividend at the cost of the independents. The intense political mobilization by the communists and socialists in favour of the responsible government expanded their sphere of influence significantly. The socialists[57] made a gain of 19 per cent in terms of their share of the total votes polled compared to 1952 election. Similarly the communists gained by 8 per cent and congress by 1 per cent. However, the independents lost by 22 per cent (Figure 2.1).

Figure 2.1: Party Position in 1952 and 1957 Elections

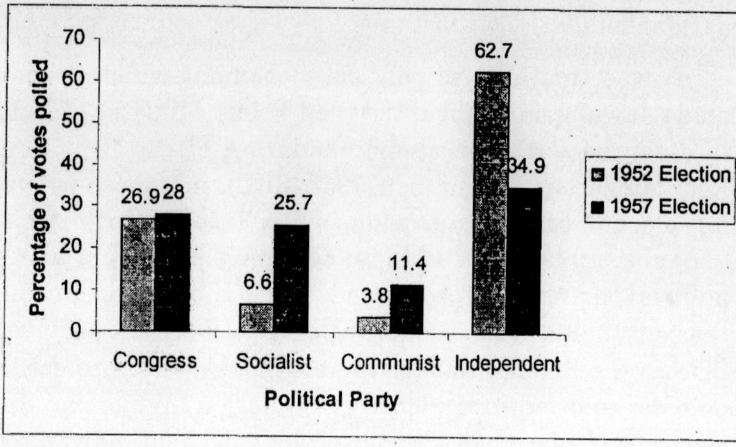

Source: Calculated from Singh, 1981: 24, 28

It may be pointed out, as a clarification, that the Independents may not necessarily mean entities without any association. In many cases, independents are the candidates of the minor political parties or ethno-social organizations which are not registered with the election commission. In Manipur, although ideology based politics were practiced in the valley, people of the hills were largely guided by the primordial loyalties. Candidates fought election on behalf of the ethno-social formations like Kuki National Association, Mao-Maram Union, Mizo Union, Manipur Zeliangrong Union, Paite National Council and Naga National League. The candidates of these ethno-social organizations are collectively shown under 'Independents'.

However, the euphoria of Territorial Council soon died down as it was realized that it was no better than the earlier Advisory Council. The members of the Territorial Council, although duly elected, had no real power and had to act virtually as the appendage of the Chief Commissioner. The second phase of the movement for responsible government and statehood began with added vigour and enthusiasm since the beginning of 1960. The socialists and communists jointly formed the Assembly Demand Co-ordination Committee (ADCC) on March 26, 1960. With the formation of ADCC, a political platform, mass base of the movement, cutting across political identities, had expanded to a large extent. The ADCC soon established frontal organizations like the Manipur Youth Assembly Demand Committee and Women's Assembly Demand Committee. Series of political programmes like road blockade, closure of markets, boycotting government office, boycotting schools, non-cooperation with the government administration, disrupting communication channels, strikes, bandhs, etc., were undertaken to achieve the political goal of attaining statehood. In order to counter these programmes the administration of the Chief Commissioner used repressive measures like the imposition of Section 144 Cr.P.C., curfew, lathicharge, firing and arrest (Snahal, 1988: 177-179). Cycles of protests and violence, actions and repressions, claims and denials, commotions and sanity reverberated the political air of Manipur throughout the 1960s. The feeling of deprivation was so intense that revival of the pre-merger representative assembly was sought from certain quarters as an alternative to the denial of the responsible government.[58] Socialists, the then parliamentary opposition, had made it a national issue and brought the matter to the notice of the Indian Parliament for redress. The MSC also drawn the attention of the central leadership and urged for statehood. It was, perhaps, due to egoistic approach of the national ruling elites, over estimation of security threats arising out of the activities of the communists and socialists in Manipur, or uncritical dependence of the leadership of the INC upon the Assam Pradesh Congress, who were lobbying for the administrative merger of Manipur with Assam, that the legitimate demand of the people of Manipur was not acceded to. The social psychology of the people of Manipur was reflected in the 1962 election. Out of 30 seats in the Territorial Council, Congress won 15, socialists 5 and independents 10 (Singh, 1997: 10). As far as the percentage share of votes is concerned, both Congress, and the socialists and communists combined together had received 29 per cent each. It appears that the rising Sino-Indian animosity over the Chinese occupation of Tibet had cast a doom spell upon the communists in Manipur which led to the shrinking of their support bases in 1962 election.

However, under the severe political unrest, Government of India passed the Union Territories Act, 1963. Following this Act, the Territorial Council of Manipur was converted into the Manipur Territorial Assembly with a Council of Ministers on July 1, 1963 (Singh, 2000: 35).

Meanwhile, to quell the 'Naga-armed-movement-for-secession' led by Naga National Council (NNC) under the leadership of A.Z. Phizo that began immediately after the Independence, which will be discussed at length in the next section, the Government of India conferred statehood to the Nagas of Naga hills in 1963. This conferment of statehood to the Nagas and the denial of the same to the Meiteis had snowballed bitter criticism against the Indian state. The perspective of the Indian state in this regard remained mystic to the perception of the people of Manipur. There had been a deep sense of deprivation and feeling of being discriminated permeated in the psyche of the people of Manipur. The national pride of the Meities was severely hurt. It was, indeed, a baffling question as to why Manipur was denied statehood in spite of the fact that the process of state formation was completed here long before it got merged with the Indian Union. While the Nagas, without any history of state formation, were conferred a state, why the Meiteis were denied of the same? This arbitrary decision of the Indian state was beyond the comprehension of any logic and the people of Manipur were shocked and dumbfounded. It may be pointed out that the Meiteis did not oppose conferring of the statehood to the Nagas, but what baffled them as to why do the Indian state deny their claim?

Let us digress a bit here to look into contemporary perspectives of the Indian state that had denied the statehood to Manipur. Firstly, as mentioned earlier, the security concern of the Indian state about her eastern border arising out of communist revolution in China, political influence of Irabot and Communist Party upon the people of Manipur, Chinese occupation of Tibet, perceived nexus between the communists of Manipur and Burma, and the propagation of the communist ideology of right to self determination and their support for secession of Manipur, had been the overriding considerations for not granting the statehood to Manipur. Secondly, there was a strong opinion at the centre against the creation of unviable states. The proposal for the creation of Purbachal including Manipur, Cachar and Tripura floated by the central congress leadership corroborates this hypothesis. Thirdly, as the socialists had a strong presence in Manipur and spearheading the statehood demand movement, according the same to Manipur might be seen as the political defeat for the congress.

Be that as it may, the intensity of the movement came down following the Sino-Indian border conflict in 1962 and Indo-Pak war of 1965. Nationalists could mould the political discourse in their favour accusing the neighbouring countries for destabilizing the Indian Union. As a result, communists and socialists were virtually routed in 1967 election while the nationalists and *primordialists*, protagonists of ethno-social identities, could fare much better (Figure 2.2).

Figure 2.2: Party Position in 1962 and 1967 Elections

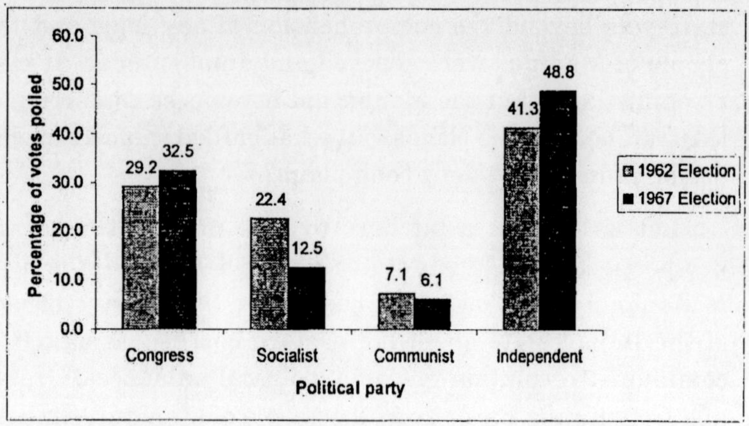

Source: Calculated from Singh, 1981: 32, 40.

The movement was revived again in 1968. Socialists and communists formed the 'All Manipur Statehood Demand Committee' on February 29, 1968, to intensify the movement for the statehood. They organized political conferences, public meetings demonstrations, etc. to mobilize the people. The Manipur Congress also organized political conferences. They submitted memorandum to the Prime Minister and urged the centre to take bold decisions. They launched dharna and hunger strike as a part of their action and even carried out the same in Delhi. With the Central Government turning a deaf ear to all these demonstrations, all the political parties decided to form a common platform. Accordingly, the 'All Parties Statehood Demand Coordinating Body' (herein after referred as Body) was formed on April 26, 1970 (Singh, 2002: 221-222).

A mighty democratic movement was launched under the Body. The leadership of the Body had adopted a strategy of disengagement with the Indian democratic framework until the goal is achieved. Accordingly, besides organizing political programmes like bandh, hartal, road blockade, rally, mass meeting, etc., the Body also called for the withdrawal of the elected members of different democratic institutions like Municipal Boards, Town Committees, Assembly and Parliament (Singh, 2002: 223-225).

Although democratic programmes had been the principal form of the statehood movement, the social frustration arising out of the refusal by the central government to pay any heed to the demand for statehood, had strengthened the alternative thoughts which advocated to go the Naga-way for achieving the goal. The left-wing extremism within the movement had led to the formation of United National Liberation Front (UNLF) in 1964.

While the depth and expanse of the movement for statehood was spreading fast, the security perception of the Indian state about the region had also undergone a sea change. The Sino-Indian border conflict in 1962 and Indo-Pak war of 1965 coupled with the cold war matrix, India was literally cordoned off by the USA-China-Pakistan axis. The East Pakistan had become the launching pad for the anti-India subversive activities. Indian intelligence had warned that in the event of simultaneous thrust from China and Pakistan, the chicken's neck might be disconnected and it would really be a difficult task for India to hold the north eastern region (Das, 2002: 539-542).

The internal security environment of the region had drastically worsened further with the formation of Mizo National Front (MNF), under the leadership of Laldenga, to launch a secessionist movement in 1966. Thus, the rising grievances of the different communities within the region were easily utilized by the destabilizing forces across the border to worsen the security environment in India's north eastern frontier.

To deal with these dual security challenges, Government of India, under the leadership of Indira Gandhi, overhauled the Nehruvian perspective of north east and came out with a more accommodative policy framework. The North Eastern Areas (Re-organization) Bill which was passed in 1971 and officially enforced in January, 1972, granted the statehood to Manipur and Tripura as well as conferred the status of Union Territory to Arunahal Pradesh and Mizoram. Thus, after 22 years of merger, Manipur became a full-fledged state on January 21, 1972, which was inaugurated by Indira Gandhi, the then Prime Minister, and in the process shaped and consolidated the idea of Meitei nationalism.

The Meitei nationalism has grown through mobilizing the people against the Indian state. A 22 year long agitation for statehood had galvanized the sense of oneness and a strong 'we' feeling in them. The binary relation between 'we' and 'they', i.e., 'we' fight for justice against 'them', help in cementing the social bond among the elements of 'we' on the one hand and a sense of distrust between 'we' and 'they' on the other. The accommodation of Meitei aspiration within the larger Indian nationalism was not easy. The present accommodation is rather hard earned. While there was widespread demand for a better accommodation, Meiteis were denied for long. This denial is standing on the way of nation-building at present. The accumulated grievances for being discriminated had led to the articulation of demand for secession by some quarters. In fact, the demand for secession is an extreme expression of wounded nationalism. The issues of militancy, insurgency, regionalism, fringe psychology and disengaging-with-mainland-syndrome all are related to this wounded nationalist feeling.

Unlike Meiteis, Nagas, the second largest constituent of Manipur's population, has hardly had any heritage to share with India. The racial origin, dialects, religion and history of belongingness of the Nagas have kept them insular and distinct from the 'other' people. As the Nagas of Manipur forms about 19 per cent (1991 Census) of the state's population, it is equally important to have a look at the growth of Naga nationalism as well. The next section will deal with this issue.

Growth of Naga Nationalism

A study of the growth of Naga nationalism in Manipur is also important for understanding the complex ethnic crisis Manipur is facing at present. As the Nagas spread across the territories of Nagaland and Manipur, such a study cannot be done in seclusion, i.e., only in case of Manipur without referring to Nagaland. Nagas are the northern neighbours of the Meiteis for ages. They spread over the northern hills of Manipur, Naga hills and in the western Sagaing Division across Indo-Myanmar border. In Myanmar, Nagas spread over from Patkai range in north to Thaungdyat in south, from Indian border in west to River Chindwin in east. However, the lion's share of the Naga population resides in the Indian side of the border. Manipur is the second home of the Nagas next to Nagaland. However, unlike the Meiteis, state formation did not take place among the Nagas. Until recently, Nagas remained secluded and embedded in their traditional way of living. It was the Baptist missionaries who ignited the light of modernity among the Nagas.

The Naga Identity

The present state of Nagaland was known as Naga Hills until the attainment of statehood on December 1, 1963. It is inhabited by various sub-tribes, who were known by different names, viz., Ao, Angami, Lotha, Sema, Rengma, Konyak, etc., until the use of the generic term 'Naga'.

The origin of the generic term 'Naga' is shrouded in mystery. Till today there is no definite answer to this question of the origin of the name 'Naga'. But many scholars have put forward different views as to the origin of the name 'Naga'. There are three prominent hypotheses regarding its origin, viz., (i) the '*Nanga*' meaning 'paucity of cloth' hypothesis of L.W. Shakespeare (1914), Robert Reid (1942), William Robinson (1841), Johnstone (2002) and E.W. Dun (1981); (ii) the '*Nok*' meaning 'people or folk' hypothesis of S.E. Peal (1894), E. Gait (1963) and V. Elwin (1960) and (iii) the '*Naka*' meaning 'pierced ears' hypothesis of R.R. Shimray (1985). Whatever may be the origin of the name 'Naga', but it is widely accepted that the name was given by the people of Brahmaputra and Barak valleys (Kabui, 1995: 24). With the consolidation of British rule and spread of Christianity, the use of the name 'Naga' has been popularized and consequently accepted by these sub-tribes as is evident from the name of the first organization among them, the Naga Club.

However, in Manipur the use of the name 'Naga' among the tribes, who are now identified as 'Naga', is a post World War II phenomena. Though the British had used the name to identify and classify the tribes of Manipur, it was not very popular. It is evident when Jadonang and Gaidinliu launched the anti-British movement in 1931 they had not termed it as Naga movement rather it was Kabui and Kutcha Naga movement. Again, Shimray (1985: 39), in his boyhood, told the Japanese forces during the World War II that they were Tangkhuls and not Nagas when the latter addressed them as Nagas. This only indicates that the Naga identity was in flux even in the mid of the 20th century.

The Traditional Naga Society

The traditional Naga society was organized centering on a village. Each village was an independent political unit governed by a sub-tribe like Ao, Angami, or Lotha, who were fiercely independent of each other. Each village was administered by a chief and the village council. The Chief performed the dual function as the religious and administrative head of the village. As such he was the religious head, judge, and leader of the community. He used to protect the interest of the community. He gave leadership at times of war and head hunting.

In most of the cases the leader of the first settlers was selected as the Chief. The Chieftainship was hereditary except among the Aos and Lothas. The Chief was assisted by the Village Council in the administration of the village. The members of the Village Council were the representatives of each clan residing in the village. Usually the eldest person in each clan was selected as representative to the Council (Shimray, 1985: 52-59, 1995: 320-325). So the Nagas had evolved a political system combining both the elements of a republic and authoritarian forms of governance.

Nagas are primarily jhumias. The Chief was the nominal owner of the land. However, each family had the right to possess paddy fields, gardens and woodlands. But the jhumming area belonged to the village. The Chief in consultation with the Village Council decided the jhum site in each rotation (Shimray, 1985: 53-54). Naga life was largely rotated centering on jhumming, hunting, gathering and fishing. Inter-village relationship was not very friendly. The practice of head-hunting[59] had restricted the expansion of social boundary beyond the village. Different dialects used by the different sub-tribes stood on the way of effective inter-village as well as inter-group interaction and hence prevented the formation of larger socio-economic formation like a state among the Nagas. The forces of market could not evolve to bind people of different villages as trade was almost non-existent among them due to internecine warfare with each other.

The Nagas, before the advent of Christianity, were animists. As animists, they worshipped spirits. Three major spirits, viz., house spirit, field spirit and jungle spirit were worshipped. Over and above these spirits, they believed in supreme creator, known by different names in different sub-tribes: the Semas called it *Alhou*, Maos - *Ora*, Tangkhuls - *Kameo* (*Arah*), Aos - *Lijaba*, Lothas called it *Potso* and so on. The Nagas were god-fearing people. They used to offer sacrifices of animals and a little food and drink before they ate to placate the evil spirit and not to harm them (Sema, 1988: 34-42; Shimray, 1985: 223-225). In addition to this they observe '*gennas*' meaning both ceremony and prohibition for the propitiation of spirits. Various *gennas* observed by them were tribal *genna*, village *genna*, crop *genna*, sickness *genna*, death *genna*, clan *genna*, household *genna*, food *genna* and individual *genna*. This, of course, differed from sub-tribe to sub-tribe and region to region (For details, Bhattacharyya, 1963: 130-132; Hodson, 2007: 164-186; Sema, 1988: 42-47).

However, with the coming of Christianity and establishment of British rule the traditional Naga society slowly degenerated and moved towards modernism.

The Tribal-Colonial Continuum

The first acquaintance of the British with the Nagas was in 1832 when Captain Jenkins and Lieutenant Pemberton along with Raja Gambhir Singh of Manipur forced a passage through these hills for a possible route to Assam (Johnstone, 2002: 41). They met with heavy resistance from these tribes. Nagas were known for their head-hunting, a practice, that took several lives of the citizens of British Indian territory adjacent to the Naga hills. Beginning from 1839, British had sent several punitive expeditions to the Naga hills, particularly to Ao, Angami and Lotha villages, to punish them for their recalcitrant behavior. In spite of several attempts to desist them from raiding the plains areas within the British territory, Nagas continued with the practice of raid and head-hunting. This had ultimately enticed the British to annex Naga hills and brought the Nagas under the close colonial surveillance. The Nagas resisted the British colonial might for couple of years and finally gave in in 1880 [For details on various expeditions, Allen, 2002: 9-28; Ghosh, 1982: 88-147; Mackenzie, 1999: 104-143; Singh (P), 1995: 11-27]. For these long 40 years, Nagas conflict with the British had, to certain extent, solidified the racial bond of the disparate groups. War had put them in equal footing and every group fought for its freedom and in the process learnt from each other.

Naga hills under the British rule since 1881 experienced a tremendous growth of Christian activities. The American Baptist missionary led by Rev. E. W. Clark, set its first step on the soil of Naga hills in 1871 among the Aos. In the initial stage the villagers opposed the new faith as it challenged the old-age customs and forbade drinking, working on Sundays, offering sacrifices, etc. Soon after the arrival of Mr. Godhula, an Assamese Christian, missionary work gained momentum and a good number of people accepted the new faith. In Kohima, Dr. S. W. Rivenburg, a medical missionary, and his wife started a school in 1885 and spread the new religion. Similarly, among the Lothas, Rev. W. E. Whittter started his missionary work in 1885. The missionaries used two main instruments viz., education and medical care to carry out their evangelistic works and proselytism. It was quite difficult for the Baptist missionaries to work in Naga hills as they were branded as British and viewed as enemies by the Nagas. The number of converts grew at slow pace initially from 211 persons in 1891 to 579 in 1901 (Ghosh, 1982: 252-255; Sema, 1988: 50-58; Singh (P), 1995: 162-174). But with the beginning of the 20th century, missionaries could create a stronghold among the Aos and also could gain confidence of the other Naga groups mainly through their medical services. For the Nagas, the system of healing and cure of illness was associated with their system of believes. Like other tribal groups, they also believed that illness is caused by the evil spirit and elaborate religious rituals were performed to propitiate the evil spirits. While the modern medicine of the western missionaries worked miraculously, Nagas realized the efficacy and supremacy of the biblical religion over their traditional faiths. Once this realization took root, their occurred a religious revolution with large scale conversion of the Nagas into Christianity (www.cbcnei.com).

By 1920s, about 100,000 Nagas had been converted (www.ltbs.org). This number went on increasing with the passage of time. By 1971, Christians form 75 per cent of the state's population (Ghosh, 1982: 254-255) and by 2001 Christians form 90 per cent of the state's population, making it one of the three Christian-majority states in India, the other two states being Mizoram (87 per cent) and Meghalaya (70 per cent) (http://mizohican.blogspot.com).

The Christian missionaries not only brought a new religion but a revolutionary change in the Naga way of living. The church was the uniting agent of these warring tribes. For the first time the new faith had brought them together and made them aware of a descent way of living beyond head-hunting, drinking, merry-making, etc. The new faith got rid of the old superstitious practices and completely changed the life-world of the Nagas. Missionaries attempted to codify the Naga dialect and introduced English as the medium of instruction in the schools. Naga elites, who have emerged out of the shadows of the church and western education, could find a common language to interact with each other. Thus, English became the common language of the educated Naga elites. Their western education had empowered them and their church education had provided them with a separate identity with which they are armed to mobilize their brethren to claim a distinct social and political space for themselves.

Emergence of Naga Nationalism

The growth of nationalism in Nagaland is a post World War I phenomena. As referred earlier, the Naga tribes were fiercely independent of each other and lived separately. The realization that they belong to the same racial stock having cultural affinity took place when they were serving as Labour Corps[60] in France during the World War I. After returning from the War, they formed the Naga Club[61] (NC) in 1918 with a view to forward the cause of the Nagas. Political consciousness grew with formation of the NC and similarly other organizations like the Lotha Council and Ao Counicl came up in 1923 and 1928 respectively to promote their interests. When the Simon Commission[62] visited Kohima in 1929, NC submitted a memorandum to the effect that the Nagas were not willing to be a part of the Reformed Scheme of India and wanted the British Government to safeguard their rights by placing the Naga hills directly under its rule. The report of the Commission was placed in 1935 before the Special Committee on Indian Bill before the House of Commons in London and subsequently, in 1937, the Naga hills was declared 'Excluded Areas' of the Province of Assam along with the North-East Frontier Tract, the Lushai Hills and Cachar Hills [Ghosh, 1982: 155-157; Horam, 1988: 37-41; Nuh & Lasuh, 2002: 111-112; Singh, 2008: 47-48; Singh (P), 1995: 79].

Shortly after, the whole of the Naga hills was engulfed by the World War II. The War had shaken the insulated psyche of the Nagas and helped in consolidating the Naga identity across the different Naga sub-tribes. Nagas had to face the onslaught of the invading Japanese force and had to bear the brunt while guarding the border of British India. Nagas stoutly stood behind the imperial forces, provided all types of logistic support to the British army, acted as the informer and courier, and stood themselves as the second line of defence (Horam, 1988: 57-58). The war efforts of the Nagas and their association with the American Baptist Missions have paid a rich dividend in terms of solid support from the British and Americans to the self-charted destiny of the Nagas. Moreover, it is believed that arms and ammunitions that the Nagas captured from the defeated Japanese also come in handy while the Naga leaders chose to go underground to fight for independent Nagaland.

Soon after the War, Charles Pawsey, the then Deputy Commissioner of the Naga hills, established the Naga Hills District Tribal Council (NHDTC) in 1945 to unite the Nagas and take up post-war reconstruction work. In its meeting held in 1946 at Wokha, NHDTC was rechristened as Naga National Council (NNC) [Horam, 1988: 41; Singh (P), 1995: 80; Stracey, 1968: 66]. The formation of NNC may be seen as the turning point in the evolution of political consciousness of the Nagas. NNC transformed the social categorization into political identity and imbued the Nagas to strive for larger calling. It may, however, be noted that NNC was mainly active among the Nagas of Naga hills. The representatives of Nagas living in Manipur, North Eastern Frontier Agency (NEFA) i.e., present day Arunachal Pradesh and Assam were not accommodated in NNC. Mainly the Angamis and Aos, the more advanced Naga groups, played the dominant role in the early phase of NNC movement.

With the British Raj coming to an end, the Nagas were caught in a dilemma of choices between 'autonomy and integration' with the India Union and 'complete independence' (Das, 1997: 171). While the integrationist faction of NNC had signed the 9-point Agreement with Sir Akbar Hyadari in June, 1947, which is popularly known as the Hydari Agreement (For full text of the Agreement, Nuh & Lasuh, 2002: 67-68), the protagonists-of-Naga-Independence under the leadership of Phizo declared the independence of Nagaland on August 14, 1947. Phizo became the president of NNC in 1949 and stepped up the campaign for independence. It is believed that Phizo had the support of the British officers like Pawsey and Clow as well as Baptist missionaries like Rev. Anderson who sympathized with the views of Nagas that their racial identity might be lost once the Naga Hills are brought under Independent India. Besides the fear of numerically vast Indians, Naga leaders also articulated their apprehensions of the religious persecution of the minority Christian Nagas in overwhelming Hindu India. Phizo claimed to have organized a plebiscite in 1951 on the question of Naga independence and won the support of 99 per cent of the people of Naga hills (Anand, 1980: 71; Horam, 1988: 49-50; Nuh & Lasuh, 2002: 116-133; Stracey, 1968: 70). NNC under Phizo also whipped up anti-India tirade and successfully boycotted the first general election in 1952 (Anand, 1980: 71; Horam, 1988: 50).

So far the Naga movement had followed the path of non-violence. Public opinion was formed and mobilized in favour of NNC demand for independence of Nagaland through two weekly newspapers, viz., the *Naga Nation* and the *Naga Herald*. NNC under Phizo adopted strategies of civil disobedience, non-cooperation with the government, mass resignation of teachers and students from schools, non-payment of house tax, surrendering the badges of authority by the village chiefs, etc. to spearhead the movement (Stracey, 1968: 72). When Jawaharlal Nehru visited the Naga hills along with U Nu, the then Prime Minister of Burma in 1953, the Nagas wanted to submit a memorandum to him demanding the secession of Nagaland from India. As they were denied to meet the Prime Minister by the Assam administration, Nagas staged a walk-out as a sign of protest (Horam, 1988: 51; Stracey, 1968: 58-59). Immediately the state security forces came down heavily on the Nagas and raided many houses including the house of T. Sakhrie, the then General Secretary of NNC. Subsequently, the two weekly newspapers were also banned (Horam, 1988: 51-55). On the face of the state onslaught, Naga movement slipped to underground.

The armed hostilities broke out in 1955 and an underground government known as Federal Government of Nagaland[63] (FGN) was set up in 1956. In the initial years of armed-struggle, NNC had the mass support. Moreover, the policy of 'one son from every family' had largely contributed to NNC army. Their finances were met by voluntary public contributions and the annual tax of Rs. 6 per family (Horam, 1988: 59-73). The state security forces took repressive measures to contain the movement and the army, which was called in 1955, also started counter-insurgency operations (Stracey, 1968: 82). During this period, the innocent villagers became the victims of repression of both the state and the undergrounds (Horam, 1988: 73). As long as Phizo was in Nagaland, the protagonists-of-Naga-Independence was dominating in NNC which, in turn, claimed to be the sole representative of Naga interest. Phizo even not hesitated to eliminate the most articulate secretary, Sakhrie, for relegating to a moderate position and singing to the tune of the integrationists (Chaube, 1999: 61; Horam, 1988: 78-79; Stracey, 1968: 79). The departure of Phizo from the scene in 1957 paved the way for the integrationists to organize Naga People's Convention[64] (NPC) in 1957 and sought for a solution to the ongoing crisis. NPC received the patronage of the Government of India and the demand for the integration of the Naga inhabited territories with that of Naga hills was partially met following the merger of Tuensang division of NEFA with that of Naga hills and formation of Naga Hills Tuensang Area[65] (NHTA) under part B tribal area within Assam. The hands of the leaders of NPC were further strengthened while Nagas were conferred statehood in 1963 as part of security overhauling measures following the Sino-Indian border conflict in 1962. The NHTA was christened as Nagaland. The leaders of NPC formed Naga National Organisation (NNO), a political party, and came out victorious in the first Nagaland state Assembly elections in 1964. This integrated the Naga society with Indian mainstream along party line politics, thus creating two poles in the Naga society: the underground government (FGN) and the Nagaland state, a constituent of Indian federation (Das, 1997: 173-174).

The polarization of the Naga society into these two camps has largely determined the dynamics of internal development of Naga inhabited areas in general and Nagaland in particular. Following NNO's coming to power, the integrationist segment of the Nagas joined the nation building exercise along with other segments of Indian population. Under the leadership of P. Shilu Ao, the first Chief Minister of Nagaland, the power elites of Nagaland could work for the people and create a mass base for them. In spite of the revolutionary callings from NNC, Nagas largely rallied behind the integrationist-nationalist leaders. It was, perhaps, due to this popularity of the integrationist-nationalist politics that compelled NNC to swallow the 1964 peace agreement[66] and Shillong Accord[67] of 1975. Following the Shillong Accord, NNO merged with the Indian National Congress in 1976 registering the culmination of integration of the Nagas with mainland India along political line.

However, the story of Naga insurgency, the militant face of Naga nationalism, has not gone with the wind following the Shillong Accord. While the NNC and FGN leadership settled the dispute and signed the Shillong Accord, some NNC cadres were in China for training. Th. Muivah, a Tangkhul Naga, and Isak Chishi Swu, a Sema Naga, were also in that group. It appears that China mentored them to revive the movement again and mobilized the logistics for them using the cold war axial relationship with Pakistan and USA leading to the formation of National Socialist Council of Nagaland (NSCN) in January, 1980.

With the formation of NSCN, the Naga nationalism took a different turn. They not only denounced the Shillong Accord but also rejected Phizo's leadership and set up a new underground government called Government of People's Republic of Nagaland (GPRN). The base of the underground movement gradually shifted to the Manipur hills, especially in the Ukhrul district, a Tangkhul dominated area. It may not be out of place to point out that Th. Muivah, General Secretary of NSCN, hails from Ukhrul district of Manipur. The demand for a unified homeland of the Nagas received a great impetus following the formation of NSCN. However, the Naga underground movement is not free from factionalism or more appropriately from localism (love for village) and tribalism (placing the tribe before large collectivity) (Verghese, 2004: 96). In 1988, NSCN split vertically only to divide the militant Naga movement into two warring camps - one under the leadership of Muivah and Swu and is called NSCN (I-M) and the other under the leadership of S.S. Khaplang, a Myanmar based Hemi Naga, and is labeled as NSCN (K). While NSCN (I-M) is blessed with the support of the Tangkhuls and Semas, its rival NSCN (K) has strong support bases across the Indo-Myanmar border particularly among Konyaks and Aos. Since 1988, militant Naga nationalists waged more wars between themselves than with the Indian security forces. The deep intra-tribal divide and distrust has largely eaten away the solidarity of the militant Naga nationalism and increasingly striving to establish a hegemonic socio-political order based on military might.

Naga nationalism is, thus, the product of the anti-India struggle of the Naga people. Assertion of Naga identity and the aspiration of the westernized Naga middle class for self-determination has been the two main edifice of Naga nationalism. Partial fulfillment of territorial unification and achievement of self-determination in terms of statehood have put the Nagas on equal footings like other nationalities in India. The ideological praxis on which the movement was initially built like 'Nagas would be run over by the huge Indian population', 'Christian Nagas might face persecution in Hindu India', etc., were unfounded as Indian democracy proved its resilience particularly in accommodating the interests of the national minorities. With the young generations of the Nagas setting out in the vast Indian expanse for decent living, orthodox Naga perception is increasingly loosing in the wilderness. In the post cold war strategic alignment of nations, while, on the one hand, it has become increasingly difficult to garner state support by the non-state actors, on the other, the forces of globalization have changed the traditional perceptions of the young generations of the Nagas who hardly agree to be the torchbearer of the age-old conflict. While, perhaps, due to this realization, NSCN (I-M) now underplays the demand for 'sovereignty', which otherwise appears to be unrealizable goal particularly following the transformation of India as a nuclear power, and focuses on the demand for unification of the Naga inhabited contiguous territories within India. Following the gesture shown by the Indian Government to accommodate the demand for unification, the severe resistance that has emerged in Manipur against Government of India's extension of cease-fire agreement with NSCN (I-M) 'without territorial limit' has led the Naga militants to single out the Meiteis as the prime obstacle on their way to achieve unification. Meiteis' demand for the preservation of the territorial integrity of Manipur stands on the way of Nagas' aspiration for unification. In fact, the demands of the Naga nationalism for 'unification' and the Meitei nationalism for 'territorial integrity' are mutually exclusive. This mutual exclusivity of national goals has stonewalled the inter community relations and made them political opponent of each other. Naga nationalism in Manipur has grown in this polemic and, under the leadership of NSCN (I-M), has distanced itself from the idea of a shared Manipur and has moved closure to demand for Naga unification. We shall deal with the growth of Naga nationalism in Manipur in the next section.

Growth of Naga Nationalism in Manipur

Nagas live in Manipur hills since time immemorial. They are the second largest group in the state. They occupy 55 per cent (approximately in 2001 Census) of the total geographical area of the state. There are 18 Naga sub-tribes in Manipur. They are: Aimol, Anal, Chiru, Chothe, Kharam, Koireng, Kom, Maring, Mayon, Monshang, Lamkang, Mao, Maram, Thangal, Poumai, Tangkhul, Tarao and Zeliangrong (Singh, 2008: 53). As referred earlier, the use of the name Naga among these sub-tribes have been popularized after the World War II.

The growth of nationalism among the Nagas of Manipur can be traced back to the first half of 20th century. Like the Nagas of Nagaland, they also started their movement against the foreign rule. After 1891, when the British took over the administration of Manipur, the whole of the hill areas were administered directly by the British with the help of the *lambus*. Along with the establishment of the British rule, the spread of Christianity also gained momentum. While the spread of Hinduism during the 18th century could not penetrate in the hills, similarly the spread of Christianity in the beginning of 20th century could not penetrate in the valley. The rigid orthodox structure of Hinduism alienated the tribals who were otherwise treated at par with any plain people. This gap was further widened with the coming of Christianity.

As mentioned earlier, the first Christian missionary, William Pettigrew, came to Manipur in 1894 and was given permission to work among the Tangkhuls in Ukhrul district of Manipur. He started schools and it served as the most important medium of spreading the new faith. However, he was opposed in the beginning by the Tangkhuls but with the help of the then British officers, especially the Political Agent of Manipur, he could peacefully carry out the evangelist works through the school (Singh, 1991; 78, 86).

The 'divide and rule' policy of the British was also another important factor for the alienation of the tribals from the people in the Imphal Valley. As has been discussed already, most of these independent tribes had developed some sort of relationship with the rulers of Manipur during the 15th century. By 18th century the king of Manipur used to exercise a great control over these tribes and even extended the system of *lallup* in the hills. Many of the Nagas were also inducted into the king's army. But Nagas were not brought under regular administration by the Meitei kings. At times, a kind of 'transient-suzerainty' was established over them. However, with the coming of the British, the administration of the hills was directly by run the British and it was not under the purview of the State Durbar.

The British rule brought many changes in the age-old traditional tribal society. As referred earlier, they had to pay a house tax of Rs. 3 per annum, which had caused hardship to the tribals as they were not required to pay any tax before the establishment of the British rule. Moreover, the spread of Christianity was a major cause of concern, though almost all the tribals have become Christians now, as it was a superimposition of foreign religion and practices over the traditional beliefs and practices. Jadonang and Gaidinliu rose in revolt against the British in 1930, which may be termed as revivalist movement of the Zeliangrongs.[68] The superimposition of the new religion, superstitious practices of the old religion and growing disunity among these tribes were the main reasons for Jadonang and Gaidinliu to rise in revolt against the British. The movement took a semi-military, semi-religious and semi-political character (For details of the movement, Kabui, 1990: 135-144; Singh, 1992: 56-67, 2002: 128-133).

The movement, however, was finally subdued with the capture of both Jadonang and Gaidinliu. Jadonang was sentenced to death by Higgins, the then Political Agent of

Manipur and the sentence was carried out on August 29, 1931 at Imphal. Gaidinlu was arrested on October 17, 1932 and was sentenced to life imprisonment but was released after Independence.

While in Nagaland, as has already been discussed, with the formation of NNC, the growth of nationalism took an anti-Indian turn, the Nagas of Manipur were not integrated with the movement. The Nagas of Manipur were neither a signatory to the memorandum submitted by NC to the Simon Commission nor took part in Phizo's plebiscite of 1951 on the question of Nagas' independence. Moreover, the Nagas of Manipur were not included in the proposed idea of 'unified Nagaland' as demanded by the NPC in 1957. The leaders of NPC only demanded for unification of the Tuensang division of NEFA and not any Naga inhabited areas of Manipur (Nag, 2002: 150).

Rani Gaidinliu, one of the leading revivalist Naga social reformer and freedom fighter, after her release from jail in 1947, opposed Phizo's demand for independence. She even went underground to organize her people to fight against the NNC militants. Under her leadership Naga nationalism in Manipur, based on traditional Naga culture, emerged as an alternative force to NNC dominated Naga nationalism based on Christianity and western culture (Stracey, 1968: 44). Thus, Gaidinliu inspired nationalistic ideas of the Nagas of Manipur came in direct conflict with the NNC inspired Naga nationalism of Nagaland. This rivalry between the two sheds of Naga nationalism, however, gradually died down following the surrender of Gaidinliu and her followers in 1966 [Singh (P), 1995: 26].

Although the Naga nationalistic territorial claim over the Naga inhabited areas of Manipur was tacitly legitimized for the first time when the 1964 Indo-Naga Cease-fire was extended to Ukhrul, Mao and Tamenglong, even then some prominent leaders of the Nagas under the banner of All Tribal Delegation[69] went to Delhi in May, 1970 to demand statehood for Manipur and stuck to the stand to remain with Manipur instead of acceding to Nagaland (Singh, 2008: 50).

However, the demand for unification of Naga inhabited areas in Manipur with Nagaland got a boost following the declaration of INC that it did not consider the Naga integration movement as anti-party, anti-national and unconstitutional activity (www.satp.org). The demand for unification was brought into the sharp focus following the establishment, and ascendance to hegemony, of the NSCN and subsequently NSCN (I-M). In fact NSCN (I-M) has bridged the Naga aspirations for unification across Nagaland and Manipur. As the Tangkhuls have become the backbone of the Naga army under NSCN (I-M), who form the majority of the Naga population in Manipur, the voice of the Nagas may be treated as equivalent to the voice of the NSCN (I-M). With the strategy of NSCN (I-M) to engage the Government of India through peace overtures and effecting the merger of Naga inhabited hills of Manipur as part of the bargain backfired on the face of stiff opposition[70] from the Meiteis, the Naga nationalism in Manipur turned assertive and restive.[71] NSCN (I-M) mobilized the Nagas of Manipur through Naga social organizations like United Naga Council, Manipur (UNCM), All Naga Students' Association, Manipur (ANSAM) and Naga Women's Union, Manipur (NWUM).[72] In fact the question of unification has put the Nagas of Manipur in a dilemma. While the Christian Nagas in general and Christian Nagas under the influence of NSCN (I-M) in particular are, explicitly or tacitly, in favour of unification, but non-Christian Nagas in general and a segment of the politically active Christian Nagas other than NSCN (I-M) are in favour of status quo.[73]

Thus, the Naga nationalism in Manipur has two dimensions. Initially, it started against the British rule and the spread of Christianity. However, in the later stage, especially after the dominance of NSCN (I-M), the aspirations of the Nagas of Manipur have tagged with the goal of unification of Nagas as professed by NSCN (I-M). This aspiration of the Nagas has led to anti-Meitei feeling and Meiteis are seen as an obstacle to their goal for Naga unification. Although a segment of the Nagas does not favour any realignment of the territorial boundary of Manipur, they are, however, awfully miniscule. Besides the Meiteis and Nagas, Kukis are the third largest group in Manipur. As the Nagas and Kukis have overlapping settlement in many parts of Manipur hills, the Naga movement for unification has a direct bearing upon the livelihood security of the Kukis. Both the perceived and real threat perception to the livelihood security has led to the politicization of the Kuki community and the emergence of Kuki nationalism. The growth of Kuki nationalism will be taken up in the next section.

Growth of Kuki Nationalism

The Kukis form the third largest group in Manipur besides the Meiteis and Nagas. They constitute about 15 per cent of the total population of Manipur according to 1991 Census. Present Churachandpur District of Manipur has been the traditional home of the Kukis besides hills in Mizoram, Chittagong Hill Tracts in Bangladesh and Somra Tract in Myanmar. With the growth of Kuki population largely due to immigration from Lushai hill areas (Mizoram), their settlement had spilled over to neighbouring Naga dominated areas. Also long back during the first half of the 19th century, British had settled a significant wandering Kuki population along the border areas in order to protect the British territory of North Cachar Hills from the frequent Naga raids and to act as guardian of exposed frontiers. In the process, Kuki settlements had sprung up in all the Naga dominated hills of Manipur, viz., Senapati, Chandel, Tamenglong and Ukhrul.

The Kuki Identity

The Kukis were a wandering race. They were first heard in 1777 during the Governor Generalship of Warren Hastings, when these tribes frequently attacked the British subjects in Chittagong (Gangte, 1993: 19; Kabui, 1995: 34). They were, however, heard in Manipur in between 1830 and 1840. In 1845, their large scale migration caused anxiety to the old Kuki inhabitants in Manipur hills (Johnstone, 2002: 45). In order to bring a solution to the problem, McCulloch, the then Political Agent of Manipur, allotted land and settled them down in such a manner that they act as guards on exposed frontiers. Following McCulloch's policy, in 1855 the British Government settled a large colony of Kukis to the east of North Cachar and beyond the Langting river to act as a barrier against the Naga raids in North Cachar (Johnstone, 2002: 45; Ray, 1990: 28).

Like the term Naga, the Kuki is also a generic term applied to the various sub-tribes, viz., Thadou, Paite, Hmar, Simte, Zou, Gangte, Vaiphei, Guite, Ralte, Sukte, etc. In Manipur, they were known as Khongjais before the use of the term Kuki. However, it is still not known for certainty as to the origin of the generic term Kuki. There are three views regarding the origin of the term Kuki: (i) it is derived from a word applied to a system of cultivation by the Bengalis (Dun, 1981: 32); (ii) it is derived from the Baluchisthan word *'Kuchis'* meaning 'wandering people' and (iii) it is derived from the English word *'Kooky'* meaning 'peculiar or unusual people' (Vaiphei, 1995: 126). Though no definite answer is found as to the origin of the term Kuki, it is widely accepted that it was given by the outsiders.

The Traditional Kuki Society

The Kuki society is marked by a unique political structure. The Kukis lived in villages, which is the highest political unit. Each village is administered by a Chief and his Council of

Ministers (Gangte, 1993: 124). The Kukis lived in peace for centuries along with the Meiteis and Nagas. Unlike the Nagas, they neither practiced head hunting nor raided the plains. Perhaps, the practice of this principle of peaceful coexistence had made their presence oblivious in an age of feudal aggression. This might be the prime reason as to why the Kukis were hardly figured in the long Meitei history.

A Kuki Chief is the ruler of the village. A Chief must be the head of the clan or sub-tribe to which he belongs (Misao, 1995: 148). He is entitled with annual tributes, free labour and other privileges like marriage fees, hind leg of an animal killed in the village, etc. (Ray, 1990: 43). In return, it is his duty to protect the village from external threats and provide social, political and economic security to the villagers. The chieftainship is hereditary and is passed on from father to his eldest son (Gangte, 1993: 125-127), which exhibits strict adherence to the rule of primogeniture.

The whole land in a Kuki village belongs to the Chief. No individual has a claim over any part of the village land. The Chief distributes the land to all the villagers for cultivation and in return he is entitled to get a tax in the form of paddy from each household (Devi, 2006: 52). The Kukis practice shifting cultivation since time immemorial. Besides paddy, they also produce cotton, maize, millet, cucumbers, sweet potatoes, watermelons, jams, beans, etc. (Lhungdim, 1995: 153-159).

The Kukis before the advent of Christianity believed in a supreme deity, who is creator of everything. He is called *Chung Pathien* or the source of 'All Creations' (Bhattacharyya, 1963: 171; Gangte, 1993: 161). They also perform various rites and ceremonies to appease the gods and to protect them from sickness and natural calamities, etc. (For details, Bhattacharyya, 1963: 171-173; Gangte, 1993: 160-220).

While the spread of Christianity started among the Tangkhuls by William Pettigrew in 1894, it had not yet penetrated among the Kukis. The Kukis were introduced to the new religion rather very late compared to the Tangkhuls. The spread of Christianity among the Kukis started in 1910, after the arrival of Watkin R. Roberts, who had his base in Aizawl, Lushai hills (Lal Dena, 1990: 109). Initially the Kukis were not in a position to accept the new religion as they saw the missionaries to be hand-in-hand with British colonialists. It is widely believed that their defeat in the Kuki Rebellion of 1917-19, which will be taken up in the next section, was the stepping stone for them to accept the new faith (Haokip, 2008).

Growth of Kuki Nationalism in Manipur

The growth of Kuki nationalism also started, like the Nagas, initially through mobilization of the Kukis against the British. The anti-British position of the Kukis in Manipur hills can be traced to at least three reasons. Firstly, it has already been mentioned that the administration of hill areas of Manipur was directly entrusted to the Vice-president of the State Durbar, who was a British subject. He was assisted by Manipuri *lambus* in the affairs of the administration. These *lambus* who were mere peons and interpreters assumed much authority during the British rule. This hurt the sentiments of the Kuki chiefs who were individualistic persons and who used to consider themselves at par with the Maharaja of Manipur. Such an administrative set up created a gap between the people and the officials. Secondly, the economic condition of the Kukis were no better off with the imposition of house tax of Rs. 3 per annum and the obligation of free labour under the system of *pothang* which they disliked. Thirdly, the conditions of the Kukis were further worsened when they were sent to France as Labour Corps during the World War I, much against their will. Then the blow came when the government gave a second calling for such recruitment. This time the Kuki chiefs did not give in easily to the British and they resisted all forms of British action towards recruitment. The British, being humiliated, burnt down a Kuki village in October, 1917, and deployed columns of Assam Rifles. The Kukis retaliated by closing roads, destroying rest houses, telegraph lines and conducted raids on neighbouring villages, especially in Naga inhabited areas. The reports of raiding villages and loss of lives came pouring in the following years as well. In order to contain the rebels British finally launched the Kuki punitive measures with a combined force of Assam Rifles and Burma military police. The Kuki chiefs finally surrendered and the rebellion subsided towards the end of 1919 (For more details of the rebellion, Lal Dena, 1990: 126-134; Ray, 1990: 63-82; Singh, 1992: 43-55, 2002: 122-128). This incident which is popularly known as 'Kuki Rebellion' in imperial historiography might be seen as the anti-colonial freedom struggle of the Kukis. This anti-colonial struggle had cemented the relationship of the Kukis across the villages and brought the Chiefs closer to each other. The Kuki identity was also widened.

With the British raj coming to an end, the Kukis formed the Kuki National Assembly (KNA), in October, 1946, to press forward the cause of the Kukis and demand for a homeland for themselves. However, with the merger of Manipur into the Indian Union in 1949, this demand was subsided. In fact the KNA, largely dominated by the Thadou chiefs, in its search for a homeland for the Kukis, switched over from the idea of an independent 'Kukiland' to a 'Kuki State' within India to a 'Kuki District' within Manipur. It has even come down to a Sixth Schedule type autonomy for the Kukis which, although they have not demanded directly but supported All Tribal Students Union of Manipur (ATSUM) who made this demand. The Kuki movement for 'homeland', which is the rallying point of all shades of Kuki sub-tribes, however, was characterized by intra-tribal split of loyalty. Right at the inception, in 1946, an alternative Kuki organization, viz., Khulmi National Union (KNU), was floated by the non-Thadou community leaders like Paite, Hmar, Vaiphei, Haokip, Kom, Maring, Chiru, Mate, Guite, Baite, Lhungdim, Lengthang, Lunkim, Changsan, Sabom, Sonte, Anal, Pakan, Lushai, etc. (Ray, 1990: 120) in order to counter the Thadou domination in the movement for homeland. The insular social structure and authoritative political structure of the Kukis did not allow the movement to break the village-based/sub-tribe-centered identity boundaries to forge a wider social boundary under the generic name 'Kuki'. As a result, the movement for homeland was caught into the cogs of intra-tribal rivalry.

However, with the Nagas and other tribal groups in the region getting their homelands, the young generations of the Kukis became restive. The sense of desperateness has increased manifold with the NSCN gaining ground in the hills of Manipur since 1980 and their demand for unification started becoming louder. With the ascendancy of the NSCN (I-M) at the driver's seat since 1988, Kukis have realized a serious threat to their livelihood. The realization that without a well-demarcated homeland the future of the Kukis is destined to be doomed has dawned into the Kuki community psyche. The failure of both KNA and KNU to address the livelihood threats faced by the community has led to the birth of a plethora of Kuki underground organizations leading to the transformation of the Kuki movement for homeland into a militant movement.

The demand for a Kuki homeland called 'Zale'n-gam: land of freedom' was spearheaded with the formation of underground government called Kuki National Organisation (KNO) and its armed wing Kuki National Army (KNA*) in 1988 under the leadership of Pu Thangkholun. The main objective of KNO is to carve out a homeland for the Kukis, i.e., 'Kukiland', one in India and the other in Myanmar

[Haokip (P), 2008: 376-377, 403]. Similarly, Nehlun Kipgen, formed the Kuki National Front (KNF) in 1988 with the objective of carving out an autonomous 'Kukiland' under the Constitution of India (Kipgen, 2006). However, the territorial claims of the Kukis overlap the territorial claims of the Nagas in Manipur. This overlapping territorial interest has brought the two communities into a conflicting situation. The Nagas see the Kukis as a barrier on the way to their long cherished goal for unification. The territorial claims of the Kukis include the districts of Churachandpur, Chandel and some portions of Tamenglong, Senapati and Ukhrul, whereas the Nagas claim the districts of Tamenglong, Senapati, Ukhrul and Chandel. Thus, the Kukis and Nagas have overlapping and conflicting territorial interests over all the hill districts of Manipur, except Churachandpur.

This conflicting territorial claim has turned into inter-tribal warfare in 1992 while the Nagas at the behest of NSCN (I-M) asserted their supremacy over the Kukis (For details of the Naga-Kuki conflict, Singh, 2008). The conflict continued for about 6 years. During 1992-97, approximately a total of 677 people were butchered only in Manipur. Of them, 470 belonged to the Kuki community and 207 were Nagas (Singh, 2008: 113). Besides deaths, thousands from both sides were injured, thousands of houses were set on fire, thousands of children were maimed and community assets like schools, hospitals, churches and other community facilities were destroyed. This Naga-Kuki conflict also spilled over to Nagaland and Assam. As per the Kukis' claim, 154 Kukis were killed in Nagaland and 21 were killed in Assam [Haokip (P), 2008: 340-373]. What is most alarming - this conflict has damaged the inter-tribal relations beyond repair. The age-old traditional rivalry between the Nagas and Kukis has reached to a point of no return. While the optimization of group aspiration calls for an accommodative attitudinal perspective, the further hardening of inter-group relations is only detrimental to the professed goals of both the partners of the game.

One important implication of the conflict is the proliferation Kuki underground organizations. The failure of the state to protect the Kukis from the onslaught of the Nagas, especially NSCN (I-M), during the conflict, gave birth to Kuki Liberation Army (KLA), Kuki Revolutionary Army (KRA), Zomi Revolutionary Organisation (ZRO) and United Kuki Liberation Front (UKLF). The failure of the KNA* and KNF to stand up to the expectation, to protect the interests of the community and to resist the onslaught of the NSCN (I-M) has sent strong signals to every Kuki sub-tribe to look for a self-defence mechanism. The multiplicity of Kuki militant organizations may be seen as the resultant reaction of this social insecurity that has arisen out of the Naga-Kuki conflict of 1990s.

Another implication is the large scale displacement of the Kukis from conflict-ridden areas and their subsequent settlement in Churachandpur district, the safe homeland of the Kukis, which has destabilized the host society. The large scale migration of the Thadous had created some unrest among the other sub-tribes of Kukis like Paite, Simte, Zou, Vaiphei, etc. for fear of being outnumbered. Intra-Kuki antagonism arising out of the dominating attitude of the Thadous is believed to be the prime factor behind the onset of Kuki-Paite clash in 1997 [For details of Kuki-Paite clash, Singh (S), 2006: 61-73] and the consequent formation of Zomi Revolutionary Army (ZRA), the armed wing of ZRO, to protect the other Kuki sub-tribes from the dominance of Thadous.

Thus, the Kuki identity, developed during the colonial rule in the north eastern hills of British India, was consolidated through anti-British rebellion during 1917-19. The Kuki identity was further consolidated while the Kukis participated in the World War II in favour of the Indian

National Army (INA). The Thadous took the lead role in mobilizing the Kukis and forging the Kuki identity. In fact, the boundary of the Kuki identity is not very well defined. A number of village based small communities having their own specificities claim allegiance to both the Kukis and Nagas at different points in time. It may be mentioned that the Anal, Aimol, Chiru, Kom, Koireng and Lamkang groups of people used to claim allegiance to the Kukis before the outbreak of Naga-Kuki conflict in 1992, but the same groups shifted their allegiance and identify themselves as Nagas rather than the Kukis immediately after the conflict.

However, the Naga-Kuki conflict has led to the further consolidation of the Kuki identity. The political mobilization of the members of the Kuki community in support of a 'Kuki homeland' has transformed itself into a nationality. The Kuki nationalism is, thus, an outcome of the search of the Kukis for a homeland of their own. In fact, the demands for 'Kuki homeland' and 'unification of Nagas' are mutually exclusive. This has given rise to a serious inter-tribal animosity between Nagas and Kukis. A deep rooted feeling of deprivation permeates the Kuki national psyche. Firstly, the Kukis feel that they have not been rewarded for their anti-British position in the post colonial arrangement. Rather, with the vivisection of their homeland into three parts falling one part each in India, Bangladesh and Myanmar, Kukis have been the net looser. Secondly, although the Kukis played a positive role in maintaining the integrity of independent India, their interest has not been taken care of by the Indian Government. Thirdly, the national sentiments of the Kukis was severely hurt as the state of Manipur utterly failed to protect the lives of the innocent Kukis on the wake of the Naga-Kuki conflict. The Kuki nationalism, thus, stands aloof in an amazingly complex ethno-political matrix in Manipur and wanders into the blind lanes of militancy in search of a homeland of their own.

The accounts of growth of nationalism among the Meiteis, Nagas and Kukis presented above indicate that the national goals of these three major groups of people do not converge. Although these three groups of people stayed together side by side for centuries, they developed their heritage parallelly under the respective ethno-social boundaries. Each group had fought against the British at different points in time. There was no attempt on the part of the tribal/feudal elites to coordinate these struggles which could have ignited the process of assimilation in pre-colonial era. The 'divide and rule policy' of the colonial administration in relation to administering the hills and plains of Manipur and the working of the Christianity had further widened cultural distance between people in the hills and plains of Manipur. Although each group shares the common political boundary of the state of Manipur with other, their political aspirations are essentially confined within the ethno-social boundary. The optimization of group interest often leads a group to choose an option that violates the territorial integrity of the present political boundary of the state, e.g., the Naga demand for unification. The diverged national goals have, thus, created faultlines along ethno-social identity.

A socio-political space studded with rival groups demanding overlapping claims is ripe for the growth and sustenance of militancy. Without any ordered and reasoned mechanism for settlement of these overlapping claims, the myopic militant movements often find their way to a cobweb of violence without any solution.

Thus, while the conflicting interests at the local level generates militant response, these could not be mediated effectively by the Indian state as it has a limited reach to the local elites. In fact, neither the Meiteis, nor the Nagas and Kukis were integrated with the mainstream Indian nationalism which took shape through struggle for Independence. This missing link has made it difficult for the

Indian bureaucracy and political managers to appreciate the aspirations of the hitherto 'excluded' people. Indeed, this lack of realization has been one of the important factors for the growth and continuation of militancy in the north eastern region in general and Manipur in particular.

The socio-political stability of Manipur will continue to elude us in near future until and unless a consociational structure is evolved to accommodate the interests of the major ethno-social groups. The ethnic movements based on conflicting and overlapping claims have a tendency to diverge. Each of the three ethnic nationalisms has two distinct trends: democratic integrationist and militant secessionist or militant separatist. A complex intra-ethnic as well as inter-ethnic network of conflict and cooperation cutting across the ideologies has created a socio-political environment in Manipur which is beyond the comprehension of not only the subjects therein but also the observers from outside as well.

The complexity of the situation may be better understood from the fact that while the Meitei insurgent groups are demanding complete independence of Manipur from the Indian 'occupation forces', they do mean to free the present territorial boundary of Manipur over which they hardly have any control, and their claim is hardly sponsored by the Meitei integrationist, Nagas and Kukis. Neither the Naga nationalists nor the Kuki nationalists share the vision of the Meitei militant nationalism. Thus the objective socio-political reality of Manipur hardly lends any support to the demand for independence of the state from Indian Union as is being claimed by the Meitei insurgent groups.

Apart from contesting nationalist goals, the weak material base of the state of Manipur is believed to have been further exacerbating the conflict situation. A section of the educated reserve army, who suffer from intense feeling of deprivation as the stunted economic growth shuts the avenues of decent living before them, is filling the pipeline to militancy which is seen as a weapon to administer social justice. We shall focus on the state of the economy in the next chapter in order to reveal the interplay between the material base and socio-political processes in Manipur.

NOTES

1. The '*Cheitharon Kumpapa*' (herein after referred as Ch. K.) is the most important royal chronicle of Manipur. It records the events relating to the kings of Manipur right from the first king Nongda Lairen Pakhangba (33 A.D.) till the last king Boddhachandra (1941-55 A.D.).

2. Nongda Lairen Pakhangba is the first chief/king of the Ningthoujas or Meiteis. According to Ch. K. he ascended the throne in the Kali age 3135 i.e. 33 A.D. and he reigned for 120 years.

3. B. H. Hodgson suggested that the Meiteis belonged to the 'Moi' section of the great 'Tai' race. According to him, Meitei is a combined appellate of Siamese "Tai' and Kochin Chinese 'Moy' (Moy + Tai = Moytei = Moitai = Meitei). T. C. Hodson rejected this 'Moi' origin and propounded that the name 'Meitei' has been derived from Mi = man and Tei = separate, meaning separate people. Though there were evidences of relationships with Mon-Khmer and Tai people, he rejected Mon-Khmer-Tai origin of the Meiteis. Ch. Budhi Singh opines that Meitei is the outcome of the ethnic blending of people of 'Mei' and 'Ti' tribes of ancient China. G. A. Grierson presumed that the ancestors of the Meiteis were the Tibeto-Burman speaking people of south west China, eastern Tibet and upper Burma thus indicating that the Meiteis migrated from these places. Pemberton, however, concluded the Meitei to be descendents from a Tatar colony which emigrated from North West borders of China. Of all these hypotheses, McCulloch's theory of different tribes/clans which subsequently got subdued under the Ningthouja or Meitei appears to be the most probable explanation. Brown also agreed with his hypothesis of tribal origin.

4. *Ningthourol Lambuba* (a more detailed chronicle of the kings, but without chronology), *Ningthourol Kumbaba* (royal chronicle of the Ningthouja dynasty), *Chakpa Khunda Khunthok* (settlement of the Chakpas), *Pakhangba Phambal* (coronation of Pakhangba), *Naothingkhong Phambal Kaba* (coronation of Naothingkhong), *Khuman Kangleirol* (geneology of the Khumans), *Moirang*

Ningthourol Lambuba (chronicle of the Moirang prinicipality), *Poireiton Khunthokpa* (migration or colonization of Poireiton), *Angomlon* (geneology of the Angom clan), *Chengleiron* (geneology of the Chenglei clan), *Khabalon* (geneology of the Khaba clan), *Sagai-Shalailon* (clan geneologies), etc.

5. The first confrontation of the Ningthoujas with other clans was with the Angoms during the reign of Naophangpa (428 A.D.). The Angoms were defeated. Moirangs were defeated during the reign of Khongtekcha (763 A.D.). The Meiteis were victorious over the Khumans during the reign of Aayangpa (821 A.D.). Luwangs were captured during the reign of Chenglei Yipan Lanthapa (910 A.D.). Yirengpa (984 A.D.) fought with both the Moirangs and Khumans (Kabui, 1991; Manikchand, 1988; Parratt, 2005; Singh, 1987; Singh, 1992; Singh & Singh, 1989).

6. The first reference of Ningthouja chiefs/kings marrying girls of other clans is found during the reign of Loiyumpa (1074 A.D.) when he addressed the chief/king of Angom as his brother-in-law. The mother of Thingpai Senhongpa (1242 A.D.) was a Khuman again referring to inter clan marriage (Kabui, 1991; Parratt, 2005; Singh, 1987; Singh, 1992; Singh & Singh, 1989).

7. During the reign of Loiyumpa (1074-1121 A.D.), a royal edict was issued. It is known as '*Loiyamba Shinyen*' and is regarded as the first written constitution of the Meitei state. He divided the land into six administrative divisions, viz., *Aangoupa Lup, Nongmai Lup, Aakong Lup, Khurai Lup, Chingcha Lup and Khaicha Lup* (Kabui, 1988: 307-311, 1991: 125; Parratt, 2005: 29-30; Singh & Singh, 1989: 20).

8. The different family surnames were assigned different activities including the worshipping of gods. For example, the *Sharang Leishangthem* should bow down to *Shorarel* (heaven), the *Sharotkhaibam* should invoke the goddess *Phouoibi* (goddess of paddy), the *Potshangbam* should glorify the *Shanglangmei* (Kangla), the *Konthoujam* should pay divine service to *Huimureima*, etc. Other activites like taking care of the bathe was assigned to the *Arambam*, supervising the grave was the duty of the *Mangshatabam*, the *Wanglenbam* beat the drum, the *Haomukpam* make the *phak* (mattress for sitting), the *Nganukappam* look after the *nganu* (duck), the *Waleppam* adore the bamboo, etc. (Chandrasekhar & N. Sanajaoba, 1988: 300-301; Sanajaoba, 1993: 3-11).

9. For example, weaving the *Mungphi* (clothe known as *Leirum*) was assigned to the *Thingujam*, weaving the *Laiphi* (clothe for the god)

to the *Lairellakpam*, weaving the *Phirel* (clothe of topmost quality) to the *Chakpram*. The *Wahengbams* weave the *Dolai*-kupphi (palanquin cover), the *Haodeijams* weave the *Heikoi-phi* (specially designed clothe), etc. (Chandrasekhar & N. Sanajaoba, 1988: 299; Sanajaoba, 1993: 3).

10. The ancestral god of the Ningthoujas is called *Pakhangba* or *Nongpok Ningthou* (King of the East). The Angoms call their ancestral god as *Purairomba* and for other clans it is *Poiraton* for the Luwangs, *Khamdingou* for the Khabas, *Thangaren* for the Khumans, *Ngangningsing* for the Moirangs, *Nungaoyumthangba* for the Chengleis and *Luangpokpa* for the Luwangs (Hodson, 2007: 99-100).

11. The Moirang principality, an abode of rich cultural heritage and human civilization, was finally defeated by the Ningthouja chief Ningthoukhomba in 1432. Many nobles were captured but the whereabouts of the Moirang chief, Sanahongba were not recorded and it is, thus, not known. The Moiang principality accepted the suzerainty of the Ningthoujas. The chief of Moirang was given the tributary status (Kabui, 1991: 188-189; Parratt, 2005: 37; Singh & Singh, 1989: 18).

12. The Meitei kings' control over the hill tribes were short lived. They could not bring the hill tribes fully under their political control once for all. Every king during his reign used to send frequent military expeditions to subjugate the hill tribes. Such type of short lived control is being denoted by the term 'transient-suzerainty'.

13. The different departments that had been created for administrative purposes were *Lanmi Yareksang* (quarter guard of the army), *Dolai Paba Loisang* (department of palanquin riders or police), *Mayang Hishaba Loisang* (department of boat makers), *Shangom Sang* (royal dairy), *Pangan Sanglen* (department of Muslim), etc. (Kabui, 1991: 218).

14. The revenue department was put under the Lourungpurel Achouba who was paid salary in kind. His salary was two *kots* (granary) of paddy (Kabui, 1991: 220).

15. The Chinese name of brick '*chek*' is included in the Meitei vocabulary (Kabui, 1991: 221).

16. Garibniwaz means 'refuge of the poor' or 'kind to the poor'. It was most probably given to him for his kind acts to the poor and suffering. But it is a Persian name and it is known for certainty how a Hindu king assumed such name. His Hindu name was Gopal Singh (Kabui, 1991: 240; Singh, 1992: 145).

17. Kabui (1991: 253-254) has given the list of 123 *puyas* that had been burnt down.

18. The Meitei traditional god and goddesses were identified with Hindu pantheon. *Soraren*, the king of Heaven, was identified with Indra, Nongpok Ningthou with Shiva, Panthoibi with Durga and Wangbaren, the water god, with Varuna (Kabui, 1991: 279).

19. The annual boat race was renamed Jal Yatra. The archery festival was converted into a Kirtan of Lord Rama. The Ahong Khongching was equated with Ratha Jatra. The offering to the ancestors was replaced by Tarpan and the Wakambung Chingung Nongombi was substituted by Dasana Kwaktanba of Durga Puja or Dusserah (Kabui, 1991: 257).

20. The seven clans of the Meiteis with their equivalent Gotras are: Ninghthouja (Shandilya), Angom (Kaushika), Sarang-Leishangthem (Bhardhwja), Luwang (Kashyap), Khuman (Madhugalya), Moirang (Aitereya) and Khaba-Nganba (Gautam) (Kabui, 1991: 256).

21. Garibniwaz fought several wars with the Burmese over a period of three decades. He carried out numerous military expeditions against Samjok in 1717, 1718, 1720, 1722, 1737 and 1748. He invaded the Burmese many times in 1717, 1718, 1723 and 1738 (Kabui, 1991: 242-247; Parratt, 2005: 118-166; Singh & Singh, 1989: 72-119).

22. Garibniwaz's sister Chakpa Makhao Ngambi was married to the king of Ava. She was ill treated at the court of Ava. He thus avenged the ill treatment by invading Burma which was also one of the wishes of his father Charairongba (Kabui, 1991: 244).

23. Any fresh reclamation of land was charged a premium of 500 *shels*; 1000 shels for one *Loukhai* (1/8 pari) and 2000 *shels* for one *Loupi* (1/4 pari) (Kabui, 1991: 261).

24. Bhagyachandra (known as Jai Singh) sensing the threat from the Burmese entered into a treaty with the East India Company in the year 1762. The British taking advantage of the weak position of the king had made the terms of treaty in their favour. The king was weak and lacked diplomacy. His successors were worse and they were only after the throne and less cared for the kingdom. Marjit Singh went to the extent of ceding the Kabaw valley and accepted the suzerainty of the Burmese for the kingship of Manipur.

25. In 1813 the Burmese force along with Marjit Singh defeated the king Chaurajit and prince Gambhir and they took refuge in Cachar.

Marjit, thus, became the king of Manipur but he was a vassal ruler under the suzerainty of the Burmese. Marjit was not satisfied with such vassal status and defied the royal summon by the king of Burma, Bagyidaw, to be present at his coronation and pay homage which was customary for any vassal ruler. This offence led to the Burmese conquest of Manipur in 1819 (Banerjee, 1934: 202; Bhattacharyya, 1963: 55; Kabui, 1991: 285-288).

26. The population of the valley was estimated at 10,000 (Singh, 1992: 248), while Brown (2001: 64) estimated the male population in the valley at 3,000, with a scanty proportion of women and children.

27. When Chandrakanta Singh ascended the throne of Assam, Purnananda, the Burha Gohain, tried to murder him. Badan Barphukan, the Viceroy of Gauhati, went in person to Burma and persuaded the court of Amarapura to send a force in aid of Chandrakanta. Consequently, in early 1817 the Burmese force appeared and crushed all oppositions and installed Chandrakanta on the throne. When Burmese learnt that Chandrakanta was again unseated, they reappeared in 1819 and reinstated the king. This time the king realized that Burma was a dangerous ally and he fled first to Gauhati and then to Bengal. Assam, thus, passed under the control of the Burmese (Banerjee, 1934: 187-190; Barpujari, 1963: 8).

28. Marjit fled to Cachar after Burmese occupation of Manipur in 1819. He reconciled with his brothers Chaurajit and Gambhir, who were already in Cachar, and invaded Cachar and ousted king Govinda Chandra, who took refuge in Sylhet (Banerjee, 1934: 202-203; Bhattacharyya, 1963: 55; Kabui, 1991: 288). Govinda Chandra entered into negotiations with the Burmese when the British did not comply with him to regain the lost kingdom from the Manipuri princes. This led to the Burmese invasion of Cachar which was made futile by Gambhir Singh and subsequently by the British (Banerjee, 1934: 206-207; Bhattacharyya, 1963: 56).

29. The eastern frontier of British India was extended upto Chittagong, Sylhet and Goalpara districts. The Burmese empire touched the border of the British frontier of Chittagong. It has occupied Assam and was proceeding towards Cachar. The occupation of Cachar would place Sylhet completely at their mercy. Moreover, one of the easiest passes from Burma into the British possessions is through Manipur and Cachar. Realizing the strategic importance of Cachar and Manipur, British changed their non-intervention policy and declared war against Burma on March 5, 1824 (Banerjee, 1934: 204; Bhattacharyya, 1963: 57-58).

30. The first Anglo-Burmese war ended with the signing of the Treaty of Yandaboo on February 24, 1826.

31. Manipur Levy is a militia group of 500 soldiers which Gambhir Singh established in order to fight against the Burmese occupation force. During the Anglo-Burmese war its strength was increased to 2000 by the Governor-General in Council and appointed two British officers, Captain F. J. Grant and Lt. R. B. Pemberton, as the Commandant and Assistant of the Levy respectively. Another officer, George Gordon, was appointed as the Adjutant of the Levy (Singh, 2002: 42).

32. The office of the Political Agent was created after the abolition of the Manipur Levy in order to preserve a friendly relation with Manipur and British India and as a medium of communication with the Manipur Government and the Burmese and more importantly to prevent border feuds and disturbances which might lead to hostilities between Manipur and Burma. Lt. George Gordon, Adjutant of the Manipur Levy, was appointed as the first Political Agent of Manipur in 1835 with a consolidated salary of Rs. 1,000 (Mackenzie, 1999: 153).

33. Gambhir Singh was succeeded by his infant son, Chandrakirti Singh, and was placed under the regent Nar Singh, a senapati of Gambhir. During his regency, Taringkhomba, son of late king Labyanachandra, revolted in 1838 but he was killed. Within the next few years, Marjit's son, Jogendra Singh made an unsuccessful attempt to overthrow the crown. Later, Tribhubanjit and Ram Singh, sons of Chaurajit, also made an attempt but both were killed. In 1844, an attempt was made on the life of the regent Nar Singh but it failed. After this incident the Maharani Kumudini fled to Cachar along with her infant king. Nar Singh declared himself Raja and shortly after Melai Romba and his brothers, descendants of Charairongba, made an attempt to invade the kingdom but they were executed. After the death of Nar Singh, his brother, Debendra Singh, ascended the throne. This time Chandrakirti Singh, who had attained the age of eighteen years, along with the sons of Nar Singh, dethroned Debendra. In 1851 the British Government recognized the kingship of Chandrakirti Singh. Very shortly after, Debendra's sons and Nar Singh's sons made an unsuccessfull attempt to overthrow the crown. After a year, two sons of Madhuchandra and Kanhai Singh, son of Marjit, made an attempt. They were captured but Kanhai escaped. In 1859, Maipak, a descendant of Garibniwaz, made an attempt but he was defeated. Kanhai made a second attempt in the beginning of 1865 but he was completely crushed. The last raid

was led by Gokul Singh, son of Debendra, in 1866, but he too met the same faith like other rebels (Brown, 2001: 65-70).

34. The Anglo-Manipur war broke out in 1891. It started with a palace coup in 1890 in which the Maharaja Surachandra Singh was ousted by a faction of his brothers. The Maharaja, instead of trying to regain his throne, expressed his desire to abdicate the throne and retire his life in Brindavan. Subsequently, Kulachandra became the new Maharaja and Tikendrajit was made the Jubraj. But the ex-Maharaja, on reaching Calcutta, asked the British government to reinstate him on the throne of Manipur. But the British government decided to recognize Kulachandra as the Maharaja on the condition that Jubraj Tikendrajit whom the British regarded as the architect of the palace coup must be banished from Manipur. It was the implementation of this decision that led to the outbreak of Anglo-Manipur War in 1819. The war finally ended with the capture of the palace by the British. The princes were either arrested or surrendered. The British also met with heavy losses especially the life of five important officers among who were Mr. J W Quinton, the Chief Commissioner of Assam and Mr. Grimwood, the Political Agent of Manipur. The British government ordered the trial of the princes and those who were involved in the war. Maharaja Kulachandra was given the sentence of transportation of life. Jubraj Tikendrajit and Thangal General were given death sentence. They were hanged on August 13, 1891 at Imphal market (Grimwood, 2003; Kabui, 1990: 48-69; Singh, 2002: 69-77). The day is being observed as 'Patriots' Day'.

35. The villagers could no longer bear the burden of *pothang* and so they carried out many protests against the system and submitted petitions to abolish it. The villagers of Thoubal, Bishnupur, Potsangbam, Thamnapokpi, Kakching, Nambol, etc. defied the orders of the Durbar and did not carry out *pothang* at different points of time. Although they were fined and forced to carry out the feudal service they did not turn back and continued to revolt against the system till its abolition in 1913 (Singh, 1998: 85-95).

36. *Lambus* were representatives and messengers of the government. They were used for the purpose of communication with the hill villages and checking taxable houses besides carrying out the duties of Police (Devi, 2000: 172).

37. The first missionary to enter the state was William Pettigrew. Initially he started his work in the capital area by establishing schools but later on he was shifted to work at Ukhrul among the Tangkhuls. This was basically due to the British neutrality policy

in religious matters after the Revolt of 1857 and the rising unrest among the Hinduised Meiteis against such activities [Constantine, 1981: 246-247; Lal Dena, 1990: 105-107; Parratt (J), 2005: 61-62].

38. The Brahma Sabha of Manipur was a storehouse of social abuse and oppression. Unlike the Brahma Samaj of Bengal which was fighting against the orthodox practices of Hinduism, in Manipur the role of the Brahma Sabha was just the opposite.

39. The bungalow of Captain Nuttall and Mr. Dunlop, Assistant to the Political Agent was burnt to the ground on the midnight of March 15, 1904. Again after three and half months, on July 6, the Khwairamband bazaar which contained 28 sheds with a seat capacity for 3000 market women was completely destroyed by fire. Then in the night of August 4, 1904, the bungalow lately purchased by the state from Mr. Mitchell, executive engineer and in occupation again of Captain Nuttall and Mr. Dunlop was totally destroyed by fire (Singh, 2006: 42).

40. The inhabitants of Imphal finally submitted to the British and carried out *lallup* to rebuild the bungalow of the Assistant Political Agent.

41. Until British arrival the market place where women used to sit for their daily transactions was an open field. Market sheds were established only after British rule in 1891 by the then Political Agent, Maxwell (Singh, 2006: 40-41).

42. The main objectives of the Mahasabha were: (i) to remove the racial differences between Meiteis and Bishnupriyas, (ii) to fill the gap of the dearth of Manipuri literature, (iii) to encourage education for all and (iv) to bring national integrity and prosperity (Singh, 1989: 48-52).

43. Export of Rice

Year	*Rice exported (maund)*	*Year*	*Rice exported (maund)*
1924	181370	1932	205287
1925	199710	1933	277389
1926	155014	1934	223523
1927	40729	1935	254619
1928	47499	1936	189608
1929	165983	1937	240625
1930	164510	1938	261716
1931	151725	1939	372174

Source: Singh, 2006: 116-117, 165

44. Price of Rice / Price of Rice

Year	*Seers per rupee (1 seer = 0.93 kg)*	*Year*	*Seers per rupee (1 seer = 0.93 kg)*
1931	22 seers	1936	21 seers
1932	34 seers	1937	26 seers
1933	46 seers	1938	20.8 seers
1934	41.5 seers	1939	32 seers
1935	32 seers		

Source: Singh, 2006: 164-165

45. By the end of the year 1939 the price of rice had risen to Rs. 2 per maund and further to Rs. 3, 4 *annas* per maund (Singh, 2006: 166).

46. The Manipur Krishi Sanmeloni was established under the umbrella of NHMM in 1936 as an organization for the peasants with its headquarters at Nambol. Its founding members were Salam Herachandra and Maimon Madhumangol [Parratt (J), 2005: 37].

47. The *Sanamahi* movement was started by Naorem Phullo, a Meitei from Cachar with the foundation of *Apokpa Marup* in 1930. In Manipur it took a definite shape with the establishment of *Meitei Phurup* in 1945 by Pukhrambam Surachand. The main objective of the movement was to revive the lost identity of the Meiteis. They opposed the Mahabharatta connection of Manipur and the Aryan origin of the Meiteis. They devoted themselves to the discovery of the ancient manuscripts and popularization of the Meitei script. The movement also took an anti-Brahmin and anti-Hindu turn as it started questioning the rigid class system and the orthodox practices of Hinduism (Kabui, 1990: 101-104).

48. The constitutional making committee was comprised of F.F. Pearson, President, Manipur State Durbar, S. Somorendra (from the Durbar), Md. Quazi Walli Ulla (from the Durbar), L. M. Ibungohal (from Chief Court), A. Ibotombi (His Highness's nominee), Dr. Lairen, S. Krishnamohan, L. Jugeshwar, I. Mera Jatra, Dwijamani Dev Sharma (deputed from the Tahsils of Imphal East, Imphal West, Mayang Imphal, Thoubal and Bishnupur), A. Daiho, Thangkhopao, M. K. Shimray, Tiankham and Teba Kilong (deputed from the hill areas Ukhrul, Mao, Tamenglong, Churachandpur and South-East area) (Singh, 1989: 189-190).

49. The full text of the Manipur State Constitution Act, 1947 is available in Sanajaoba (1993: 358-369).

50. The Interim Council was formed with the following members: M. K. Priyobrata Singh, K. Gouro Singh, Bashiruddin Ahmad, S. Krishnamohan Singh and R. K. Bhubansana Singh.

51. A mammoth public meeting of the people of both the valley and hills of Manipur was held on 18.9.1948 in which it was resolved that they will strongly protest against the move for and attempt at the creation of a new administrative province fondly called Purbachal comprising Manipur, Cachar and Tripura (*Resistance*, July 18, 1978: 6).

52. Earlier in a special meeting of the Manipur State Council held on 3.9.1948 it was resolved that the activities of the Krishak Sabha (communist) were becoming subversive of law and order and in the interest of the public security and maintenance of public order such activities should be prohibited. It was hereby notified that the holding of processions, meetings or assemblies by the said organization and its members were prohibited unless a written permission was procured from the S.P. prior to holding of such processions, etc. The Sabha had already obtained the prior permission from the S.P. for the said meeting on 21.9.1948. But the police met some people at Pungdombam on their way to the venue and actually prevented them from going towards the venue. There occurred a scuffle and unfortunately firing had taken place and killed one Naren Baran, S.I. on the spot. The police then resorted to lathi charge and many were severely hurt. Day after day the police with arms in entered the villages in the area and searched from house to house looking for members of the Sabha, thereby causing destruction to the household properties of the people (Singh, 1989: 311-326).

53. The appointment of a Dewan came as a result of the Agreement signed on July 2, 1947. In the agreement, it was expressly provided that an Agent of the Indian Dominion should remain at Imphal and exercise certain specific functions. Accordingly, the Dominion Agent would be abolished and in place, a Dewan would be appointed so that the relations of the State with the Dominion might be conveniently conducted. Accordingly, Major General Rawal Amar Singh was appointed as the Dewan on 16.4.1949 with the following powers: (a) the administration of Manipur state should be carried on under the general superintendence, guidance and control of the Dewan, (b) the Dewan should hold direct charge of the portfolios of law and order, administration of Hill tracts, state forces and relations with the Government of India (*Resistance*, July 3, 1979: 6).

54. When the INA force entered Manipur it could not get mass support from the people. The Maharaja, Durbar members and other state officers allied with the British. Even Irabot, who was in exile in Cachar, requested the Chief Secretary to the Government of Assam to allow him to enter Manipur so that he could raise volunteers to fight against the INA force. However, after hoisting the National Flag at Moirang in April 14, 1944, many members of the NMM started working for the INA. The people of Bishnupur and Miorang area also strongly supported the force (Singh, 1998: 172-175).

55. On November 25 and 26, 1954, there was a clash between the agitators and the police at the gate of the office of the Advisory Council and in these incidents about 85 persons were injured. Again on December, 17, 1954, police opened fire at the agitators injuring 3 persons and arrested 150 of them (Singh, 2002: 206).

56. Many leaders of the movement, viz., S. Somorendra, Rishang Keishing, Dr. Lairen, Paokhohang, S. L. Luneh and Paolen were arrested under the Preventive Detention Act (Singh, 2002: 206-207).

57. The socialists comprises of MSP and Praja Socialist Party (PSP). A group of defectors from the Congress Socialist Party formed the PSP after the 1952 general election by merging with Kisan Mazdoor Praja Party.

58. The Executive Committee of the PSP demanded for this pre-merger status (Singh, 2002: 217).

59. The practice of head-hunting prevalent in the old Naga society had religious sanction, economic utility, political considerations, social value and justice. [For details, Hodson, 2007: 115-122; Shimray, 1985: 71-97; Singh (P), 1995: 35-40].

60. During the World War I, many people were recruited, especially the Nagas and Kukis of Naga hills and Manipur to carry out the works of a coolie in France. They were known as Labour Corps.

61. Naga Club was formed in 1918. It was formed by the people who had returned from France after serving as Labour Corps during World War I. Its members also included Christian educated government officials, village chiefs and Dobashis (interpreters). Initially it was a social organization and ran a co-operative store and formed a football club. Gradually it became politically conscious and emerged as a strong political organization (Ghosh, 1982: 155; Sema, 1986: 80).

62. The Indian Statutory Commission was a group of seven British Members of Parliament that had been dispatched to India in 1927 to study constitutional reform in the colony. It is commonly referred to as Simon Commission after its chairman, Sir John Simon (http://en.wikipedia.org).

63. The Federal Government of Nagaland (FGN), the underground government was set up by NNC. The rulers of the government like the president, prime minister, governor, commissioners, deputy commissioners, etc. were either selected or appointed from NNC, the only political party of FGN.

64. The first Naga People's Convention (NPC) was held from August 22 to 26 in 1957 at Kohima. Its members consisted of underground sympathizers, members of NNC who differed from Phizo and the integrationists. Dr. Imkhongliba Ao, an active worker of NNC, was the President of NPC until his assassination in 1961(Horam, 1988: 82; Stracey, 1968: 95).

65. The Naga Hills Tuensang Area (NHTA) was formed on December 1, 1957, by combining the Naga Hills District and the Tuensang division of NEFA. It was placed under the part B tribal area within Assam. Under this category, the post of a commissioner was created to assist the Governor in the administration of NHTA. The Governor appointed deputy commissioners for the districts within NHTA, to function under the supervision of the commissioner (Chaube, 1999: 162).

66. The Suspension of Operations Agreement was signed on August 15, 1964 which was christened as 'Cease-fire' with effect from September 16, 1964 (For details of the Cease-fire, Nuh & W. Lasuh, 2002: 233-268).

67. The Shillong Accord was signed on November 10, 1975 between the Government of India and the representatives of the underground organizations of Nagaland. Accordingly, the underground organizations accepted the Constitution of India, without condition, and agreed to deposit the arms at appointed places (For more details, Nuh & W. Lasuh, 2002: 331-357).

68. The use of the term Zeliangrong was only in 1947 and before that Zemei and Liangmei were known as Kutcha Naga and Rongmei as Kabui (Singh, 1992: 59).

69. Some of the Naga members of the All Tribal Delegation were: Daiho (Ex-Finance Minister, Manipur Assembly), Stephen Angkang (Ex-president, Tangkhul Long), K. Kalanlung (President, Zeliangrong Regional Council) (Singh, 2008: 50).

70. In 2001, the Government of India, 'in order to extend the area of peace in the northeast', extended the cease-fire with the NSCN (I-M) 'without territorial limits' (www.satp.org). This had created a lot of trouble in the valley districts of Manipur. The All Manipur United Clubs' Organisation (AMUCO) and All Manipur Students' Union (AMSU) spearheaded the movement against the cease-fire extension by organizing rallies, sit-in-protests, calling bandhs, blockades, strikes, etc. The movement was further strengthened with the formation of a common body called United Committee Manipur (UCM). The movement took a violent turn and the buildings of Assembly Secretariat, Chief Minister's Secretariat, political party offices and MLA quarters were set on fire and in the process 18 innocent lives were lost (www.e-pao.net).

71. In 2005, the Government of Manipur declared June 18 as 'State Integrity Day' and a state holiday in commemoration of the 18 innocent lives lost while agitating against the cease-fire extension 'without territorial limits'. The decision was retaliated by imposing a 52-day long economic blockade on NH 39 and 53 by ANSAM.

72. The Naga social organizations of Manipur, viz., UNCM, ANSAM and NWUM submitted a joint memorandum to the Prime Minister of India in June, 2001, where they held the cease-fire extension and made clear that they are not a party to any of the organizations made by the valley based organizations on the territorial integrity of Manipur. Similarly, the NPC held in June, 2001 at Senapati district, Manipur, declared that the agenda of territorial integrity of Manipur by Meitei community is a move to deny the rights of the Naga people (www.satp.org).

73. However, some mixed reactions also came from the Nagas. Rishang Keishing, former Chief Minister of Manipur and Prof. Gangmumei Kabui, MLA questioned the move of the centre and stood for territorial integrity of Manipur. The Zeliangrong United Clubs' Association, Manipur and All Colleges Tribal Students' Union, Manipur opposed the cease-fire extension and pledged to protect the territorial integrity of Manipur (www.e-pao.net).

3

Economy of Manipur: The Dynamics of Development

Having discussed the socio-political background of Manipur in the previous chapter, let us now look into the economy of the state. A study of the economy will help us in deeper understanding of the complex political crisis of the state. As it is the material conditions of life that shapes the political destiny, it is important to understand the interplay between eeconomic and political forces. Socio-political movements are often the direct manifestations of economic deprivation and, at times, economic conditions play crucial indirect role in either mitigating or aggravating social tensions. It is from this perspective that we attempt to trace the development of the economy of Manipur. The emergence of nationalistic feelings among the dominant groups in Manipur that has already been discussed in chapter 2 is conditioned by the growth of her material well being of the people concerned. We shall juxtapose these socio-political and economic growth trends in chapter 4 in order to analyze the emergence of militancy in the state.

The Feudal Economy

The feudal economy was basically agrarian in nature.

Agriculture was the mainstay of the economy. The state was known for its rice economy. The inhabitants of the valley had specialized in the art of wet rice cultivation while the hill people widely practiced jhum cultivation. But the technique of shifting cultivation appeared to have been used for wet rice cultivation as the method of transplantation of paddy and use of plough were introduced in the valley only after the arrival of the Muslim war captives in the beginning of 17th century.

The valley, being blessed with fertile land, rivers, streams and lakes, had a stable food economy. Though the size of cultivated land is not known for certainty, it is widely believed that about one-fourth of the valley area was cultivated (Brown, 2001: 85). Prior to the first Census in 1881, a rough estimate showed that the area of Manipur was about 7000 sq. miles (17920 sq. km.) and the valley area was about 650 sq. miles (1664 sq. km.) (Brown, 2001: 1; McCulloch, 1980: 1; Pemberton, 1966: 23), which forms about 9.29 per cent of the total area. The population was also estimated at around 139000 persons, of which the valley population was 65000 (46.76 per cent) and hill population was 74000 (53.24 per cent) (Brown, 2001: 1). The valley, thus, registered a population density of 39 persons per sq. km. compared to 4 persons per sq. km. in the hills. According to the first Census of Manipur in 1881, the population was 221070 persons (Allen, 2002: 45).

With a very low population to support, the valley with its rich land had a surplus production. A rough estimate of the yield rate showed that on worst land the paddy yield was 100 baskets[1] or 2700 kg. per pari (2.5 acre or 1 hectare) and 4320 kg. (160 baskets) to 5400 kg. (200 baskets) on the best land. So, the average yield was 4050 kg. (150 baskets) per hectare (Brown, 2001: 86).

The structure of feudal agrarian economy is also well defined by the land holding pattern of the prevailing period.

As already been mentioned in the previous chapter, the king had the sole ownership right over all the land. He distributed the land to the subjects on the basis of the system of *lallup*. In other words, every male who served as *lallup* was given 1 pari of land for cultivation. Besides, land was given to officials and nobles. An official named *Phunan Selungba* (Land Settlement Officer) looked after all the matters connected with land (Brown, 2001: 85). All the land under cultivation was taxed according to the category of land[2] and taxes were paid in kind. These taxes ranged between 1 per cent to 6 per cent of the total produce on the best land and 2 per cent to 12 per cent of the total produce on the worst land. So, the land relationship system was non-exploitative if rent is a criterion (Singh, 2005: 151).

Since people in the valley practiced wet rice cultivation, they had also developed a crude form of irrigation. They used to dredge the course of river and make channels near the foot of the hills to carry the hill streams to the fields. However, a good harvest was still dependent on timely monsoon and the role of irrigation was minimal. A severe flood or drought often led to failure of crops. But food scarcity was a rare phenomenon during this period of time. As has already been mentioned in the previous chapter, the kings of Manipur had established granaries known as *kei*, which was built in each village. All the villagers had to contribute a share of 12 pots[3] per pari and the village chief used to look after all the matters connected with *kei*. At times of crop failure and whenever a situation of food scarcity arises, kings used to distribute paddy from these *keis*.

Besides rice production, the other agro-based products of the valley were potatoes, sweet potatoes, brinjals, cucumber, pumpkins, onions, pepper, tobacco and different varieties of dhal. English vegetables like peas, cabbage, cauliflower, beans, etc, were also raised. In the hills, rice, cotton, oil seeds, pepper, tobacco, vegetables of various kinds, potatoes, sweet potatoes, ginger and yam were produced (Brown, 2001: 84). However, except rice and cotton, other products were raised mainly for household consumption and they hardly had any importance from commercial point of view.

The state was also blessed with a rich forest resource. Of the varieties of trees found in these forests mention may be made of teak, bamboo, nagesar, jarul, India-rubber, tun, oak, etc. (Brown, 2001: 5). The timber obtained from these forests had a ready market in Surma Valley.

The people in both the valley and hills had also developed animal husbandry. Among the animals raised were cow, buffalo, goat, fowl, duck, geese, pigeon, pig, cats and dogs. Besides rearing animals, fishing was another activity of the people. It is said that about 22 different kinds of fish were found in the rivers and lakes, especially Loktak, Ekop and Waithou lakes (Brown, 2001: 8-9, 85-86).

Though Manipur excelled in agriculture, its manufacturing base was extremely weak. Its manufactures were few and subsistence in nature. It comprised of coarse clothes, leather, cooking pots, pottery, jewellery, iron and steel, carpentry, etc. (Brown, 2001: 89). Weaving was the most important industry of the state. Raw cotton was ginned and spun into thread by women. Cotton in large quantity was raised by hillsmen and so the supply of raw cotton came mostly from the hills. The clothes produced were of excellent quality and extraordinarily cheap (Allen, 2002: 87). Another very important manufacture was salt. The state was blessed with a large number of salt springs. There were four principal salt-wells, viz., Ningail, Chandrakhong, Sikhong and Waikhong. The salt obtained was quite pure and free from smell. Its wholesale price was about Rs. 6 a maund (Brown, 2001: 9-10). Salt was an important item of trade as well as a source of revenue. Hill people mainly took salt in return for raw cotton and firewood. The bazaars in the Cachar valley, adjacent to the hills were also supplied.

Besides manufacturing coarse cloths and salt, other manufactures of the state included leather manufactures. The skins of deer and calf were used and the products included saddles, shoes, belts, pouches, etc. Brass, copper and bell metal were used for making cooking pots. But clay was used for ordinary pots and water jars. Jewellery was another important craft and the products included rings, bracelets, necklets, armlets, etc. These items were chiefly made of brass and bell metal (Brown, 2001: 89). Gold imported from Calcutta were also used (Allen, 2002: 90). In iron and steel works, the manufactures included daos, spears and arrow heads. Iron was available in valley and a small quantity was also found in the hills. Another important activity of the people was carpentry. The valley people were much praised for their artistic carpentry works and could exactly imitate English works (Brown, 2001: 90).

The state was not very open to trade. Major trade of the state was carried on with Cachar. Major items of export included cloths, yarns, buffaloes and ponies. In return, Manipur imported betel nut and pan, cloth, yarn, brass and other metals and hukas. The state enjoyed a positive trade balance with Cachar. In 1868-69 the total exports from Manipur to Cachar was Rs. 3533 and total imports from Cachar was Rs. 1975 (Brown, 2001: 88), leading to a positive balance of Rs. 1558.

The state, being a closed agrarian economy, had a very limited source of revenue. Moreover, the economy was not fully monetized. Although a currency called *Sel* was in circulation, most of the taxes were paid in kind. The only important source of revenue was the Kabaw valley compensation of Rs. 6000 per annum received from the Imperial government by the kings of Manipur. The other sources of revenue were taxes on fishing, exports and imports, transit duties and tributes from the outcast communities

(McCulloch, 1980: 36). A rough estimate, although not reliable, showed that the revenue of the valley was in between Rs. 12000 to Rs. 15000 per annum (Brown, 2001: 89).

The feudal economy of Manipur may, thus, be characterized as self-sufficient and self-contained system largely insulated within the Imphal valley without much interaction with outside world. The ruling aristocracy, no doubt, used to enjoy higher social status but without much economic inequality. The agrarian base of the economy and egalitarian approach towards resource mobilization, particularly in relation to collection of taxes, had made the feudal state economically weak. The feudal authority hardly had resources to strengthen its armoury even while the neighbouring powers were gaining strength. With the rise of Ava in the east and imperial British in the west, the balance of power tilted against Manipur. Instead of gaining strength in order to face the new challenges and order the surrounding political environment, the feudal state of Manipur had to come to terms with these powers at the cost of her own interest. This had ultimately led Manipur to slide into the grips of British colonial power.

The Colonial Economy

As has been discussed in the previous chapter, Manipur came under the indirect colonial rule after the Anglo-Manipur War of 1891. This had led to the transformation of the traditional socio-economic and political structure. The feudal services like *lallup* and *pothang* were replaced by a uniform tax. The land holding system also underwent a major change. The Rayatwari system of land holding, which bestows private ownership, was introduced. As a result, the king was deprived of the traditional rights over land. With the monetization of the economy and introduction of private property, the feudal economy began to give way to commercialization of agriculture.

Under the new land system, the nobles and influential people began to apply for land on a mass scale. The colonial government issued pattas for as many as 14,000 paris (35000 acres) during 1892-93 only and in the next year for 24,887 paris (62218 acres) (Singh, 1998: 51), registering an annual increase of almost 78 per cent patta . In 1901, the area under paddy was 42283 paris (105708 acres). It further increased to 71316 paris (178290 acres) and 75370 paris (188425 acres) in 1931 and 1941 respectively (Singh, 2005: 158). Thus, in 40 years time the area under cultivation increased by 78 per cent in the valley area only. Indeed, the introduction of Rayatwari system had revolutionized the agricultural sector of Manipur. The sense of ownership had encouraged people to invest in agriculture as well as provided recognition of their bona fide.

Alongside the increase in demand for land, population also started growing. The 1891 Census reports were lost in the Anglo-Manipur War and so no data is available for the said year. Table 3.1 shows the growth of population since 1901.

Table 3.1
Growth of Population in Manipur
(1901-1941)

Year	*Population (persons)*	*Growth Rate (percentage)*
1901	284465	-
1911	346222	21.70
1921	384016	10.92
1931	445606	16.04
1941	512069	14.92

Source: Statistical Abstract Manipur 2005.

In 40 years time, the population of Manipur increased by 80 per cent. Though the absolute population figure increased over the years, the decadal growth rate was in fact low and insignificant. The decadal growth rate declined from 21.70 per cent in 1911 to 10.92 per cent in 1921. It slightly increased to 16.04 per cent in 1931 but again declined to 14.92 per cent in 1941. We may safely conclude that Manipur was in the first stage of demographic transition, i.e., a stage of high growth potential but of low actual growth, during the colonial period.

As is expected of being in the first phase of economic transition, the vast populace of the state was engaged in agriculture. Table 3.2 shows the occupational distribution of Manipur in 1901.

Table 3.2
Occupational Distribution of Manipur in 1901

Occupational classification	*No. of Persons*	*Percentage Share*
Pasture & agriculture	207265	73
Preparation and supply of materials	62988	22
Services[4]	14212	5
Total Population	284465	100

Source: Allen, 2002: 66.

In 1901, the colonial government conducted a census in Manipur along with British India. It appears that the format of the census used in Manipur had not been tailored made to suit the conditions of the state. In spite of the limitations of the one-size-fit-all approach[5] of the colonial government, one can have some rough idea about the occupational structure of the people of Manipur at the beginning of the 20th century. It may be noted that 73 per cent of the population was engaged in pasture and agriculture. Another 22 per cent of the population was engaged in 'preparation and supply of substances'. These activities include weaving and other subsidiary activities which people, especially women, used to take up during the after harvest off-season. Although 'preparation and supply of substances' invariably indicate non-farm activities, but in most cases, these were either subsidiary or complementary activities. In fact, manufacturing and processing activities in every traditional society initially grew out either as subsidiary or complementary activities before graduating into a whole time profession. Thus, manufacturing and processing activities began as an embodiment of an agrarian society. A labeling of the 'preparation and supply of substances' as secondary activities may lead to an erroneous conclusion. Looked from this perspective, the percentage of people engaged in agriculture in Manipur in 1901 would be much higher than what Allen made us to believe (73 per cent). As is expected, a 5 per cent of the population was engaged in services.

The closed agrarian economy of Manipur was opened to free trade during the colonial period. There was not only change in export basket but this period also witnessed the emergence of a new dominant business class, the Marwaris, who entered into Manipur as comprador to colonial authority. In no time, Marwaris, armed with huge market network, established their hegemony over both the external as well as the internal trade. The opening of cart route to Dimapur via Mao Thana in 1896 further added impulse to the ongoing trade (Allen, 2002: 112).

Table 3.3
Exports from Manipur to the Surma and Assam Valley

(Value in Rs.)

Name of Articles	*Average value of Exports during the three years 1902-1904, via*			
	Jirighat (1)	*Mao Thana (2)*	*Total (1) + (2)*	*Percentage*
Cattle	27022	2610	29632	11.02
Timber	85577		85577	31.83
Rice husked	731	93998	94729	35.23
Others[6]	41617	17341	58958	21.92
Total Export	154947	113949	268896	100

Source: Allen, 2002: 111.

Table 3.3 shows the average value of exports from Manipur to the Surma and Assam Valley during the three years 1902-04, via the two trade routes, viz., Jirighat and Mao Thana. While Jirighat route connects Imphal Valley with Surma Valley, Mao Thana route connects her with Assam Valley. As it is seen from Table 3.3, colonial Manipur was a source of rice, cattle and timber. Rice was the main item of exports, its value averaging at Rs. 94729 in three years, i.e., 35.23 per cent of the total exports. Timber and cattle were the other two main items, with their values averaging at Rs. 85577 (31.83 per cent) and Rs. 29632 (11.02 per cent) respectively in three years. Thus, rice, timber and cattle were the principal exports items of Manipur.

Table 3.4
Imports to Manipur from the Surma and Assam Valley

(Value in Rs.)

Name of Articles	*Average value of Imports during the three years 1902-1904, via*			
	Jirighat (1)	*Mao Thana (2)*	*Total (1) + (2)*	*Percentage*
Cotton twist, yarn and piece goods	9687	54161	63848	26.31
Dry fish	19636	211	19847	8.18
Salt	1418	19353	20771	8.56
Betel nuts	57532	2850	60382	24.89
Others[7]	15628	62162	77790	32.06
Total Import	103901	138737	242638	100

Source: Allen, 2002: 112.

While the state was a source for rice and forest products like timber, it served as a market for the manufactured goods produced outside. Among the main items of imports, cotton twist, yarn and piece goods contributed the highest share, its value averaging at Rs. 63848 for three years, i.e., 26.31 per cent of the total imports. Betel nuts and salt are the two other major items of import with their value averaging at Rs. 60382 (24.89 per cent) and Rs. 20771 (8.56 per cent) respectively.

The colonial trade policy had a backwash effect for the emerging manufacturing activities in Manipur. The worst affected were the traditional weaving and salt industries. The hand made products of Manipur could not compete with the cheap machine made products of Britain. As a result the traditional weaving faced gradual extinction. Besides price competition, cultural competition between tradition and modernity had also caused a shift of the preference of the people towards British made cloths. The traditional salt making was also gradually heading towards extinction due to import of cheap foreign salt. The local salt which was priced at four annas a seer could not compete with the imported salt which was priced at seven Pisa a seer (Allen, 2002: 94). This had led to gradual disappearance of the local salt from the market. The traditional metal industry was another victim which declined due to increasing import of aluminium and enamel products.

Thus, colonial commercial policy stood on the way of emerging manufacturing activities in Manipur. The natural transition of Manipur from agrarian to industrial society had not only been shunned but the natural process of social transition had also been put to reverse gear by way of setting a de-industrialization process that even routed the traditional manufacturing and processing activities.

With the coming of the British and subsequent monetization of the economy, the revenue of the state had also increased. As has already been discussed in the previous chapter, the system of *lallup* was abolished and substituted by a house tax of Rs. 2 per annum in the valley and Rs. 3 in the hills. The house tax in the valley was, however, replaced by a uniform homestead tax of Rs. 5 in 1900 due to irregularities and tax evasion. A uniform land tax of Rs. 5 per pari was also realized in lieu of kind tax. This was raised to Rs. 5.15 per pari in 1913 following the abolition of *pothang*. With the introduction of foreigner tax, the revenue of the sate had further increased. The revenue[8] of the state under different heads is given below (For absolute figure: Annexure V).

Table 3.5
Revenue Receipts of Manipur (Percentage Share)

Categories	*1893*	*1901*	*1902*	*1903*	*1904*
Land revenue	57.87	65.51	65.15	65.21	71.08
Foreigner's tax	0	1.16	1.08	1.26	1.47
Hill house tax	14.30	13.78	16.32	15.13	11.76
Fisheries	6.76	7.31	7.46	8.28	6.11
Salt revenue	6.17	1.83	2.19	1.93	1.50
Forests	1.88	8.50	6.54	5.93	6.69
Others	13.02	1.91	1.26	2.26	1.39
Total Revenue	100	100	100	100	100

Source: Calculated from Allen, 2002: 139.

One can observe from table 3.5 that land revenue formed the major source of revenue of the state. The share of land revenue to total revenue was more than 65 per cent during these years. Increasing land revenue and increasing number of patta holders while read along with increasing export of rice lead us to conjecture that the commercialization of agriculture was taking place at a faster rate.

Hill house tax was another main source of revenue contributing about 15 per cent. The revenue from forests and fisheries also increased during this period of time contributing about 7 per cent and 8 per cent respectively. However, the revenue from salt declined from about 6 per cent in the beginning of colonial period to about less than 2 per cent in 1904. The increasing share of revenue from land and forests and decreasing share of revenue from salt indicates the essence of colonial economic policy–promotion of the primary resources and destruction of the traditional industry.

With the introduction of money tax, there was a sudden need for surplus cash. But cash was very hard to obtain during this period of time owing to very low price of rice. The average price of rice during the 1930s was around 30 seers per rupee (price list of rice in different years is already given in previous chapter, Note 44), the major source of money income of the people. Coupled with this factor was the non-availability of any gainful job in other sectors during the post-harvest off-season. The manufacturing sector was dying and trade was largely controlled by the Marwaris. Export of rice by the Marwaris (figure on rice export is already given in previous chapter, Note 43) was flourishing during this period. We have already discussed in previous chapter as to how the unprecedented export of rice by the Marwaris had led to the outbreak of *Nupi Lan* in 1939. According to Singh (2005: 153), after paying the land tax of Rs. 5, which was increased to Rs. 5.15 in 1913, a farmer was left with Rs. 8 and 15.65 annas as surplus cash.[9] Out of this he had to pay the house tax of Rs. 2 per annum which was increased to Rs. 5 since 1990. Under such conditions, not only the position of the farmers began to deteriorate but they also began to borrow money from rich moneylenders, mainly the Marwaris, at a high interest rate which subsequently led to the surrender of their lands.

Thus, the British colonial power had established a kind of diarchy in Manipur. While the administration of the state and the maintenance of the law and order was the responsibility of the king, collection of revenue was under the control of the British officials. Although Manipur was not annexed to British India, the economy of the state was integrated with the colonial market. The trade potentials in rice, timber and cattle had been fully exploited. The benefit from enhanced agriculture went to the Marwaris as they used to control the rice trade. The benefits from enhanced revenue went to the colonial masters. However, the benefits arising out of the transition from feudal agrarian relations to colonial agrarian relations had, to some extent, gone to the ordinary people in that that they had been bestowed the ownership of land. Of course, this benefit had been accrued to people only at a high cost as the colonial master had raised land taxes considerably. To be precise, while the people of Manipur were better off socially with the abolition of obligatory feudal services like *lallup* and *pothang*, they were not benefitted economically as far as rise in real income is concerned. The higher tax rate and larger tax base had robbed the surplus generated by the peasantry.

Production in agriculture increased due to fresh private initiative following the introduction of Rayatwari system. Of course, colonial government refrained from modernizing agriculture which would have called for state investment in agro-inputs particularly irrigation. Colonial commercial policy although revolutionized agriculture by way of synchronizing land ownership, marketing of rice and rice export, it routed the emerging manufacturing activities in Manipur by way of substituting local manufactures by cheap imported ones. While the people were experiencing export-led-retardation, the economy was experiencing some sort of deindustrialization with a feeble trend towards tertiarization due to the little expansion in trade and commerce.

The independent Manipur, thus, inherited a monetized and market oriented agro-based economy which was subsequently merged with the planned economy of India after its merger with the Indian Union in 1949.

The Post-Independence Economy

As has already been discussed in previous chapter, with the lapse of paramountcy on August 15, 1947, Manipur also became independent but she merged with the Indian Union in 1949. With the merger, her economy also came under the purview of the national planned economy. As the agriculture sector has been the driver of the economy of the state, it is only expected that a significant size of the planned investment will flow in this sector in order to remove the institutional, infrastructural and market rigidities associated with the production and marketing of agricultural produce. In this section, we intend to focus on the strategy of the state of Manipur towards the development of the economy of the state and also intend to assess the soundness of this strategy based on the performances of the different sectors.

Strategy of Planned Development

An analysis of the plan expenditure reveals the relative weightage that the state gives to various sectors of the economy. Since inception, planned development in Manipur emphasized the importance of three sectors, viz., transport and communications, social and community services and agriculture where 72.33 per cent, 18.58 per cent and 4.22 per cent of the total 1st Plan expenditure had been made respectively (table 3.6). This trend continued till the end of the 4th Plan (1969-74). Thus before Manipur was granted the statehood, the strategy was to establish the physical infrastructure in order to integrate the hitherto isolated kingdom with the Indian mainland. Higher expenditure had been made on social and community services in order to bring immediate relief to the people of the state so that they could enjoy the benefits of freedom directly. The importance of developing the real sectors of the economy—agriculture and industry—was overlooked during the initial years of independence.

This trend was, by and large, continued even after Manipur was graduated to a state in Indian Union in early 1970s. Besides the three focus areas mentioned above, a significant share of plan resources was also allocated for the development of water, power and irrigation. Following the initiation of economic reforms during the early 1990s, the share of agriculture in total plan expenditure has drastically reduced. The share of agriculture sector in the total expenditure was only 9.22 per cent and 5.14 per cent in the 8th and 9th Plan respectively (table 3.6). The percentage allocation of plan resources has been further declined to 3.47 per cent and 4.73 per cent in the 10th and 11th Plan respectively (Annexure - IX).

Thus, the strategy of planned development of the economy of Manipur has focused on the growth of the tertiary sector instead of the real sector of the economy. Agriculture, even being the driver, did not receive the top priority. The transition of the economy has charted from agriculture to tertiary sector bypassing the industrial sector. Before we question the resiliency of such a development strategy, a sectoral analysis of the economy is in order.

Table 3.6
Plan Expenditure under different heads in Manipur (% share)

Plan	*Agriculture & Allied services*	*Irrigation & flood control**	*Industry & mining*	*Transport*	*Social services*	*Others (*)*
1st Plan	4.22	4.18	0.66	72.33	18.58	0.03
2nd Plan	16.12	7.01	2.02	34.99	37.85	2.01
3rd Plan	12.63	4.57	2.75	39.28	38.39	2.38
4th Plan	11.95	12.39	6.94	40.65	26.25	1.82
5th Plan	16.06	30.87	7.13	22.22	18.48	5.24
6th Plan	18.72	25.54	5.56	15.25	30.48	4.45
7th Plan	12.62	18.14	5.47	14.79	29.75	19.23
8th Plan	9.22	16.78	4.31	16.42	29.62	23.65
9th Plan	5.14	13.07	5.09	13.87	33.69	29.14
10th Plan	3.47	16.65	5.89	9.41	37.99	26.59

Source: Annexure VI, VII, VIII, IX

* Irrigation & flood control was given a separate head since 7th Plan. Prior to the 7th Plan, this was included in Water & Power Development.

(*) Others include Co-operation, Rural Development, Energy, Science & Technology, General Economic services and General services.

Performance of Primary Sector

Although Manipur is rich in agriculture, she has only limited land for cultivation. The cultivable land forms only 7.34 per cent (164000 hectare) of the total geographical area (22327 sq. km.) of the state in 1999-2000. The net shown area forms 85.37 per cent (140000 hectare) of the cultivable area in 1999-2000 (*Economic Survey Manipur 2007-08*). As the valley area is about 10 per cent (2238 sq. km.) of the total geographical area where wet rice cultivation is practiced and the remaining 90 per cent (20089 sq. km.) is the hills where shifting cultivation is practiced, agriculture is mainly concentrated in the Imphal valley.

Predominance of rice cultivation has all along been observed. Out of the total cultivable area, 95.76 per cent (157050 hectare) land comes under rice cultivation in 1999-2000. Due to little diversification that has taken place over the years, growth of rice cultivation alone represents the condition of agriculture in Manipur.

It might be noted (Table 3.7) that during the decade following the grant of statehood, the area under rice suffered a negative growth rate. The race towards urbanization and implementation of infrastructural projects as well as other development activities had led to a squeeze on the cultivable land particularly in the valley. During the subsequent decades, there has been some expansion of area under rice perhaps due to the decline in the jhum cycle on the face of mounting population growth as well as expansion of area under multiple cropping particularly in the valley.

Table 3.7

Decennial Compound Growth Rate of Area, Production and Yield Rate of Rice in Manipur (%)

Year	*Area*	*Production*	*Yield Rate*
1981-90	-0.68	1.39	2.08
1991-2000	0.22	2.92	2.69
2000-07	1.23	1.12	-0.10

Source: Calculated from Economic Survey Manipur 2007-08 & Statistical Handbook of Manipur 1992.

The gain in production outweighed the gain in area during the 1980s and 1990s. Adoption of modern inputs appears to have caused this production as well as gain in productivity (table 3.7). However, these gains have largely been petered away as the state patronage in the form of subsidy was gradually withdrawn following the India's entry into World Trade Organization (WTO). It has already been mentioned that Plan outlay for agriculture has been gradually reduced since 8th Plan.

With the rise in population over the years there is an increasing pressure on land especially in the valley. The population growth rate has increased from 12.80 per cent in 1951 to 29.29 per cent in 1991. In 2001 it slightly declined to 24.86 per cent (table 3.8) against the national population growth rate of 21.54 per cent. Manipur registered a population density of 103 persons per sq. km. according to 2001 Census, against the national figure of 313 persons per sq. km. The valley area registered a density of 631 persons per sq. km. against the density of 44 persons per sq. km. in the hills.

Table 3.8
Growth of Population in Manipur (1941-2001)

Year	*Population (persons)*	*Growth Rate (percentage)*
1941	512069	
1951	577635	12.80
1961	780037	35.04
1971	1072753	37.53
1981	1420953	32.46
1991	1837149	29.29
2001	2293896	24.86

Source: Statistical Abstract Manipur 2005

According to 2001 Census, the valley population is 1411766 whereas the population in the hills is 882130 persons. The land-man ratio in the valley has been more or less constant around 0.2 hectare in 2001 since 1981 but the same for the hill areas declined from 4.1 hectare in 1981 to 2.3 hectare in 2001. The state which was once the net exporter of rice has now become the net importer (Table 3.9).

Table 3.9: Foodgrain Production and Shortfall in Manipur

(in '000 tonnes)

Year	*Production*	*Requirement*	*Shortfall*
1996	347.58	404.30	56.72
1997	393.31	413.76	20.45
1998	368.02	423.33	55.31
1999	395.06	433.01	37.95
2000	378.92	442.80	63.88
2001	395.75	448.34	52.59
2002	400.39	458.01	57.62
2003	347.07	467.35	120.28
2004	392.01	477.02	85.01
2005	449.32	486.74	37.42
2006	398.39	496.54	98.15

Source: Economic Survey Manipur 2007-08.

The growth of population besides worsening the food security of the people of Manipur has also foreclosed any technological solution to the stunted growth of food production by way of delimiting the institutional arrangement in agriculture. The impact of population growth on the average size of holding bears one such testimony.

Table 3.10 shows increasing marginalization of operational holdings over the years. The marginal and small holdings account for about 83 per cent of the total holdings and occupy about 60 per cent of the total area operated. About 30 per cent of the area operated is held by semi-medium holders which account for about 15 per cent of the total holdings. The number of medium holdings is very low and they account for about 2 per cent of the total holdings and occupy about 8 per cent of the total area operated. The size of the large holdings is very low and their share is negligible and they also occupy a negligible share of the area operated.

Table 3.10
Percentage Distribution of Operational Holdings in Manipur

Category/ size class (in Hect.)	*Marginal (below 1.00)*	*Small (1.00–1.99)*	*Semi-medium (2.00–3.99)*	*Medium (4.00–9.99)*	*Large (10..00 & above)*
1971					
No. of holdings	40.887	42.88	14.99	1.22	0.03
Area operated	18.9	44.18	31.76	4.67	0.42
1981					
No. of holdings	47.77	34.97	15.16	2.08	0.02
Area operated	21.00	38.38	31.53	8.87	0.22
1991					
No. of holdings	48.29	34.53	15.10	2.05	0.03
Area operated	21.61	38.37	31.37	8.35	0.30
2001					
No. of holdings	50.34	32.88	14.77	2.01	Negligible
Area operated	23.26	36.63	31.97	8.14	Negligible

Source: Calculated from Statistical Handbook of Manipur 2002 & Economic Survey Manipur 2007-08.

A comparative picture of Manipur and India is given in Table 3.11.

Table 3.11

Percentage Distribution of Operational Holdings in Manipur and India

Category/size	*1991*				*2001*			
class(in Hect.)	*No. of holdings*		*Area operated*		*No. of holdings*		*Area operated*	
	Manipur	*India*	*Manipur*	*India*	*Manipur*	*India**	*Manipur*	*India**
Marginal (below 1.00)	48.29	59.44	21.61	15.04	50.34	62.88	23.26	18.70
Small(1.00 – 1.99)	34.53	18.84	38.37	17.42	32.88	18.92	36.63	20.16
Semi-medium(2.00 – 3.99)	15.10	13.06	31.37	23.19	14.77	11.69	31.97	23.95
Medium(4.00 – 9.99)	2.05	7.11	8.35	27.04	2.01	5.48	8.14	23.97
Large(10.00 & above)	0.03	1.55	0.30	17.31	Negligible	1.03	Negligible	13.22

Source: Calculated from *Statistical Handbook of Manipur* 2002; *Economic Survey Manipur* 2007-08; Agricultural Census Division, Ministry of Agriculture, New Delhi; Singh, 2007: 60

* Excluding Jharkhand.

Like Manipur, the all India pattern of operational holding exhibit the same trend. The share of marginal and small holdings account for about 78 per cent and occupy about 32 per cent of area operated in 1991 compared to about 83 per cent and 60 per cent respectively in case of Manipur. However, in case of India, the number of marginal and small holdings increased to about 80 per cent in 2001 occupying about 38 per cent of area operated. The increase in the share of marginal and small holdings is largely due to the decrease in the medium and large holdings. The medium and large holdings which accounted for about 8 per cent in 1991 declined to about 6 per cent in 2001. Similarly the share of medium and large area operated declined from about 44 per cent in 1991 to about 36 per cent in 2001. In case of Manipur, there is no significant change in the size of marginal and small holdings as well as area operated in 2001, though there is a marginal increase in both marginal and small holdings and area operated corresponding to a marginal decline in both medium and large holdings and area operated. Thus, there has been a gradual but positive shift in favour of marginal and small holdings and concentration of land with very large landowners is coming down in both Manipur and India.

Table 3.12
Average Size of Operational Holdings in Manipur and India

Category/size class (in Hect.)	*1991*		*2001*	
	Manipur	*India*	*Manipur*	*India*
Marginal (below 1.00)	0.55	0.39	0.53	0.40
Small(1.00 – 1.99)	1.37	1.43	1.29	1.42
Semi-medium(2.00 – 3.99)	2.56	2.76	2.50	2.72
Medium(4.00 – 9.99)	5.01	5.90	4.67	5.81
Large(10.00 & above)	12.16	17.33	Negligible	17.13
All holdings	1.23	1.55	1.15	1.33

Source: Calculated from Statistical Handbook of Manipur 2002; Economic Survey Manipur 2007-08; Agricultural Census Division, Ministry of Agriculture, New Delhi; Singh, 2007: 62.

The average size of all holdings in Manipur is smaller than the national average except in case of marginal holding. The average size of all holdings declined from 1.23 hectares in 1991 to 1.15 hectares in 2001 in Manipur, a decline of 6.5 per cent during the decade. Similarly, the all India average size of all holdings also declined from 1.55 hectares in 1991 to 1.33 hectares in 2001, a decline of 14.19 per cent. One may attribute the declining trend to the growth of population over the years and reduction of agricultural land due to urbanization.

The growth of population in tandem with the social institution of male line inheritance is one of the main causes of increasing marginalization of operational holdings. The size of the holding gets fragmented as it passes hand from father to sons. This is a universal phenomenon across societies. This process of defragmentation makes the marginal holdings economically unviable when the size of the holding gets reduced below the threshold limit. Besides this institutional factor, with the rise in population, the demand for land has increased over time. Supply being fixed; the forces of market have added further fuel to the process of marginalization of holdings. Furthermore, the state does not have a uniform land tenure system. The legal land tenurial framework applicable for the valley land does not apply in case of the hills. The land tenure system in the hills is governed by the traditional tribal customs. Further, there is no uniform tribal customs. The customs varies from tribe to tribe. The Nagas and Kukis follow different customs. What is more perplexing is that even the customs that govern the land tenure system of a particular tribe again varies at the sub-tribe/clan level. Thus, the tribal customary laws provide a shield against forces of market. Land market in the hills is subject to socio-political rigidities leading to factor immobility. The impact of the market forces on the marginalization of land is basically concentrated in the valley. The increasing pace of urbanization, rural-urban migration, and expansion of non-farm activities—all are putting pressure on the valley land.

The process of marginalization of land holding pushes the marginal holders to the status of agricultural labourers. Rise in the numbers of agricultural labourers over time bears a testimony of this.

Table 3.13
Percentage share of Cultivator and Agricultural labour to total Main Workers in Manipur

Classification of Workers	*1961*	*1971*	*1981*	*1991*	*2001**
Cultivator	65.43	67.00	63.60	61.77	43.35
Agricultural labour	0.61	3.65	4.99	6.69	6.34

Source: Statistical Abstract Manipur 2005
* Figures for 2001 exclude Mao-Maram, Paomata and Purul sub-divisions of Senapati District.

Table 3.13 exhibits a continuous rise in the number of agricultural labourers in Manipur. In fact, their number has increased from 0.61 per cent in 1961 to 6.34 per cent in 2001 leading to an increase by about 1815 per cent over the 40 years. Thus, the marginal and small farmers and agricultural workers together constitute about 50 per cent of the main workers of Manipur in 2001.

With about half of the people engaged in agriculture being marginalized, the condition of agriculture has hardly improved over the years. The increasing marginalization of holding is an indication of increasing pauperization of peasantry. Since they hold a meager size of land, it is difficult to make out a descent living. The result is the decline in agricultural income which is shown in table 3.14.

Table 3.14
Contribution of Primary Sector to total NSDP in Manipur (% share)

Year	*Agriculture*	*Forestry & Logging*	*Fishing*	*Total Primary*
1961	52.82	2.11	0.76	55.69
1970	55.68	0.95	0.75	57.37
1980	46.24	0.73	2.07	49.04
1990	32.01	2.18	4.07	38.26
2000	25.90	1.64	3.59	31.13
2007	20.31	1.39	1.27	22.96

Source: Calculated from EPW and CSO.

From Table 3.14 it is clearly seen that the contribution of primary sector to total net state domestic product (NSDP) in Manipur is declining over the years. While the primary sector was contributing more than 50 per cent of the total state income during the 1960s and 1970s, its share has declined to less than 50 per cent since 1980s. It has further declined from 38.26 per cent in 1990 to 31.13 per cent in 2000 and further declined to 22.96 per cent in 2007. Another important feature is that within the primary sector, agriculture is the only main activity. Out of the total primary sector share of 55.69 per cent in total NSDP in 1961, agriculture alone contributed 52.82 per cent. This trend is observed for all the reference years. In 2007 out of the primary sector share of 22.96 per cent, the share of agriculture is 20.31 per cent. The other activities like forestry and logging and fishing are almost negligible.

Table 3.15
Percentage Share of Various Components in Primary Sector in Manipur

Year	*Agriculture*	*Forestry & Logging*	*Fishing*	*Total*
1961	94.86	3.78	1.36	100
1970	97.85	1.65	1.30	100
1980	94.29	1.49	4.22	100
1990	83.67	5.69	10.63	100
2000	83.20	5.28	11.52	100
2007	88.45	6.03	5.52	100

Source: Calculated from EPW and CSO

Table 3.15 shows the contribution of various components to primary sector income. It is seen that agriculture is the main activity in this sector. Its share is more than 88 per cent throughout the years. Other activities like forestry and logging and fishing contribute around 12 per cent respectively whereas that of mining and quarrying is nil.

The all India trend also shows that agriculture is the main activity in primary sector. Like Manipur, the share of agriculture in primary sector in India is more than 80 per cent throughout the years. However, mining and quarrying is another main activity in India with its share of around 8 per cent unlike Manipur where this activity is nil (For India's figure: Annexure X).

The component-wise break up of primary sector income indicates the potential for the development of animal husbandry, pisciculture, social forestry, floriculture and horticulture in the state. Diversification of primary activities can open up new opportunities for the rural people. The strategy of agricultural development in the state needs to factor into this aspect. This will simultaneously serve two purposes: arrest the drain of resources that go out of the state for their procurement as well as create new opportunities for employment and trade. Moreover, diversification of primary sector activities also provides security of income to the rural people. In case of a crop failure, farmers will have alternative options to bank on. Indeed, Manipur has to think out of the box solution for the stagnation that has gripped its rice cultivation.

Although the share of the primary sector in NSDP has declined from 55.69 per cent in 1961 to 22.96 per cent in 2001, a whopping decline of about 33 percentage point, the decline in the number of people engaged in the primary sector has not been proportional. The occupational distribution of main workers bears testimony to this.

Table 3.16
Occupational Distribution of Main Workers in Manipur (% share)

Sector	*1961*	*1971*	*1981*	*1991*	*2001**
Primary	66.26	71.30	69.60	70.00	49.69
Secondary	23.05	12.23	13.35	9.66	6.55
Tertiary	10.69	16.47	17.05	20.33	43.76

Source: Calculated from Statistical Abstract Manipur 2005
* Figures for 2001 exclude Mao-Maram, Paomata and Purul sub-divisions of Senapati District.

It may be noted that for two decades 1970-90, while the percentage share of primary sector to total NSDP was declining (table 3.14), the percentage share of population engaged in this sector remained more or less stagnant (table 3.16). This trend may be interpreted as an indication of declining labour productivity in agriculture which has been the main component (table 3.15) of the primary sector of the economy of Manipur. Thus, the economy of Manipur was undergoing a retrogressive change during these two decades. However, 2001 Census figures exhibit a sudden decline of the percentage of people engaged in the primary sector to the tune of more than 20 percentage points while the share of this sector in NSDP has declined by about 7 percentage points. Although trade and commerce activities have received a boost following the signing of the Indo-Myanmar Border Trade Agreement in 1994, transport and communication services also expanded following the adoption of the 'New Initiative Towards North East' by the Union Government as well as creation of the central pool system for financing the infrastructural projects for the states of the north eastern region, but the ground experiences about the economy of Manipur do not provide adequate support to this significant shift of labour force from the primary sector.

As such, the reduction of the work force in primary sector from 70 per cent in 1991 to 49.69 per cent in 2001 should be viewed as a progressive structural change desirable and inevitable for the development of the economy of Manipur. But this shift of workforce has not resulted from the dynamics of the forces of economic development rather it appears to exhibit a movement of the workforce under compulsion. We attempt here to provide a plausible explanation.

During the 1990s, insurgency related activities had escalated beyond control. This had created a sense of insecurity particularly in the minds of the people living in rural areas. It appears that insurgency and counter-insurgency operations have strengthened the push factors and accelerated rural-urban migration in the state. Much of this migrant population has been absorbed in the urban informal sector. The growth of the construction activities in the state about which we shall discuss shortly seems to corroborate this hypothesis.

However, this view does not get invincible empirical support as far as comparative growth of population in rural and urban areas is concerned. A further investigation in this area can only ascertain the validity of this proposition.

What is important to note is that during the 1980s and 1990s about 70 per cent of the workforce was engaged in agriculture while the literacy rate in the state was 50 per cent and 60 per cent respectively indicating a sizeable segment of educated people tied up with the primary sector. In fact the strategy of emphasizing the social sector in all the plans and ignoring the real sector of the economy has led to widening the gap between the expectation of the educated class to be absorbed in white collar jobs and the creation of opportunities in the modern sectors. While the objective of economic reality demanded a Lewis-type transformation of the economy, it remains steadfastly agrarian. This lagging real sector growth has been at the core of the rising social frustration particularly among the educated youths in the state about which we shall occasion to discuss later in this chapter.

People of Manipur being poor in industrial experiences the responsibility of the transformation of the economy has to be bored by the state. In the next section we shall detail out the strategy of the planned development of the industrial sector in the state.

Strategy of Industrialization

We have seen that the state was experiencing some sort of de-industrialization syndrome during the colonial period.

However, even in the post independence period, no appreciable progress has taken place in this sector. As the state is not blessed with natural resources except meager cultivable land in the valley, industrializing the economy of Manipur has been viewed as a daunting challenge. As Manipur does not have an indigenous entrepreneurial class of her own, industrialization has not been considered as an option for the development of the economy of the state in the initial years. The state did not have an industrial policy until 1982. The first industrial policy was framed exactly after 35 years of independence and after 10 years of statehood. It is followed by three more revised policies in 1989, 1990 and 1996.

Government of Manipur initially decided that the state should act as the entrepreneur for the development of the industrial sector in Manipur (Industrial Policy of Manipur 1982). While the state will undertake the medium and large industrial projects, it will encourage small scale industries to grow under private initiative. The 1982 policy identified bamboo based industries, starch and glucose factory, mechanized dye house, cement factory, plywood factory and sugar factory for establishment under public sector.

Weaving, sericulture, traditional handicrafts and production of various electrical goods are encouraged under the private sector. In order to accelerate the process of the growth of the indigenous entrepreneurial class, the government of Manipur committed itself to arrange industrial training to select people in these areas.

In order to encourage the entrepreneurs to establish industries in Manipur, the government adopted an incentive package that include octroi relief, exemption from stamp duty and registration charges, allotment of government land at subsidized rate, government purchase, interest subsidy, exemption of sales tax, equipment subsidy and exemption of water tax (Industrial Policy of Manipur 1982).

The 1982 policy, however, could not bear immediate fruit. The late 1980s saw the materialization of the policy as most of the public sector units came up during this period. We shall be dealing with these units later. But, the feasibility of these large and medium scale industries was questionable and it was soon realized that the small industries had more potential in the state rather than large and medium units. Thus, the government shifted its focus to small scale and agro-based industries in the 1990 industrial policy. Although government of Manipur had adopted an industrial policy in 1989 but it was soon replaced without any trial in 1990.

The 1990 policy shifted the focus from large and medium scale industries to small and agro-based industries. The main strategy of the policy was to set up small scale industries based on available local raw materials and local demand. It also focused on employment generation among the local people. As such, it identified the areas like agro-based industries, handloom and handicrafts, development of electronics, petro-chemical based industries and forest based industries which do not involve extensive felling of trees as priority areas. It also emphasized tourism industry as one of the promising areas of development. It was also mentioned that the state government will urge the central government to establish central public sector units.

As an incentive package, the government rendered land allotment, allotment of shed to SSI units, manpower development, state capital investment subsidy, state transport subsidy, interest subsidy, power subsidy, subsidy on drawal of power lines, subsidy for feasibility study and project report preparation, subsidy for technical know-how, government purchase, reimbursement and exemption of local sales tax and reimbursement of stamp duty and registration fee (Industrial Policy of Manipur 1990).

It was expressly mentioned that the industrial policy of 1990 would be valid only for a period of 5 years and, thus, a new industrial policy was framed in 1996. The 1996 policy was framed keeping in mind the changing economic scenario in the post-1991 liberalization era and the post-1994 era of border trade agreement with Myanmar. The state government decided to adopt a multi-dimensional strategy which depends not only on subsidy/incentive regime but which optimizes the state's potential and offsets her disadvantages. In the meantime, the government realized that the development of infrastructure as well as creation of business environment are a *sine qua non* for industrial development in the state. The Industrial Policy of 1996 emphasized on 'creation of an integrated investor-friendly environment', 'infrastructural development', 'maximizing resource utilization', 'quality improvement and skill upgradation', 'revival of sick industries' and 'promotion of Indo-Myanmar border trade'.

The 1996 policy sought for the establishment of a special monitoring cell to asses and to provide requisite security to all major industrial investment in the state. It also sought the intervention of the central government in the industrialization of special category states like Manipur and urged for establishing central public sector units. To meet the infrastructural needs, the state, in addition to upgradation of facilities at Takyelpat Industrial Estate, sought to take up a phased development of Integrated Infrastructural Development Centre at Moreh in Chandel District, Export Promotion Industrial Park at Kakching in Thoubal District, Export Processing Zone at Moreh in Chandel District, Industrial Growth Centre at Kanglatongbi in Senapati District and four additional industrial locations viz., Jiribam (Imphal), Litan (Ukhrul), Noney (Tamenglong) and Nambol (Bishnupur) to catalyze balanced dispersal of industries.

The major thrust areas identified are agro-based industries, industries based on locally available raw materials, including minerals and waste, products with local/regional demand, all units which take advantage of the Indo–Myanmar border trade, handloom and handicraft, electronics, petro-chemical based industries, forest based industries not involving depletion of the tree population, export oriented activities/industries, all non-polluting labour intensive units, units using non-conventional energy devices/systems/technology and tourism. Besides identifying new areas, the government also sought for the revival of sick industrial units by way of disinvestment and joint ventures (Industrial Policy of Manipur 1996).

In order to promote Indo-Myanmar border trade, the government sought to set up an export cell in the Directorate of Commerce and Industries which will be the nodal agency which will educate, train and guide traders/entrepreneurs in international trading, conduct an export potential survey, undertake measures to promote trade-motivated industrial activity, optimize use of agriculture/horticulture/forest resources across the border, and facilitate setting up of trade centres with integrated and in-house basic facilities (Industrial Policy of Manipur 1996).

The government, in order to materialize the above objectives, rendered an incentive package which includes land allotment, allotment of shed to small scale units, manpower development, state capital investment subsidy, state transport subsidy, interest subsidy, power subsidy, subsidy for feasibility study and project report preparation, subsidy for technical know-how, government purchase, reimbursement and exemption of local sales tax and reimbursement of stamp duty and registration fee, quality control and subsidy for modernization/expansion/diversification (Industrial Policy of Manipur 1996).

Thus, we can see from the above that the strategy of the government of Manipur towards industrialization of the state has two facets. Till 1990, the government assumed the role of an entrepreneur and tried to industrialize the state. Having failed in this objective, as we shall see in a short while, the government after 1990 took a u-turn and bestowed the whole responsibility of industrialization of the state upon the shoulder of the people who hardly have any entrepreneurial skill. Since 1990 the government assumed the role of a manager and focused on providing suitable business environment and industrial infrastructure. However, the absence of indigenous entrepreneurial class and with the gradual disappearance of the state from the scene, the process of industrializing Manipur has taken a back seat. Moreover, the strategies laid out in policy statements are not substantiated on the ground in terms of financial allocation. The plan expenditures made in industrial sector in the five year plans bears testimony to this.

The plan expenditure in industrial sector was very low to the tune of less than 3 per cent of the total plan expenditure up to the 3rd plan. During the 4th and 5th plan the expenditure had increased slightly to about 7 per cent. Since the 6th plan, expenditure has declined to less than 6 per cent of the total expenditure (table 3.6). The outlays for the industrial sector in 10th and 11th plans are 11.87 per cent and 8.05 per cent of the total outlay respectively (Annexure - IX). With such a meager expenditure and outlay, it is hard to make any dent for the improvement of the industrial sector in the state. Moreover, given the geographical location, topography and the resource base of the state, the cost structure of setting up an industry and running it viably outweighs the incentives offered by the state.

Having discussed the strategy of industrialization of the Government of Manipur, let us now see the performance of this sector.

Performance of Secondary Sector

As has already been mentioned above, following the 1982

industrial policy, the government of Manipur took the initiative of establishing large and medium industries. However, there is no public sector unit worth mentioning and whatever had been established are now in the process of liquidation.

Table 3.17
Public Sector Undertakings in Manipur

Sl. No	*Name of the Units*	*Year of Incorporation*	*Share Capital (Rs. Lakhs)*
1	Manipur Agro Industries Corporation Ltd. (MAICL)	1982	200
2	Manipur Cement Ltd. (MCL)	1988	350
3	Manipur Cycle Corporation Ltd. (MCCL)	1985	100
4	Manipur Electronics Development Corporation Ltd. (MANITRON)	1987	300
5	Manipur Handloom & Handicrafts Development Corporation Ltd. (MHHDCL)	1976	40
6	Manipur Industrial Development Corporation Ltd. (MANIDCO)	1987	1300
7	Manipur Plantation Crops Corporation Ltd. (MPCCL)	1981	200
8	Manipur Spinning Mills Corporation Ltd. (MSMCL)	1974	1300

Source: Government of Manipur, Planning Department, 1994.

Table 3.17 gives a list of the public sector undertakings in the state. It is seen that most of the units have come up in the post-statehood period. However, in the late 1980s, a number of units have come up. But, one can see that the efforts towards industrialization in the state started after about 40 years of Independence. In spite of the planned strategy of development since 1950, the state has not been able to materialize the process of industrialization until 1980s. While the India's efforts towards industrialization started with the 2nd Plan (1956-61), it was yet to make any headway in case of Manipur. However, one will see that even after the establishment of these units, Manipur is still an industrially backward state owing to the non-performance of these industries.

Table 3.18 gives the profit/loss, return on equity and return on investment of the public sector undertakings in Manipur in 1989, 1991 and 1993. It may be seen that most of the units are loss making units except MANITRON. It was making a profit of Rs. 20.19 lakhs, Rs. 16.55lakhs and Rs. 21.49 lakhs in 1989, 1991 and 1993 respectively. In case of MAICL, it kept on fluctuating and though it registered a loss of Rs. 9.13 lakhs in 1991, it was making a profit of Rs. 6.17 lakhs in 1993. Though MANIDCO was making a profit of Rs. 33.65 lakhs in the initial years of establishment, it lost significance in the subsequent years and was running on a loss. However, MHHDCL was running on a loss throughout the years despite having a comparative potential in the state.

In case of return on equity, except MANITRON all the units were making a negative return on equity. However, the return on equity in case of MANITRON also declined over the years from 33.72 per cent in 1989 to 9.59 per cent and 7.23 per cent in 1991 and 1993 respectively. MAICL also made a positive return on equity of 5.24 per cent in 1993 despite its negative return of 15.67 per cent in 1991. MANIDCO though made a positive return on equity of 7.03 per cent in 1989 registered negative return in the subsequent years.

Table 3.18
Performance of Public Sector Undertakings in Manipur

Sl. No.	*Name ofthe Units*	*Profit (+)/Loss(-) (Rs. Lakhs)*			*Return on Equity (%)*			*Return on Investment (%)*		
		1989	*1991*	*1993*	*1989*	*1991*	*1993*	*1989*	*1991*	*1993*
1	MAICL	0.82	-9.13	6.17	2.62	-15.67	5.24	6.67	-47.90	31.11
2	MCL	0	-40.65	-37.50	0	-10.79	-11.36	0	-11.15	-11.01
3	MCCL	-7.49	-6.33	-5.67	-22.52	-28.21	-36.94	-29.25	-32.28	-38.21
4	MANITRON	20.19	16.55	21.49	33.72	9.59	7.23	-153.89	-100.24	-50.80
5	MHHDCL	-37.65	-22.54	-39.88	-20.54	-11.66	-70.28	-18.44	-58.93	-107.73
6	MANIDCO	33.65	-100.59	-36.18	7.03	-8.29	-2.50	30.31	-50.43	-17.71
7	MPCCL	-186.89	-18.54	-18.58	-77.50	-4.94	-4.06	-91.55	-7.89	-6.05
8	MSMCL	-159.79	-95.07	-172.98	-25.14	-12.35	-18.42	-52.50	-39.59	-87.67

Source: Government of Manipur, Planning Department, 1994

However, all the units made a negative return on investment. Only MAICL registered a positive return on investment of 31.11 per cent in 1993 despite making a negative return of 47.90 per cent in 1991. MANITRON, which was making profit and having a positive return on equity throughout the years, however, registered a negative return on investment to the tune of 153.89 per cent, 100.24 per cent and 50.80 per cent in 1989, 1991 and 1993 respectively. MANIDCO which was making a positive return on investment of 30.31 per cent in 1989 registered negative return of 50.43 per cent and 17.71 per cent in 1991 and 1993 respectively.

Thus, we see that the public sector undertakings are not viable and all are making losses. All the units registered a negative return on equity and on investment. Because of the non-performance of these units, the government has taken up steps of winding up the sick units. According to the Annual Administrative Report 2008-09 of the Directorate of Commerce and Industries, all the units are in active process of winding up except MANITRON, MANIDCO and MHHDCL. All the staffs of the units which are under the process of winding up had already been retrenched, except 12 employees retained to complete the updating of accounts of these units. With the failure of the state in her efforts to industrialize the state by setting up large and medium scale industries, the government focused on small scale industries since 1990. Let us now see the performance of the small scale industries.

Table 3.19 gives the growth of small scale industries in Manipur. The number of small scale units increased from 6319 in 1990 to 9415 and 9690 in 2000 and 2007 (upto 31-03-2007) respectively. So, in about 17 years time the small scale units grew at the rate of about more than 50 per cent. However, the average number of employment per unit is

Table 3.19

Growth of Small Scale Industrial Units (Both SIDO and Non-SIDO) in Manipur

Year	No. of Units	No. of Employment	Average no. of employment per unit	Investment in Plant & Machinery (Rs. Crore)	Average investment per unit (Rs. Thousand)	Production (Rs. Crore)	Average production per unit (Rs. Lakh)
1990	6319	31500	4.98	19.20	30.38	89.11	1.41
2000	9415	48514	5.15	33.19	35.25	150.69	1.60
2007*	9690	51829	5.35	39.91	41.19	170.77	1.76

Source: Economic Survey Manipur 2002-03; Government of Manipur, Directorate of Commerce and Industries
* Upto 31-03-2007.

around 5 persons and the average investment in plant and machinery is around Rs. 40,000. Similarly, the production per unit is below Rs. 2 lakh. But there is an increasing trend in all the parameters from 1990 to 2007. The average number of employment increased from 4.98 persons in 1990 to 5.15 persons and 5.35 persons in 2000 and 2007 respectively. The average investment in plant and machinery increased from Rs. 30.38 thousand in 1990 to Rs. 35.25 thousand and Rs. 41.19 thousand in 2000 and 2007 respectively. Similarly, the average production per unit increased from Rs. 1.41 lakh in 1990 to Rs. 1.60 lakh and Rs. 1.76 lakh in 2000 and 2007 respectively.

From the above observation one can deduce the nature of small scale industries in Manipur. It appears that the small scale industries in Manipur are more or less demand based units which are operating at household level. There is no huge employment or huge investment. Even the productions in these units are not very high. These are basically need based industries which are run by few people and are somewhat more or less subsistence in nature. No doubt, these are important agents of an economy but they will not be in a position to lift Manipur to a developed industrial state.

The Khadi and Village Industry (KVI) is also another category where traditional small industries are grouped. In Manipur, the KVI was constituted in the year 1966 following the establishment of KVI Commission by the Government of India in the year 1957.

Table 3.20 gives the performance of the Khadi and Village industries in Manipur. During the late 1990s, the production was growing at a rate of around 50 per cent. This has declined to less than 1 per cent in 2003-2004. The sales which were growing at a rate of around 46 per cent during 1998-1999 declined to about 7 per cent in 2003-2004. Similarly, the earning of the KVI which was growing around 43 per cent

Table 3.20
Performance of Khadi and Village Industries in Manipur

Item	*Unit*	*1998*	*1999*	*Growth rate (1998-99)*	*2003*	*2004*	*Growth rate (2003-04)*
Production	Rs. Lakhs	2978.57	4457.27	49.64	6000.85	6029.24	0.47
Sales	Rs. Lakhs	3151.84	4602.41	46.02	5661.92	6069.88	7.21
Earnings	Rs. Lakhs	962.13	1385.01	43.95	2632.68	2690.18	2.18
Employment	No. Lakhs	0.42	0.42	-	0.61	0.62	1.64

Source: Economic Survey Manipur 2002-03; Basic Statistics of NER 2006.

Table 3.21

Number of Enterprises and Workers According to Economic Census

Economic	*Agricultural Enterprises*					*Non-Agricultural Enterprises*				
Census	*Rural*	*Urban*	*Total*	*Persons usually working*	*Hired workers*	*Rural*	*Urban*	*Total*	*Persons usually working*	*Hired workers*
1980	1765	552	2417	4839	360	17097	15231	32328	100120	55355
1990	3787	1190	4977	9701	548	30034	26253	56287	147667	75972
1998	4235	1938	6173	12867	1017	38785	35531	74316	187859	102904
1980-1998 Growth Rate (%)								129.88	87.63	85.90

Source: Statistical Handbook of Manipur 2002; Fourth Economic Census 1998 Manipur.

in 1998-1999 declined to about 2 per cent in 2003-2004. However, the employment has increased during 2003-2004 and is growing at the rate less than 2 per cent. The KVI is, thus, facing a retrogressive change.

Given the above nature of industries in Manipur, we may safely conclude that the secondary sector in the state is basically non-agricultural activities of very low scales. The Economic Census gives an idea of non-agricultural activities of the state.

The non-agricultural enterprises increased from 32328 in 1980 to 56287 and 74316 in 1990 and 1998 respectively. So, in 18 years time the non-agricultural enterprises have grown by about 130 per cent. The number of persons usually employed in these enterprises has increased from 100120 persons in 1980 to 147667 persons and 187859 persons in 1990 and 1998 respectively. The employment in these enterprises has grown by about 88 per cent in these 18 years. In case of hired workers, it has increased from 55355 persons in 1980 to 75972 persons and 102904 persons in 1990 and 1998 respectively, registering a growth of about 86 per cent. One can observe that the growth of number of enterprises outweighs the growth in employment. Moreover, the average number of persons working in these enterprises was about 3 persons per enterprise in 1980. But in the 1990 and 1998 Census, the average number of persons employed was less than 3 persons per enterprise. In case of hired workers, the average was less than 2 persons per enterprise throughout the census years.

Thus, the non-agricultural enterprises in Manipur are basically household based enterprises. They are very small in size and are neither labour nor capital intensive. As a result there is absence of externalities in the non-agricultural enterprises in the state (Yumnam, 2005: 93).

As is expected of such low performance of industries, the contribution of secondary sector to the total income of the state is also low. Table 3.22 gives the percentage contribution of secondary sector to total NSDP in the state.

Table 3.22
Contribution of Secondary Sector to total NSDP in Manipur (% share)

Year	*Manufacturing*				*Electricity,*	*Total*
	Regd.	*Unregd.*	*Total*	*Construction*	*Gas & Water Supply*	*Secondary*
1961	-	-	8.34	1.68	0.25	10.28
1970	-	-	6.57	1.89	0.40	8.86
1980	0.48	6.24	6.72	11.67	-0.23	18.16
1990	0.08	5.68	5.76	7.91	-4.18	9.48
2000	0.06	8.20	8.26	11.54	0.31	20.12
2007	0.14	4.25	4.39	36.83	0.89	42.11

Source: Calculated from EPW and CSO.

From table 3.22, it is seen that the share of secondary sector to total NSDP in Manipur has increased over the years. While the share was very low to the tune of 10.28 per cent and 8.86 per cent in 1961 and 1970 respectively, it has increased to 18.16 per cent in 1980. However, its share declined to 9.48 per cent in 1990. Since then, the share of secondary sector has increased and it share was 20.12 per cent and 42.11 per cent in 2000 and 2007 respectively, thus becoming the major contributor to the state's income. However, a further break up of the components of the secondary sector will give us a true picture of the nature of growth in this sector.

Table 3.23
Percentage share of various components in Secondary Sector in Manipur

Year	*Manufacturing*			*Construction*	*Electricity, Gas & Water Supply*
	Regd.	*Unregd.*	*Total*		
1961	-	-	81.15	16.36	2.46
1970	-	-	74.16	21.35	4.49
1980	2.65	34.35	37.00	64.29	-1.28
1990	0.85	59.85	60.70	83.41	-44.10
2000	0.29	40.77	41.06	57.38	1.57
2007	0.34	10.09	10.43	87.47	2.11

Source: Calculated from EPW and CSO.

In the secondary sector construction is the leading activity. Though its share before 1970 was very insignificant, contributing around 20 per cent, it has been the major activity of growth after 1970s. Its share which was 64.29 per cent in 1980 increased to 83.41 per cent in 1990. However, the share declined to 57.38 per cent in 2000 but improved to 87.47 per cent in 2007.

The manufacturing unit whose share was more than 70 per cent before 1970 lost its significance. Its share which stood at 81.15 per cent and 74.16 per cent in 1961 and 1970 respectively declined to 60 per cent in 1980. Since then its share has been declining and its share stood at 41.06 per cent in 2000. It has further declined to 10.43 per cent in 2007.

A very interesting observation within the secondary sector is that the share of registered manufacturing unit is insignificant. Its share varied between 1 per cent and 2 per cent over the years. Since 1990 its share has dropped below 1 per cent. Same is the case with electricity, gas and waster supply. Its share which stood once at 4.49 per cent in 1970 has gone negative to the tune of -44.10 per cent in 1990. But it has shown some sign of improvement in the preceding years and contributed 1.57 per cent and 2.11 per cent in 2000 and 2007 respectively.

The national growth trend of secondary sector is in contrast with the state growth experience. In case of India, major share of secondary sector comes from manufacturing which contributes around 60 per cent throughout the years. Within the manufacturing the major share comes from registered unit contributing around 40 per cent and the rest 20 per cent comes from unregistered manufacturing units. The share of construction, which is the main contributing component in case of Manipur, is around 35 per cent. The share of electricity, gas and water supply is low around 5 per cent (For India's figure: Annexure - XI).

Though the share to the total income of the state keeps on fluctuating, the share of working population in this sector is declining. Table 3.24 gives the distribution of main workers in secondary sector.

Table 3.24
Distribution of Main Workers by Industries in Secondary Sector in Manipur (% share)

Classification	*1961*	*1971*	*1981*	*1991*	*2001**
Mining & quarrying	0	0.02	0.04	0.03	NA
Manufacturing, processing, servicing & repairing in household industry	22.12	9.34	9.68	5.80	6.55
Manufacturing, processing, servicing & repairing other than household industry	0.31	1.65	1.80	2.31	NA
Construction	0.62	1.25	1.88	1.55	NA
Total Secondary	23.05	12.23	13.35	9.66	6.55

Source: Calculated from Statistical Abstract Manipur 2005
*Figures for 2001 exclude Mao-Maram, Paomata and Purul sub-divisions of Senapati District.
NA – Not Available.

A major portion of the working population in secondary sector is engaged in manufacturing, processing, servicing and repairing in household industry. It may be noted that in 1961, the share of main workers engaged in manufacturing, processing, servicing and repairing in household industry accounts for 22.12 per cent. But in the following years it declined to 9.34 per cent and 9.68 per cent in 1971 and 1981 respectively. It further declined to 5.80 per cent and 6.55 per cent in 1991 and 2001 respectively. The main reason for a high percentage share in 1961 is that in 1961 Census, subsidiary activities like weaving was included in this category which was subsequently dropped in the following census (IDBI, 1972: 5). The share of main workers engaged in manufacturing, processing, servicing and repairing other than household industry gradually increased from 0.31 per cent in 1961 to 1.65 per cent, 1.80 per cent and 2.31 per cent in 1971, 1981 and 1991 respectively. Similarly, the share of main workers engaged in construction increased from 0.62 per cent in 1961 to 1.25 per cent, 1.88 per cent and 1.55 per cent in 1971, 1981 and 1991 respectively. However, the share of main workers engaged in mining and quarrying is very low and negligible.

The share of main workers in the secondary sector as a whole declined from 23.05 per cent in 1961 to 12.23 per cent in 1971. It slightly increased to 13.35 per cent in 1981. Since then it declined to 9.66 per cent and 6.55 per cent in 1991 and 2001 respectively (table 3.16).

Thus, one can observe that the working population engaged in real sectors of the economy is declining over time. Moreover, the planned strategy of development has not given major thrust to the real sectors. The resultant is the non-performance of these sectors, which are the major engines of growth of an economy. The planned development has focused more on providing social services and infrastructural facilities. Let us now focus on the tertiary sector.

Strategy of Development of the Tertiary Sector

As has already been mentioned above, the planned strategy of development of the government of Manipur has laid more emphasis on providing social services and infrastructural facilities. The plan expenditure was very high to the tune of 72.33 per cent in case of transport in the 1st Plan. The expenditure on social services was 18.58 per cent in the same plan (table 3.6). These two heads continue to receive the same loyalty in the subsequent plans as well. However, the expenditure on transport keeps on declining and expenditure of social services keeps on increasing over the years. Upto the 4th Plan the expenditure on transport was around 40 per cent of the total plan expenditure. In the 5th and 6th Plan the expenditure has declined to 22.22 per cent and 15.25 per cent respectively. Since then, the plan expenditure on transport has declined and it was 14.79 per cent, 16.42 per cent and 13.87 per cent in 7th, 8th and 9th Plan respectively (table 3.6). The plan outlay on transport in 10th and 11th Plan is 7.97 per cent and 4.94 per cent respectively (Annexure- IX).

The expenditure on social services has increased since 2nd Plan. This particular head received much attention in the succeeding plans as well. The expenditure increased from 18.58 per cent in 1st Plan to 37.85 per cent and 38.39 per cent in 2nd and 3rd Plan. It, however, declined to 26.24 per cent and 18.48 per cent in 4th and 5th Plan respectively. But in the 6th Plan the expenditure has increased to 30.48 per cent. Since then, the expenditure on this head more or less remained around 30 per cent till the 9th Plan (table 3.6). The plan outlay on social services in the 10th and 11th Plan is 36.21 per cent and 39.60 per cent respectively (Annexure- IX).

Thus, the government of Manipur has focused more on providing better social service and infrastructure since Independence. As the performance of the social services could not be quantified in economic terms, the performance is unlikely to match the investment that has gone into the tertiary sector.

Performance of Tertiary Sector

Since independence the focus of the government has been to provide social service and infrastructural facilities. Given the geographical location and topography of the state, road is the only means of transport. As such, transport and social service were given more emphasis during the plan strategies as we have already seen.

The total road length in Manipur was 11434 kms. on March, 2002. The total surfaced road length was 3863 kms. and the rest 7571 kms. were unsurfaced. So, the percentage of surfaced road length to total road length was 33.79 per cent compared to all India figures of 57.82 per cent. The road per 100 sq. km. was 42.65 km. in Manipur against the national figure of 74.73 km (Basic Statistics NER 2006).

Table 3.25 gives the contribution of tertiary sector to total NSDP of Manipur. It is seen that the share of tertiary sector keeps on fluctuating over the years. The share declined from 34.04 per cent in 1961 to 33.76 per cent and 32.80 per cent in 1970 and 1980 respectively. It increased to 52.25 per cent in 1990. Since then, the share of tertiary sector has declined to 48.75 per cent and 34.93 per cent in 2000 and 2007 respectively. A further break up of the various components of the tertiary sector will give us clear idea of the nature of growth in this sector.

In the tertiary sector, the major growth in this sector is the result of public administration. The share of public administration increased from 9.90 per cent in 1961 to 16.37 per cent and 23.32 per cent in 1970 and 1980 respectively. It further increased to 32.34 per cent and 34.48 per cent in 2000 and 2007 respectively. Trade, hotels and restaurants which contributed 42.82 per cent and 35.69 per cent in 1961

Table 3.25

Contribution of Tertiary Sector to total NSDP in Manipur (% share)

Year	*Transport, Storage & Communication*	*Trade, Hotels & Restaurants*	*Banking & Insurance*	*Real Estate, Ownership & Business Services*	*Public Administration*	*Others*	*Total Tertiary*
1961	1.60	14.57	0.93	6.15	3.37	7.41	34.04
1970	1.64	12.05	0.95	6.03	5.53	7.57	33.76
1980	3.02	5.81	1.33	0.93	7.65	14.06	32.80
1990	4.73	4.01	2.31	13.44	12.40	15.37	52.25
2000	3.46	11.22	1.72	3.39	15.77	13.19	48.75
2007	1.95	7.18	1.72	1.77	12.04	10.26	34.93

Source: Calculated from EPW and CSO.

Table 3.26

Percentage share of various components in Tertiary Sector in Manipur

Year	*Transport, Storage & Communication*	*Trade, Hotels & Restaurants*	*Banking & Insurance*	*Real Estate, Ownership & Business Services*	*Public Administration*	*Others*
1961	4.70	42.82	2.72	18.07	9.90	21.78
1970	4.87	35.69	2.80	17.85	16.37	22.42
1980	9.20	17.73	4.04	2.84	23.32	42.87
1990	9.05	7.68	4.42	25.72	23.73	29.41
2000	7.09	23.02	3.53	6.96	32.34	27.06
2007	5.58	20.55	4.93	5.08	34.48	29.38

Source: Calculated from EPW and CSO.

and 1970 respectively declined to 23.02 per cent and 20.55 per cent in 2000 and 2007 respectively. The share of banking and insurance is low with 2.72 per cent and 2.80 per cent in 1961 and 1970 respectively. But it has increased to 3.53 per cent and 4.93 per cent in 2000 and 2007 respectively. The share of transport, storage and communication is also low with 7.09 per cent and 5.58 per cent in 2000 and 2007 respectively. Similarly the share of real estate, ownership and business services is 6.96 per cent and 5.08 per cent in 2000 and 2007 respectively.

In case of tertiary sector too, the national experience is in contrast with the state experience. In case of India, trade, hotels and restaurants is the main activity contributing around 30 per cent throughout the years. A significant share of about 20 per cent comes from transport, storage and communications. The share of banking and insurance and real estate, etc. and public administration is around 13 per cent each (For India's figure: Annexure - XII).

Alongside the increase in the share to the total income of the state, the share of working population engaged in tertiary sector has also increased. Table 3.27 gives the distribution of main workers in tertiary sector.

Table 3.27
Distribution of Main Workers by Industry in Tertiary Sector (% share)

Classification	*1961*	*1971*	*1981*	*1991*	*2001**
Trade & Commerce	3.32	3.55	3.37	3.83	NA
Transport, storage & communication	0.85	1.09	0.90	1.21	NA
Other services	6.52	11.83	12.78	15.30	43.76
Total Tertiary	10.69	16.47	17.05	20.33	43.76

Source: Calculated from Statistical Abstract Manipur 2005
* Figures for 2001 exclude Mao-Maram, Paomata and Purul sub-divisions of Senapati District.
NA – Not Available

There is a continuous increase in the share of working population in the tertiary sector. The share of main workers engaged in other services but not as cultivators or agricultural labourers or manufacturing, processing, servicing and repairing, increased from 6.52 per cent in 1961 to 11.83 per cent, 12.78 per cent and 15.30 per cent in 1970, 1980 and 1990 respectively. However, the main workers engaged in trade and commerce is below 4 per cent throughout the years. Similarly, the main workers engaged in transport, storage and communication is around 1 per cent of the total main workers throughout the years.

The share of main workers in the tertiary sector as a whole increased from 10.69 per cent in 1961 to 16.47 per cent in 1971. It further increased to 17.05 per cent and 20.33 per cent in 1981 and 1991 respectively. Then in 2001 its share sharply increased to 43.76 per cent.

The distribution of the occupational pattern shows that there is a shift of the working population from the primary sector to the tertiary sector bypassing the secondary sector. It may be pointed out that the increase in the share of main workforce in the tertiary sector is mainly due to the increase in the number of government jobs which alone constitutes about 25 per cent of the total workforce employed in this sector. Out of 288272 main workers in the tertiary sector in 2001, which forms 43.76 per cent of the total main workers, 71508 have been engaged in government jobs. Besides government jobs, another significant size is engaged in urban informal sector.

Sectoral Share

The sectoral share gives the relative performance of the different sectors of the economy. It is a road map showing how the economy is growing over time.

Table 3.28
Sectoral Share of NSDP of Manipur (% share)

Year	*Primary*	*Secondary*	*Tertiary*
1961	55.69	10.28	34.04
1970	57.37	8.86	33.76
1980	49.04	18.16	32.80
1990	38.26	9.48	52.25
2000	31.13	20.12	48.75
2007	22.96	42.11	34.93

Source: Calculated from EPW and CSO.

The sectoral share of the NSDP of Manipur shows that the percentage share of primary sector is declining and that of tertiary sector is increasing over the years. While the contribution of secondary sector to NSDP is insignificant, its share is increasing at a low rate over the years.

Agriculture, being the mainstay of the state, has a major contribution to total NSDP. Upto 1980, the share of primary sector in NSDP has been above 50 per cent. It was 55.69 per cent in 1961 which has gone up to 57.37 per cent in 1970. However, the share of primary sector is continuously declining over the years. In 1980, its share was 49.04 per cent which declined to 38.26 per cent in 1990. In 2000, its share was 31.13 per cent which further declined 22.96 per cent in 2007.

Manipur has a very low manufacturing base. It has virtually no industries. As a result the share of secondary sector to NSDP is very low. The share of secondary sector kept on fluctuating up to 1990s. Its share declined from 10.28 per cent in 1961 to 8.86 per cent in 1970. It increased to 18.16 per cent in 1980 but declined very sharply to 9.48 per cent in 1990. From 1990 onwards its share has increased to 20.12 per cent and 42.11 per cent in 2000 and 2007 respectively, mainly due to spurt in construction activities.

The tertiary sector, driven by the growth of government jobs, is playing an important role in the economy of Manipur.

Its contribution to the growth of the economy has been very significant throughout the years. At present its share is more than the primary sector. Initially its share declined from 34.04 per cent in1961 to 33.76 per cent and 32.80 per cent in 1970 and 1980 respectively. Since then its share has increased to 52.25 per cent in 1990. Again the share fell to 48.75 per cent and 34.93 per cent in 2000 and 2007 respectively.

Thus, while the contribution of the primary sector is on the decline, it is mainly compensated by the growth of construction activities in the state, the main driver being the centrally sponsored development schemes, and government jobs, mainly funded by the centre. There has not been any significant increase in the productive capacity of the state. These weak sectoral performances have been reflected in the NSDP of Manipur.

State Income

The state domestic product and per capita income indicate the performance of an economy. The state domestic product is one of the most important indicators of the growth and structural change in the economy. Similarly per capita income is considered as the most effective indicator for ascertaining the economic welfare of people. It is an indicator of the change in the standard of living of the people.

Table 3.29
Decennial Compound Growth Rate of NSDP and Per Capita Income in Manipur

Year	*NSDP*	*Per Capita Income*
1961-70	7.37	4.16
1971-80	6.84	3.81
1981-90	4.80	2.14
1991-2000	4.68	2.36
2001-07	11.30	9.06

Source: Calculated from EPW and CSO.

The decennial compound growth of NSDP is declining over the years. It has declined from 7.37 per cent in 1961-70 to 6.84 per cent and 4.80 per cent in 1971-80 and 1981-90 respectively. It further declined to 4.68 per cent in 1991-2000 but increased to 11.30 per cent in 2001-07.

The growth pattern of state income corroborates the growth pattern of the three sectors of the economy. Up to 2000, we have seen that there was virtually no growth in the real sectors of the economy. The share of primary sector was declining and the share of secondary sector was not steady and kept on fluctuating. Since 2000, there is a sudden improvement in the growth of state income. As has already been indicated, the main driver behind the growth since 2000 is the rise in the share of construction. This is the resultant of the various development projects and economic packages that have been granted by the centre at the wake of the escalating tensions in the state especially during 2001 and 2004.

Similar trend is also found in case of per capita income. The decennial compound growth rate of per capita income declined from 4.16 per cent in 1961-70 to 3.81 per cent and 2.14 per cent in 1971-80 and 1981-90 respectively. But it has improved to 2.36 per cent and 9.06 per cent in 1991-2000 and 2001-07 respectively.

Table 3.30
Decennial Compound Growth Rate of NDP and Per Capita Income in India

Year	*NDP*	*Per Capita Income*
1961-70	3.16	0.92
1971-80	3.23	0.93
1981-90	5.11	2.89
1991-2000	5.97	3.90
2001-07	7.31	5.62

Source: Calculated from CSO.

In case of India, the decennial compound growth of both NDP and per capita income are increasing with the passage of time. The decennial compound growth rate of NDP increased from 3.16 per cent in 1961-70 to 5.11 per cent in 1981-90. It further increased to 7.31 per cent in 2000-07. Similarly, the decennial compound growth rate of per capita income increased from 0.92 per cent in 1961-70 to 2.89 per cent and 5.62 per cent in 1981-90 and 2000-07 respectively.

Thus, we see that the economy of Manipur is experiencing a low growth syndrome. There is virtually no growth in real sectors of the economy. In fact, the economy was stagnant and undergoing a retrogressive change up to 2000. Since 2000, the economy has grown suddenly. But this growth, as we have seen, is brought about mainly by construction. This is the result of government development projects through the central funding. As a Special Category State (SCS), Manipur enjoys the favour of 90 per cent plan assistance as grant and 10 per cent as loan, whereas other states other than SCS get 30 per cent plan assistance as grant and remaining 70 per cent as loan.

What is more important is whether this growth is leading to employment opportunities in the state or not? The employment elasticity of real NSDP will show the employment content of growth. The sectoral elasticities are derived by dividing the percentage change in employment by percentage change in real NSDP at 1993-94 prices originating in the sector.

Table 3.31 shows the job creating character of economic growth. During the year 1987-88 to 2004-05, the employment elasticity of real NSDP is 0.67. The sectoral variation shows that trade (1.508) is the most employment elastic sub-sector followed by agriculture (1.34). Construction (0.839) and transport (0.734) are fairly elastic sub-sectors but manufacturing (0.189) and services (0.133) have the least elasticity.

Table 3.31
Sectoral Employment Elasticity in Manipur

Sector	*1987-88 to 1993-94*	*1993-94 to 1999-2000*	*1999-2000 to 2004-05*	*1987-88 to 2004-05*
Agriculture	1.057	1.93	1.589	1.34
Manufacturing	0.296	-0.42	1.437	0.189
Construction	3.66	-0.282	2.078	0.839
Transport	1.15	0.25	0.85	0.734
Trade	1.785	0.643	1.661	1.508
Services	0.758	-0.189	0.209	0.133
All	0.794	0.303	1.322	0.67

Source: Singh (B), 2009: 497.

Employment and Unemployment

The poor economic growth and sectoral elasticity of employment have led to the escalation of the problem of unemployment in the state. The Employment Exchange and National Sample Survey (NSS) provide data for unemployment.

Table 3.32
Registration and Placing done through Employment Exchanges in Manipur

Year	*No. of Registrants on the live register*	*No. of persons placed in appointments*	*3 as % 2*
1985	194581	638	0.33
1990	254310	292	0.11
1995	249910	1085	0.43
2000	387890	69	0.02
2005	491476	-	-
2006	548704	489	0.09
2007	583653	357	0.06

Source: Statistical Handbook of Manipur 1992 & Economic Survey Manipur 2007-08.

Table 3.32 shows the number of persons on the live register and number of appointments made through the employment exchange. The number of live registrants on the live register increased from 194581 in 1985 to 583653 in 2007, an increase of about 200 per cent.

But the data on appointments gives a grim figure. The percentage of persons appointed was 0.33 per cent in 1985. In the recent years the condition is more pathetic with the percentage of appointments amounting to 0.09 per cent and 0.06 per cent in 2006 and 2007 respectively.

However, the data provided by the employment exchange suffers from many demerits like, non-renewal by the card holders, non-deletion of names of persons who are placed by some other agencies other than employment exchange, non-deletion of names who are in private jobs, self-employment, non-registration by the unemployed persons, etc. In spite of these drawbacks, it, no doubt, gives an overall picture of the precarious condition of educated unemployment in Manipur.

The NSS estimates on educated unemployment are shown in Table 3.33.

Table 3.33
Educated Unemployed aged 15 and above per 1000 in Manipur

Category	*Year*	*Rural*			*Urban*		
		Male	*Female*	*Persons*	*Male*	*Female*	*Persons*
Usual	1993-94	65	61	64	102	101	101
Status[10]	1999-00	63	131	75	114	193	130
	2000-05	65	86	69	85	146	82
Usual	1993-94	46	37	44	89	86	88
Status	1999-00	51	90	60	106	123	110
Adjusted	2000-05	43	47	45	84	119	95
Current	1993-94	57	45	54	94	89	93
Weekly	1999-00	52	160	73	101	131	108
Status[11]	2000-05	57	64	59	85	141	103

Source: Singh (B), 2009: 484.

The rate of educated unemployment is rising in all categories of unemployment over the years. The current weekly status unemployment rate in urban area rose from 93 per 1000 in 1993-94 to 103 in 2000-05. In rural, it rose from 54 per 1000 in 1993-94 to 59 per 1000 in 2000-05. Among the females in rural area, the current weekly status unemployment rate rose from 45 per 1000 in 1993-94 to 64 per 1000 in 2000-05, whereas in urban, it rose from 89 per 1000 in 1993-94 to 141 per 1000 in 2000-05. The rise is more pronounced in urban areas and among females. Thus, educated unemployment is a cause of serious concern in the state [Singh (B), 2009: 485].

The NSSO estimates on the dimension of youth unemployment, aged between 15-29 years per 1000, are presented in table 3.34.

Table 3.34
Youth Unemployment aged between 15-29 years per 1000 in Manipur

Category	*Year*	*Rural*			*Urban*		
		Male	*Female*	*Persons*	*Male*	*Female*	*Persons*
Usual	1993-94	69	25	52	180	80	154
Status	1999-00	52	72	58	226	242	231
	2000-05	51	23	39	197	185	193
Usual	1993-94	40	14	28	163	60	120
Status	1999-00	49	45	41	199	150	182
Adjusted	2000-05	35	14	26	192	146	174
Current	1993-94	58	18	39	168	65	133
Weekly	1999-00	56	72	62	203	154	186
Status	2000-05	48	21	36	202	199	210
Current	1993-94	65	24	49	173	83	145
Daily	1999-00	57	75	62	216	168	200
Status[12]	2000-05	49	23	38	204	201	202

Source: Singh (B), 2009: 486.

It may be seen from table 3.34 that youth unemployment in all categories of unemployment is rising in case of urban areas while it is declining in case of rural areas. In urban areas, the increase is more pronounced among the females than the males. Even in rural areas the decline is not very significant among the females. The current weekly status unemployment rate in rural declined from 39 per 1000 in 1993-94 to 36 per 1000 in 2000-05, whereas in urban in increased from 133 per 1000 in 1993-94 to 201 per 1000 in 2000-05.

Thus, the educated unemployment in general and youth unemployment in particular are a serious problem in Manipur. With the avenues of gainful employment getting closed with the poor growth performance of the economy, the level of frustration among the educated youths is getting higher and higher. The underdeveloped material base acts as a driver in accentuating the feeling of neglect and deprivation among the educated youths of the state. The demand for autonomous homeland, articulated by the ethno-national groups, as has been analyzed in the previous chapter, get further intensified due to this feeling of economic deprivation. The logic of separation or secession of the underdeveloped regions gets strengthened while seen from the view point of economic deprivation. The perceptions of political and cultural marginalization while added up with economic deprivation often transform the regional ideology into the ideology of secession and militancy is opted as a means to achieve the goal. Thus, although economic underdevelopment may not be the fundamental cause for the growth of militancy in the northeastern region in general and Manipur in particular, but nonetheless, it helps in aggravating the problem.

Further, whatever development has taken place in Manipur is largely concentrated in the valley districts. Although the valley constitutes of only 10 per cent of the geographical area of the state, being plains, densely populated and seat of administration; urban amenities, economic activities including agriculture, trade and commerce, social and community services—all are concentrated here. The disparities in development between the hills and plains, whatever economic logic it might have, have strong bearing on the inter-ethnic relations due to the coincidence of geography and ethnic boundary in the state. Thus, competitive ethno-national goals assume an altogether new orientation while perceptions of development disparities between hills and plains are juxtaposed with them making the 'Manipuri' nation building all the more difficult. The implications for policy interventions to deal with this inter-ethnic competition for independent national accommodation will be taken up in the concluding chapter.

NOTES

1. One basket contains about 60 pounds. 1 pound ≐ 0.45 kg. So, one basket contains about 27 kg.
2. The cultivated land was categorized into nine types, viz., (i) *Tauna Lou*, (ii) *Sarkari Lou*, (iii) *Pham Lou*, (iv) *Sepoy Lou*, (v) *Mana Lou*, (vi) *Brahmin Lou*, (vii) *Temple Lou*, (viii) *Royal Family Lou* and (ix) *Pangal Lou* (For more details, Singh, 1998: 14-20).
3. 60 pots = 2 *sangbai*; 1 *sangbai* = 29.86 kg. (approximately 30 kg.) So roughly 1 pot = 1 kg.
4. Services include government service, personal service, commerce, transport, storage, professions, unskilled labour not agricultural, means of subsistence independent of occupation (Allen, 2002: 66).
5. According to 1901 Census, the occupational distribution was divided into not less than 520 different heads. Such an elaborate classification was not suitable for a state like Manipur. But the British had applied the one-size fit all approach and used the same criteria in conducting the census in Manipur without any merit (Allen, 2002: 65).
6. Other exports include canes, rattans, cotton twist, yarn, piece goods, ghee, dry fish, spices other than betel-nuts, bamboos and other articles (Allen, 2002: 111).

7. Other imports include horses, ponies, mules, wheat, grams, pulses, liquors, brass, copper, mineral oils, ghi, sugar refines and other articles (Allen, 2002: 112).

8. The revenue out of Kabaw Valley compensation is excluded due to differences in the amount between different authors. Brown & McCulloch used Rs. 6370, Allen used Rs. 6270 and according to the treaty it was Rs. 6000.

9. Singh (2005: 153) assumed that one pari (1 hectare) of land gave farmer 37.9 maunds of paddy and after deducting his subsistence requirements for five persons he would be left with 10.65 maunds which would give him Rs. 13 and 15.65 annas.

10. In this approach the status of activity on which a person spent relatively longer time of the preceding 365 days from the date of survey is considered as the principal usual status activity of the person. Accordingly, a person is considered 'working or employed' if the person was engaged for a relatively longer time during the past year in any one or more work related activities (economic activities) including seeking or being available for work. The person is considered as 'seeking or available' for work or 'unemployed' if the person was not working but was either seeking or was available for work for a relatively longer time during the past year. If the person was engaged in any non-economic activities for a relatively longer time of the reference year he/she is considered as 'out of labour force'. The specific activity category is determined on the basis of time spent criterion i.e., the activity on which major time was spent being assigned as the usual status activity. A person categorized as 'worker' or 'employed' on the basis of the principal status is called a 'principal status worker' or 'principal status employed'. A person categorized as a non-worker (i.e. unemployed or out of labour force) who pursued some economic activity in a subsidiary capacity is called a 'subsidiary status worker' or 'subsidiary status employed'. These two groups, viz., principal status workers and subsidiary status workers together constitute 'all workers' according to the usual status classification (NSSO).

11. For classification of persons according to current weekly status approach, they are assigned a unique activity status with reference to a period of 7 days preceding the date of survey. Using this procedure in the current weekly status a person is considered working or employed if the person was engaged for at least one hour on any one day of the previous week on any work related (economic) activity. A person who had not worked for even one hour on any one day of the week, but had been seeking or had been

available for work at any time for at least one hour during the week was considered 'seeking/available for work'. Others were considered 'not available for work' or as out of labour force (NSSO).

12. In the current daily status (CDS), up to two activity statuses were assigned to a person on each day of the reference week. The unit of classification was thus 'half day' in the CDS. In assigning the activity status on a day, a person was considered working for the entire day if he had worked 4 hours or more during the day. If he had worked one hour or more but less than 4 hours, he was considered working (employed) for half day and seeking/available for work (unemployed) or not available for work (not in labour force) for the other half day depending on whether he was seeking / available for work or not. On the other hand, if a person was not engaged in any work even for one hour but was seeking or available for work for 4 hours or more, he was considered unemployed for the entire day. If he was available for work for less than 4 hours only, he was considered unemployed for half day and not in labour force for the other half of the day. A person who neither had any work to do nor was available for work even for 'half' of the day was considered not in labour force for the entire day and was assigned one or two non-economic activity status codes (NSSO).

4

Dynamics of Growth of Militancy in Manipur

Socio-political aspirations of the different ethno-national groups, as has already been discussed in chapter 2, coupled with stunted economic growth, discussed in chapter 3, have led to the growth of deep sense of frustration which in turn has given birth to militancy in Manipur. It has already been pointed out that a strategy of growth based on the expansion of the service sector without any corresponding programmes for the growth of the real sector has raised the aspiration of the people in the state far more than her material condition could support. The gap between the peoples' aspiration and opportunities being offered by the material condition of the economy has led to the accumulation of the sense of relative deprivation and has provided socio-political justification for joining in the alternative movement in the form of militancy.

In this chapter we intend to look into the dynamics of the growth of militancy in Manipur. We see the emergence of militancy as the product of a complex interplay of socio-political and economic processes. We also intend to analyze the symbiotic relations between the militant movements and the electoral politics. It is also of interest to investigate as to how the interests of seemingly different entities are depended on each other that act as drivers for the growth of militancy.

It is also of no less important to peruse the efficacy of the counter-insurgency strategy of the state in Manipur. We also intend to analyze the external factors that have provided the logistics for the growth of militancy and finally we make an attempt to assess the extent of degeneration of militancy in Manipur overtime.

Dynamics of Growth of Militancy

The growth of militancy in Manipur can be traced back to the days of Irabot. As has already been mentioned in chapter 2, Irabot and some of his close associates had gone underground after the Pungdombam incident in 1948. He organized the 'Red Guard' army during March, 1950, in collaboration with the Burma Communist Party (BCP). Their demand included, among others, the establishment of a popular government, withdrawal of Indian army from Manipur, equal status of men and women, provision of adequate food and clothing for all and conferment of land ownership to landless peasants (Singh, 1989: 389). But the untimely demise of Irabot on September 26, 1951 left the movement in its pregnancy period.

It may not be out of place to recall the political environment during this period of time. As has already been discussed in chapter 2, the air during this period was tense due to possible merger of Manipur into the Indian Union or formation of Purbachal Pradesh comprising the territories of Manipur, Tripura and Cachar. We have also seen how there emerged two opposing ideas—one in support of the merger and the other against the merger. However, the merger was effected on October 15, 1949 against all odds.

With the merger, the pre-merger democratic institutions suffered a setback. We have already discussed at length the after effects of merger in chapter 2. But it may not be out of place to note that with the merger, the elected assembly was dissolved and a bureaucratic form of government was imposed by reducing Manipur to the status of Part 'C' state. Since then a 22 year long political movement started in the state until it graduated to a full-fledged state on January 21, 1972. It was during these 22 years that the seeds of desperation, deprivation, dispossession, frustration, etc. were sown in the fertile soil of the Manipur valley. As the Naga hills was granted statehood in 1963, in order to appease the militant movement of Naga National Council (NNC), this had sent a wrong signal to the people of northeast in general and Manipur in particular. It left the impression that nothing will come on the way unless the path of armed rebellion is being followed. Although Manipur had a long history of state formation and a better socio-economic and political condition, the denial of her rightful place in the newly formed Indian Union had aggravated the situation. Moreover, the major population of the state was more attached to the mainland people by virtue of being Hindus, unlike the tribal counterparts who are predominantly Christians.

The sense of deprivation was deep rooted in the psyche of the people, especially among the educated youths and middle class elites. With their voices going unheard, the only way out was the armed rebellion. The legacy of Irabot was soon followed by some leftist radicals after his death.

The Manipur National Union (MNU), as has already been discussed in chapter 2, was spearheading an intense movement for statehood. They even met the then Prime Minister Jawaharlal Nehru and served an ultimatum for establishing an administrative set up accountable to the people. Having failed in their democratic efforts, some leftists of the MNU like Sagolsem Indramani, R K Maipaksana, Yangmasho Shaiza, etc., formed the Revolutionary Nationalist Party on April 19, 1953. Their main objective was to create a buffer state of Manipur under the United Nations

(UN) Trusteeship Council. But the party was short-lived as most of the ring leaders were arrested within 24 hours of formation of the party [Constantine, 1981: 94; Parratt (J), 2005: 133; Sanajaoba, 2000]. Though the party died right at its birth, but it left a trail for the future generations to seek justice through armed struggle.

The militant initiative, however, momentarily died down. But the step-motherly treatment of the India government once again lit the fire of militancy as Jawaharlal Nehru, during his visit in Naga hills along with U Nu, the then Prime Minister of Burma, in 1953, handed over the Kabaw valley to Burma. It may be noted here that the Kabaw valley was handed over to Burma in 1834 by the British colonial government and Manipur was compensated for the loss of the valley by granting a sum of Rs. 6000 per annum. The India government continued to pay this compensation amount even after Independence. But following Nehru's step of 1953 the payment of this compensation amount was stopped (Verghese, 2004: 114). Again, the conferment of statehood to Naga hills, thence Nagaland in 1963, was a major source of desperation. Nagaland was carved out of Assam and granted statehood to appease the militant movements of NNC bypassing the status of Part 'C' state and Union Territory. These steps had deeply hurt the sentiments of the people of Manipur, especially the nationalists who were all along clamouring for statehood through democratic means.

Meanwhile, the air was very tense as the demand for statehood had reached its height with all the political parties joining hand together and started mass movement as has already been discussed in chapter 2. Moreover, the Nagas under Phizo, not content with statehood, were engaged heavily in armed struggle for independence. Sensing a right moment during this situation, some communist followers of Irabot contacted the Naga underground members and discussed their desire to launch an armed movement against the India government. The Nagas readily gave a green signal. Consequently, the Meitei State Committee[1] (MSC*) was formed under the leadership of W. Tomba Singh, a close associalte of Irabot. The main objective of MSC* was to establish an independent Manipur and carry forward the movement of Irabot. The members were not only trained by the underground Nagas but were also supplied some small firearms and ammunitions to start the movement at the initial stage. A few cases of robbery conducted by the committee to collect money and arms by using firearms were reported [Singh (J), 2005: 54-63]. The committee, however, met with little success. With the arrest of its top leaders, the MSC* faced extinction.

The Red Guard army, the Revolutionary Nationalist Party and the Meitei State Committee were, thus, the forerunners of the underground movement in Manipur. Although these organizations did not have a wide network, mass support and lacked in their organizational skills and revolutionary ideas, they left a trail for the future generations. These organizations kindled revolutionary ideas and sense of nationalism among the young generations who foresaw their future in armed struggle. These movements articulated the national interests of the Manipuris in general and Meiteis in particular against the interest of the Indian state and had created an impression that the only solution to the ongoing struggle in the state was armed rebellion. In fact they had greatly shaped the future course of militancy in the state.

The impact of the above mentioned movements was soon visible on the ground. Some educated youths of the valley formed the non-violent organization—United National Liberation Front (UNLF) on November 24, 1964. Arambam Somorendra was the founder General Secretary of UNLF. A post-graduate from Poona University, Somorendra comes from a very well-to-do family of Sagolband Meino Leirak, Imphal. The main objective of the organization was the restoration of the lost sovereignty of Manipur. According to Somorendra, the causes of the rebellion were unemployment, economic backwardness, exploitation by the non-Manipuri business classes, denial of top posts to Manipuris, surrender of Kabaw valley to Burma and extension of cease-fire agreement between India government and Naga undergrounds in three sub-divisions of the hill districts of Manipur. His objectives were 'liberation' of Manipur and restoration of Kabaw valley (Constantine, 1981: 95). Initially UNLF did not opt for armed struggle but first wanted to make people 'conscious' about the changing conditions within Manipur since merger and their aims and objectives. It is widely believed that UNLF ran a frontal organization called the Pan Manipuri Youth League (PANMYL) and floated an English weekly newspaper called *Resistance* through it. The PANMYL through *Resistance* campaigned against corruption and other societal evils and sought for hill-valley cooperation and restoration of Kabaw valley.

So, UNLF was concentrating more on awareness campaign in its initial stage. But it did not rule out the strategy of armed struggle. It tried to establish links with outside powers especially the then East Pakistan (now Bangladesh). Somorendra personally paid a visit to East Pakistan in 1967 along with Sudhir Kumar, foreign secretary of UNLF (Hemanta, 2007: 127).

However, Somorandra came overground when the state government announced general amnesty to all militants after attaining statehood in 1972. He was succeeded by R.K. Sanayaima, popularly known as Meghen. A post-graduate degree holder from Jadavpur University, Meghen is the great grandson of Bir Tikendarjit, a prince cum patriot who was hanged on August 13, 1891 by the British after the Anglo-Manipur War. Even after his succession, the same strategy of revolution was continued and followed the trail of Somorendra. Besides keeping in touch with East Pakistan,

Meghen also contacted the Naga undergrounds for a unified struggle against the India government. Having spent a significantly long time in mobilizing the masses, UNLF decided to launch armed struggle against the India government by forming its armed wing—Manipur People's Army (MPA). The announcement was made on the 27th anniversary of its existence on November 24, 1991 (Tarapot, 1996: 67). Since then UNLF is engaged in a continuous scuffle with India government agencies. But in February 2, 2005, UNLF while responding to the appeal of S.S. Sidhu, Governor of Manipur, to all militant groups to come to the negotiation table, had come up with a four-point proposal to 'end the conflict satisfactorily once and for all'. The four proposals are: (i) a 'plebiscite' under the supervision of the UN, (ii) deployment of a UN peacekeeping force, (iii) surrender of all weapons to the peacekeepers and (iv) transfer of political power in accordance with the outcome of the plebiscite (www.satp.org). So far no positive development has come up over this issue.

However, the organization is not free from factionalism. Right from its early days it was suffering from intra-group differences. We have mentioned above that Sudhir Kumar, foreign secretary of UNLF, went to East Pakistan along with Somorendra to seek help. Sudhir, a graduate hails from Singjamei, Imphal. Their tour to East Pakistan in 1967 met with some positive response. Sooner, Sudhir, without any prior permission, landed in East Pakistan with some 200 members for training. This extreme left oriented reaction of Sudhir was not appreciated by Somorendra and he was subsequently disconnected with UNLF. But a determined Sudhir set up an organization under the banner of Revolutionary Government of Manipur (RGM) in 1969 along with some leftist radicals of UNLF like N. Bisheswar. But the RGM could not make its presence as they were arrested while coming back from East Pakistan following the war of 1971 which gave birth to Bangladesh (Tarapot, 1996: 41-44).

With the attainment of statehood on January 21, 1972 and subsequent announcement of general amnesty by the new government of Manipur the underground movement momentarily died down. Many came overground including Somorendra and the arrested underground personals were released. They were given an opportunity to start a new life in the newly formed state. However, the revolutionary ideas had already been crafted in the minds of these people. Moreover, it was soon discovered that the new state was only a change in nomenclature and that the state which they had dreamt for was yet to be established. We shall have occasions to deal with this issue later.

After being released from jail with the announcement of general amnesty in 1972, Bisheswar, the former home affairs secretary of UNLF, established a co-operative society along with Sudhir. Bisheswar, a resident of Naorem Leikai, Imphal, comes from a very poor family. However, he could manage to study upto B.A. 1st year and took up a training course in ceramics in Calcutta. After returning from Calcutta, he joined UNLF probably because he was disillusioned for not having secured a government job [Nepram, 2002: 76; Singh (J), 2005: 135].

While working together in the society, they discussed about reviving the revolutionary movement. But there developed some difference between Bisheswar and Sudhir over the choice of foreign power for help—while Bisheswar preferred China, Sudhir preferred USA. In spite of the differences, Bisheswar could manage to reach Lasha, capital of Tibet in 1975 with about 16 youths (Tarapot, 1996: 54-55).

After coming back from Lasha, Bisheswar launched an armed propaganda campaign for secession of Manipur under the banner of People's Liberation Army (Eastern Region) [PLA] on September 25, 1978 (Tarapot, 1996: 58).

Indoctrinated with Maoism, PLA launched a strong campaign against the India government by engaging in ambush, loot, kidnappings, etc. They even eliminated Sudhir on January 14, 1979 on the grounds that he had become an agent of both the India and state government [Singh (J), 2005: 83]. Meanwhile the security forces came down heavily on these militants following the declaration of Manipur as 'disturbed area' in 1980. We shall discuss this issue later.

However, PLA was suffering from two main disadvantages—lack of arms and communication equipments. With the counter-insurgency operations gaining ground, PLA suffered a setback during 1980s. Coupled with these factors was the ill health of Bisheswar, who was suffering from asthma. On July 5, 1981, Bisheswar was captured alive after a fierce gunbattle at Tekcham camp in Thoubal district [For more details, Singh (J), 2005: 88-90; Tarapot, 1996: 87-102].

Since then, the activities of PLA had been declined to a large extent. But in February 1989, some of the members of PLA gathered together and revived the organization with the formation of Revolutionary People's Front (RPF), the political wing of PLA under the leadership of Irengbam Bhorot, popularly known as Chaoren. Since then, PLA/RPF has stepped up their activities in order to materialize their demand for secession of Manipur from the yoke of the 'Indian colonial power'. In 1999, a memorandum was submitted to the Secretary General, UN and the Chairman, Decolonisation Committee (Committee of 24), Geneva/New York Headquarters, for 'granting and restoration of independence and de-colonisation of the state of Manipur from the present colonial administering power of India, which has occupied Manipur since October 15, 1949 till today' (RPF, 1999). PLA/RPF has not, so far, shown any interest for any kind of talks with the government. President Chaoren, in a statement issued on February 24, 2008, stated that "The more than 30-year-long battle aims to win back the lost freedom of the

Manipuris. India's army is killing the Manipuris. No Indian leader takes the issue of Manipur's freedom seriously. Under these circumstances, how can we enter into peace talks?" (www.satp.org).

Before a year of formation of PLA, another organization under the banner of People's Revolutionary Party of Kangleipak (PREPAK) was formed on October 9, 1977 under the leadership of R.K. Tullachandra. A resident of Thangmeiband, Imphal, Tullachandra holds a post-graduate degree from the Jawaharlal Nehru Centre for Post Graduate Studies, Imphal (now Manipur University). He was associated with All Manipur Students' Union (AMSU). Before going for an underground organization he first established an organization called Young Manipur Universe in 1976 in order to prepare the ground. Then after about a year he formed PREPAK along with some ex-RGM members [Sing (J), 2005: 140-142]. The main objective of PREPAK is to restore the lost sovereignty of Manipur and establish a classless society. It also pledged to expel the outsiders (Indians), who are known by the generic term 'mayang'. Since then it is engaged in long war with Indian forces. PREPAK, however, suffered a setback after Tullachandra was killed in encounter on November 12, 1985 [Sing (J), 2005: 101]. At present Achamba is the Chairman of the organization. PREPAK, on October 15, 2007, made an announcement stating that 'it sets on itself the deadline of 2015 to fight with all its might to achieve its cherished goal of restoring independence to Manipur, failing which it will leave the path of armed struggle forever' (www.satp.org).

The period of 1980s is the most crucial year for Manipur. It was during this period that many organizations started launching armed struggle against the India government. Besides, PLA and PREPAK, another organization under the banner of Kangleipak Communist Party (KCP) came up on April 13, 1980 under the leadership of Y. Ibohanbi, former active volunteer of MSC*. The main objective of KCP is restoration of the lost independence of Manipur and preservation of the Meitei culture. In April 2005, KCP pressed for the introduction of the Manipuri script, *Meetei Mayek*, in educational institutions in the state. KCP, however, is the most faction ridden party. After the death of Ibohanbi in an encounter on July 1, 1995, the party split into four groups, viz., KCP (City Meitei), KCP (Prithivi), KCP (Mangang) and KCP (Noyon). But following a decision taken during a five-day central committee meeting held during May 4-8, 2006, the KCP factions are reported to have merged together (www.satp.org). However, on August 3, 2006, another faction of KCP under the banner of KCP [Military Council (MC)] was formed under the leadership of L. Khuman. On its third rising day, Khuman lamented that factionalism in the party is the result of race for leadership and KCP (MC) was formed with a view to build a common platform for all the factions of KCP (IFP, August, 2 & 3, 2008). So far, KCP has not been able to unite itself and fight collectively.

The forces of factionalism are not only present within KCP. We have seen as early as 1969 how RGM broke away from UNLF. These forces of factionalism resurfaced during 1990s again. In January 1994, an organization under the banner of Kanglei Yawol Kanna Lup (Organization to save the revolutionaries in Manipur) (KYKL) was formed by the splinter groups from UNLF, PREPAK and KCP. Achou Toijamba is the Chairman and N. Oken is the head of Military Commission. The main objective of the organization is to unite all the revolutionary organizations operating in Manipur and fight together in the struggle for independence. Another objective of the organization is to rebuild the Manipuri society by clearing it of all vices like drug trade and addiction, corruption and immoral activities. But in 1996 KYKL split into two factions, viz., KYKL (Toijamba) and KYKL (Oken). However, both the factions reconciled together somewhere in February 2001. Towards the end of 2001, the outfit launched 'Operation New Kangleipak' (ONK), an 'anti-corruption' campaign to 'clean up' the educational system in Manipur (www.satp.org).

Thus, one can observe that militancy movement, for a moment, died down with the conferment of statehood in 1972. But it resurfaced again in the late 1970s and early 1980s. While the political aspirations were fulfilled, to some extent, with the conferment of statehood, what basically ignited the movement was the economic underdevelopment coupled with failure of the state to fulfill the aspirations of the young educated people in the newly formed state. As seen from above, most of the organizations are headed by educated youths. What basically transpired these youths to take up arms was the losing credibility of the power elites in the state and their failure to fulfill the aspirations of the people. They feel that the state power elites in connivance with the Indian state is robbing the state and hence causing deprivation, dispossession, distrust, etc. They see independence as a solution to all the problems in the state. Their objectives clearly suggest that they want a radical change in the society which will be marked by equal opportunities without any discrimination, preservation of culture and traditions and a peaceful co-existence among all the ethnic communities in the state. But the question is why so many organizations have come up to fight for the same cause. While the objective of independence could be easily pressed forward by fighting collectively, their proliferation into many groups have shattered their credence and given them a bad name. Initially, when RGM was formed as a breakaway faction of UNLF, it was basically guided by difference in ideology over armed struggle. While UNLF was not in favour of armed struggle, RGM wanted armed rebellion. Again, PLA, PREPAK and KCP were formed with the same motive of launching armed rebellion against the Indian state. The attitude of UNLF against armed struggle might be one reason for the formation of other organizations. One may observe that PREPAK, PLA and KCP have come up in quick succession within a period of two-three years. Though PREPAK and PLA have some connections with UNLF and RGM, KCP was formed by ex-members of MSC*. Even after UNLF opted for armed rebellion since 1991, there was no effort on the part of these organizations to work under one umbrella. KYKL, formed by splinter groups of UNLF, PREPAK and KCP to unite all the revolutionary organizations had also failed to fulfill its objectives. One may observe that all the organizations are ridden with factionalism except PLA. However, in March, 1999, UNLF, PREPAK and PLA formed a common front called Manipur People's Liberation Front (MPLF) with an aim 'to remove the slow progress of liberation struggle because of lack of unity among the revolutionary parties' (Tarapot, 2005: 179-180).

Thus, the differences of opinion over the war strategy, differences in ideology and race for leadership are the main reasons for proliferation of underground organizations in the valley.

Besides the Meiteis, other ethnic groups like Nagas, Kukis and Meitei Pangal (Muslim) have also organized themselves to press forward their demands. But Naga underground organizations are basically based in Nagaland. As we have already mentioned in chapter 2, with the formation NSCN, the base of Naga undergrounds gradually shifted to the Naga inhabited areas of Manipur. The split of NSCN into NSCN (I-M) and NSCN (K) in 1988 further strengthened the hold of NSCN (I-M) in the hills of Manipur especially among the Tangkhuls as it is led by Muivah, a Tangkhul from Ukhrul district of Manipur. With the growth of NSCN (I-M), the demand for unification of Naga inhabited areas into a single administrative unit gained momentum and Nagas of Manipur have also tacitly supported the movement. However, factionalism among the Nagas did not end with the split of NSCN into NSCN (I-M) and NSCN (K). On November 23, 2007, NSCN-Unification (NSCN-U) was formed with the objective of uniting the warring factions of NSCN by some members of both NSCN (I-M) and NSCN (K). Azheto Choppy of NSCN (I-M) is the convener. However, Issac and Muivah accused Choppy of defection and recently NSCN (I-M) and NSCN-U were engaged in internecine clashes (www.satp.org). Although, the antagonistic relationship between NSCN (I-M) and NSCN-U does not have much bearing on the Manipur scene, the impact of rivalry between NSCN (I-M) and NSCN (K) on the proliferation of ethnic insurgencies in the region in general and Manipur in particular needs to be worked out.

It has already been mentioned in chapter 2 that KNA* and KNF, formed in 1988, spearheaded the demand for Kuki homeland. It has also been noted that Naga-Kuki conflict of 1992 gave birth to a plethora of Kuki underground organizations like KLA, KRA, UKLF and ZRA. KLA was formed in 1992 under the leadership of Paozangam Letkholun with the objective of securing an independent Kukiland. KRA was formed in 1999 under the leadership of Thangkeng Hangshing with the objective of securing a separate state for Kukis and unifying all the scattered Kukis in the new homeland. UKLF was formed in 2000 under the leadership S. S. Haokip in order to uphold the interests of the Kuki community and form a separate Kuki state called 'Kukiland'. ZRA, an armed wing of ZRO, was formed in 1997 and is the fallout of Kuki-Paite clash in 1997, under the leadership of Phanznianpau Guite. The main objective of ZRA is to protect the interests of the Paite community against the 'onslaught of any community or group' and 'to bring all the Zomi people under one administrative unit, Zogam, which means 'land of Zomi' under the Indian Union (www.satp.org).

However, the Kukis are the most divided among themselves. It may not be out of place to point out that the traditional set up of a Kuki society, where each sub-tribe of a Kuki lives in a village under its own chief, appears to be the main reason for the failure among the Kukis to come under one umbrella. The multiple authority structure of the traditional Kuki society appears to stand on the way of development of the 'we' feeling among them. While all the organizations aim to secure a separate homeland for themselves, the intra-tribal conflict has left them in total disarray. The Kuki-Paite clash of 1997 is one point.

Some members of the Meitei Pangal[2] community, a minority group in the valley, formed People's United Liberation Front (PULF) in 1993 following the clash with the majority group in 1993. At present the outfit is headed by Kaji Ibrahim, general secretary and Raffisuddin, home secretary. Under the disguise of protecting the communal interest of the minority Muslim, it appears that PULF is more like a racketeering group dealing with narcotics and arms trade. In April, 2005, a huge consignment of arms and explosives belonging to PULF was caught at Behara railway station of Cachar district of Assam (www.satp.org). Again in April, 2008, PULF activists were caught with a large quantity of SP tablets, a potent analgesic, used by intravenous drug users, in Guwahati (Hussain, 2008). PULF utilizes the Muslim community network across the Indo-Myanmar border and plays a feeder role in arms and drug trade in the region.

Thus, ethno-national ideology seems to be the driving force behind the growth of militancy in the state. The trajectory of the growth of Meitei insurgency, Naga insurgency and Kuki insurgency evidently speaks for this. The goals of these ethno-insurgent groups do not converge as the fulfillment of one is only possible at the cost of the other. As a result, apparently there is no common ground of cooperation among these militant outfits. Rather these groups often work for cross purposes. The competitive ethno-national interests may lead to ethnic flare ups as has happened in case of Naga-Kuki clash.

It may be reminded that much of the problem of ethnic-insurgency has been the creation of the Naga militant movement. In their bid to transform the war of the Nagas to the war of the ethnic groups against the Indian state, the Naga militant leadership had popped up ethno-insurgent movements involving the other communities in the region as this will simultaneously create multiple war fronts for the Indian army and as a result ease out the attack on the Nagas. Besides this strategic motive, resource mobilization from the areas beyond the sphere of influence has been another driving force for the proliferation of insurgency in the region. The Naga insurgent groups provided the logistics for the operations conducted by the smaller satellite ethno-insurgent groups and claimed a major share of the booty.

In spite of conflicting goal orientations, different ethnic-insurgent groups cooperate with each other against the operation of the Indian security forces. As much of the elements of cooperation are priced, for example, there are rates for training per head, arms per piece, shelter per head, etc., there is enough incentive for cooperation. It is, indeed, not possible to fathom out in detail the structured shades of cooperation and conflicts among the various ethnic-insurgent groups operating in the region in general and Manipur in particular.

Besides inter-group relationships within the region, external linkages of the ethno-insurgent groups particularly with entities and agencies across the border have further strengthened the dynamics of growth of militancy in the state. We shall turn to this dimension in the next section.

External Factors Facilitating Militancy

Although unlike Jammu and Kashmir, external forces

are not the primary factors behind the growth of insurgency in the north eastern region, militant movements that primarily grew out of the internal contradiction often get entangled with the external forces and the extent of outside support is largely determined by the dynamics of global politics in general and the politics of the South Asian region in particular. States in the international system often sponsors or supports anti-state movements in opponent domain in order to achieve competitive advantage in global power politics. Strategic partnership among the states forged for reordering the global political space often plays crucial role in encouraging separatist and secessionist movements in each other's territory. The Indo-Pak animosity, Sino-Indian rivalry for regional leadership, cold war stratagem—all have created an environment, which lasted till the dismemberment of erstwhile USSR, conducive for militancy to thrive and proliferate within the South Asian region.

We have already mentioned in chapter 2 that the security perspective of the Indian state had undergone a sea change following the Sino-Indian border conflict of 1962 and Indo-Pak war of 1965. We have also mentioned that the newly formed USA-China-Pakistan axis in the cold war era has threatened the security environment of India in general and north eastern region in particular. China and East Pakistan had become the safe heavens for the militant outfits operating in this region.

We have already mentioned above, Somorendra (UNLF) and Sudhir (RGM) went to East Pakistan as early as 1967 to seek help. The Pakistan authorities, under Yahya Khan, responded positively. Then Sudhir led a group of some 200 members and landed in Pakistan. This hasty act of Sudhir was not appreciated and many of them were deported back by handing them over to Indian army by the Pakistan army itself. But a few of them who were allowed to stay back were given training. They in fact took part in the 1971 war which gave birth to Bangladesh in favour of Pakistan army (Tarapot, 1996: 41-45).

However, with the creation of Bangladesh, the northeast insurgents were no longer safe in that country. But the cordial relation with India ended with the assassination of Mujibur Rahman, the first President of Bangladesh, in 1975. Since then Indo-Bangladesh relation soared. The situation was further aggravated by the Pakistani Intelligence—Inter-Services Intelligence (ISI) that was looking for an opportunity to revive the old networks with the northeast insurgents and avenge their defeat in 1971 war.

As a result, the north east militant organizations found safe sanctuaries in this soil. The PLA reportedly formed its political wing RPF in 1989 in Sylhet district of Bangladesh (Egreteau, 2006). A joint committee of PLA, PREPAK and KCP known as Revolutionary Joint Committee (RJC) was also established there (Tarapot, 1996: 143). Moreover Chittagong and Cox' Bazar in southeastern region of Bangladesh have become the largest weapon supermarket of the Indo-Burmese region. The route for 'long marches', the technical term used for arms and arms procurement route by northeast rebels, originate from Cox's Bazar and pass through Chittagong hill tracts and Mizoram and then to other parts of northeast India (Nepram, 2004: 48-49). With the active connivance of Bangladesh intelligence, the militant outfits in north eastern region also procure sophisticated weapons from Thailand (Gopal, 2007: 185).

We have also mentioned above that Bisheswar, founder of PLA, went to Lasha in 1975 to seek help from China. After returning from Lhasa, he formed PLA in 1978, exactly the same acronym of the Chinese Army, People's Liberation Army of China (PLAC).

China has been the old patron for the northeast insurgents. The formation of People's Republic of China (PRC) on October 2, 1949 under the leadership Mao Tse-tung launched an ideological campaign and helped all political parties and underground outfits. It became the patron of revolutionary insurgencies and political rebellions across the world. The Chinese government along with its powerful army, PLAC helped the insurgent groups in return for promoting the Maoist ideology and to check the western imperialism, the thrust of Soviet revisionism in Asia and to contain the rise of Nehruvian India by defending its southern borders. Chinese help for the northeast insurgents was guided by the region's fragile ethnic framework and to destabilize the pro-Soviet India. Another important factor is to keep India busy with its northeast insurgencies so that it can check any move in favour of Tibet's struggle for autonomy. The Cultural Revolution (1966-68) of Mao further strengthened the underground relations of the insurgents with the PRC (Egreteau, 2006).

However, with the death of Mao Tse-tung in 1976 and Deng Xiaoping coming to power, the position of China towards the rebels of the northeast underwent a change. Xiaoping committed himself to economic development of the country and subsequently cut off all the direct connections with the northeast rebels. But China has not completely disconnected with the militants of the northeast. It is widely believed that NSCN (I-M) has 'full-fledged liaison officer' in the territories in China across the border with Arunachal Pradesh and pleading the Chinese for major arms consignment (Ramana, 2002: 104).

Besides Bangladesh and China, Burma[3] (now Myanmar) is the most important external factor that facilitated the growth of militancy in this region. Burmese connection with the north east militants is in fact the outcome of the serious wave of insurgency that hit Burma right after her independence on January 4, 1948. This has been further strengthened by the close ethnic affinities that are shared by the people inhabiting both sides of the region.

Like the north eastern part of India, the new Republic of the Union of Burma consisted of a large area of rugged hill tracts inhabited by diverse ethnic groups. These groups, who were otherwise independent, resisted firmly when the new government tried to establish its authority. Coupled with this factor were the communist undergrounds who were looking for an opportunity to seize power. This had resulted in various underground insurrections by the small ethnic groups at the periphery and mutinies by the armed forces. The first sign of such insurrection was visible in 1949 when the Karens under the banner of Karen National Union began its struggle for independence. Other ethnic groups like the Kachins, Arakans, Chins, Was, Shans, Poas, Lahus, etc. soon followed trail (For details of Burma insurgency, Lintner, 1994; Smith, 1999).

Burmese Prime Minister U Nu, sought help from UK and India to fight the ethnic insurrections. Jawaharlal Nehru extended full support and a close relationship developed between these two countries. However, this arrangement was short-lived as the military junta under General Ne Win overthrew Nu's government in 1962. Since then Burma followed the policy of 'autarchic diplomacy' and deliberately isolated the country. However, there was no end to despair. Ne Win's military rule was widely condemned and opposed for its failure to address the economic downtrend. Moreover, the ethnic insurrections had increased manifold. With the Great 8888 (August 8, 1988) Uprising, Ne Win's Burma Socialist Program Party (BSPP) was replaced by General Saw Maung's new military government under the banner of State Law and Order Restoration Council (SLORC) (For more details, Egreteau, 2003). With the military junta coming to power, India's bilateral relationship with Burma deteriorated and provided a safe room to the north east rebels.

The Burmese connection with the north east militants can be traced back to the days of Irabot. We have already mentioned that Irabot's Red Guard army was established with the help of the Burma communists. Soon the Naga and Mizo militants joined the track and started operating their bases from Burma with the help of the Burmese outfits. The formation of NSCN in 1980 and the consequent split of NSCN in 1988 into two groups—one under Indian Naga [NSCN (I-M)] and other under Burmese Naga [NSCN (K)]—came as a blessing to other outfits of this region. Sooner, on May 22, 1990, the Indo-Burma Revolutionary Front (IBRF) was formed by NSCN (K), UNLF and ULFA with the objective to 'build up a united struggle for the independence of Indo-Myanmar (Tarapot, 1996: 69). Both PLA and PREPAK also have camps in Somra hills and are being trained and armed by Kachin Independence Army (KIA) (Egreteau, 2006).

The external linkage of the north east militant outfits is, in fact, guided by different motives. While Bangladesh, ISI and China's support to north east militants are guided more by the motive of destabilizing India, Burmese motive is altogether different—financial and other crimes like drug smuggling, arms trafficking, counterfeit currency, etc. to sustain the insurgency. While Bangladesh, ISI and China provide training and weapons free of cost, Burmese charge a huge sum for these services (Bhaumik, 1997: 97). India also responded to these developments and played the Chakma[4] card and helped KIA to set up and train underground groups like KNF loyal to Research and Analysis Wing (RAW) (Egreteau, 2006). However, one may note that in case of Bangladesh and China, it is the state actors that are providing logistics to the northeast rebels, but in case of Burma, it is the non-state actors fighting against the Burmese state that is providing logistics.

Thus, the concern of all these countries was more inclined towards settling scores rather than tackling the situation jointly. However, with economic concerns coming to the forefront with the onset of globalization, the situation seems to be have improved to a certain extent.

State Response

The geographical location, topography, race, religion, culture, customs, traditions, etc., had greatly shaped the policy making of the Indian state towards this north eastern region. The policy of the Indian state towards this region in general and Manipur in particular appears to have been informed of strategic and peripheral location, Mongoloid racial identity that spreads across the international boundary, cross-border ethnic affinities, lack of emotional integration of people living along the border and cross border synergies in militant movements. Coupled with these factors, the territorial security concerns of the Indian state about her easternmost border, lying between Tibetan region of China and East Pakistan, the fear of Indian intelligence about the viability of defending the territory in the event of simultaneous thrust from China and Pakistan had greatly shaped her policy towards this region particularly in the initial years of her independence.

The denial of statehood in the initial years of independence that had spurred Meitei nationalism may be viewed from these security predicaments of the Indian state. Indian security concerns which denied statehood to Manipur for a long time had greatly shaped the future course of militancy in the state. Because of the denial of her rightful place in the newly formed Indian Union, the Merger Agreement of 1949 became the rallying point of all militant groups in the state. The Indian state, instead of accommodating the nationalist sentiments of Manipur in general and Meiteis in particular, has viewed the problem of militancy as mere law and order problem. The state-centric security approach of the Indian state in dealing with the aspirations of the bordering people has, thus, aggravated the situation.

The state-centric and law and order skewed outlook of the Indian state has led to the use of iron hand in dealing with the militancy problems of the region instead of addressing the core issues of empowerment and development. The military approach towards polity management has led to the frequent imposition of President's Rule and other anti-terrorism laws like Armed Forces (Special Powers) Act, 1958 (AFSPA) as de-escalation measures to contain militancy. The short term repressive measures became counterproductive as these are allowed to continue for indefinite period. Long term political economy measures to redress the grievances of the people have never been outlined. The myopic and ad hoc state responses allowed the internal social, political and economic factors to continue to act as the source of militancy.

In September 1980, the whole area of Manipur was declared as 'disturbed area'.[5] It may be noted here that the power to declare an area to be a 'disturbed area' was conferred only upon the state governments. However, by Act 7 of 1972, such a power was conferred concurrently upon the central government (GoI, 2005). It may not be out of place to recall the circumstances during 1980s that has resulted in the imposition of AFSPA. It was during 1980s that armed struggle against the Indian government has just started by PREPAK, PLA and KCP. It was only miniscule compared to the then Naxalite movements in West Bengal and Bihar. Simultaneously, Assam and Tripura, besides the Naga and Mizo insurgency which started in 1950s and 1960s respectively, had also taken up arms in the 1980s against the Indian government. Thus, the north east was on the boil during the 1980s. Though the circumstances were alarming, but it was viewed as a law and order problem rather than trying to understand the socio-political and economic dynamics of the problem. The outcome was the imposition of AFSPA in the north eastern states and not in West Bengal and Bihar.

With the imposition of AFSPA, Manipur has been transformed to a police state. The rule of army with wide powers under AFSPA has, in fact, nullified the existence of the state with her judicial and legislative powers. The security forces do not come under the purview of the state law and as such they often go scot free. The basic freedom and individual rights are not honoured, the right of the nations for self-determination, the cardinal principle of any federal association, has become the mockery once AFSPA is promulgated. It is not the representative of the people any more who govern and manage the polity; instead, it is the security forces, armed with AFSPA, who govern the affairs of the state.

The Act, however, instead of curbing insurgency has rather put more oil in the fire. The army's uncontrolled actions often leading to human rights violation had created a fear psychosis among the people in general and youths in particular. This has further escalated the feeling of hatred against the Indian state (represented by the Indian army and other security forces) and fomented the anti-outsider or anti-mayang feelings. This has in a way motivated the youths to join the rank and file of militancy in Manipur (Bisheswar, 1986: 48-49). We shall take up this issue further in the next chapter.

Excessive use of army and central paramilitary forces to contain insurgency in the region in general and Manipur in particular has, to a large extent; weaken the combat capability and intelligence gathering capacity of the state police forces. The high level of distrust between the army and police often leads them to act for cross purposes. Instead of the formation of a United Command Structure combining the army, paramilitary forces, state police and state and central intelligence agencies, much success could not be achieved due to the inner fissures among the constituent organizations. What is worse is that the local power elites who are supposed to work for the polity management are often not taken into confidence by the counter-insurgency forces and hence hardly strive for achieving the goal of the state. Many of them, as a result, sit on the fence and happy to seek personal aggrandizement at the cost of the people and the state.

The failure of the democratic conflict resolution mechanism in a poly-ethnic society often motivates the smaller ethnic groups to adopt violence as a means for political discourse. In democracy, if the grievances of the people are not met, people intervene in the decision making process by way of electing the representatives of their choice who seek to redress the same. But in a multi-ethnic society, smaller ethnic groups, even if they act collectively, can hardly influence the institutions of democracy as they do not make up the required number needed to affect a change in the system. Out of 545 seats in the Lok Sabha, the lower house of Indian parliament, Manipur has only 2 seats. Out of this two, one seat is from the valley and the other from the hills. Thus, aspirations of the Meitei nationalism hardly get reflected in Indian parliament. Even if the community votes en bloc, it can in no way influence the institutions of Indian democracy. Thus, the democratic conflict resolution mechanism hardly works to resolve the grievances of the Meiteis vis-à-vis Indian state. As a result, militancy is often adopted as a strategic means to reach out to the Indian state. This logic also holds good at local level where different ethnic groups are striving for conflicting political goals. In Manipur legislature, out of 60 seats, 41 come from the valley and another 19 from the hills. Even if the Nagas or Kukis act as a homogenous political group, they can not affect any change in the institutions of democracy. The number based electoral democracy, thus, has a built in bias against the smaller ethnic groups in a poly-ethnic social space. The state machinery has to invent a way out to this endemic problem which motivates the smaller groups to take up arms to redress their grievances. Up till now, the state response in this front is utterly inadequate and habitual in nature. North eastern states of India in general and Manipur in particular have to find out-of-box solution to this problem.

The state response manifested in the formulation of the surrender policy, which is supposed to encourage surrender and discourage new recruitments, has been designed in such a way that the policy hardly has any demotivating elements in it. As such it is laden with more sops. With the new surrender policy which has come into effect from January 14, 2008, the government has doubled the stipend money to Rs. 4000 per month from the existing amount of Rs. 2000 per month. The stipend will be paid for a period of 30 months against the existing 2 years period. The lump sum grant has also increased to Rs. 5 lakhs from the old rate of Rs. 2 lakhs. Moreover, they will be provided accommodation including family accommodation in a safe and secured complex. Under the new policy, a militant is allowed to surrender before any unit of army, central paramilitary forces, sub-divisional magistrates, sub-divisional police officers, district magistrates, district superintendent of police and above rank officers of the state police department. It also allows a militant to surrender before a unit of the army or central paramilitary force outside the state (IFP, January 17, 2008). The policy does not contain any elements to fix accountability for the offences committed by the surrendered militants. Once a person surrenders, all his offences are pardoned and he is allowed to spring back to normal life. This encourages many to venture a short cut route to success by joining the militancy and later on surrendering to the authority for power and position. We have taken up this dimension further in the next chapter.

As the anti-insurgency political response of the Indian state towards the insurgency in the region is guided more by the concerns of the Naga movement, the search for the political solution of the Naga insurgency has overlooked the interests of the other ethnic communities in the region and resulted into further deterioration of militancy situation in Manipur. As part of negotiation, Indian state has extended cease-fire agreement with the NSCN (I-M) 'without territorial limits' in 2001 which has undermined the authority of the state of Manipur and has tacit support in favour of unification of Naga inhabited contiguous areas across the North Eastern states. This agreement between the Indian state and NSCN (I-M) has directly gone against the interest of the Meiteis who have been demanding to protect the territorial integrity of the state of Manipur. The people of Manipur in general, of course, except a section of the Nagas, and the Meiteis in particular have been deeply hurt and the feeling of deprivation has been intensified manifold. In the face of mass upsurge of public protest cutting across political domains, the Indian state has reverted back and made commitment to maintain the territorial integrity of Manipur. This incident has further widened the distrust between the society and the state in Manipur. Indian government, while agreed to barter the autonomy of state of Manipur, did not bother to consult the people in the first place and in the process added further fuel to Manipur inferno.

While the military approach of the Indian state, as short term measures, failed to contain militancy in Manipur, the political initiatives towards conflict management particularly in relation to Naga militancy have aggravated the situation further. The initiatives towards economic development, viewed as long term measures to contain militancy, could hardly make any dent due to the failure of the delivery mechanism. The transfer of resources to the state in the form of grants-in-aids, creation of central pool to fund the development projects in the region, attempts towards the integration of the border economies with their counterparts across the border—all failed to strengthen the productive capacity of the local economy primarily due to the non-performance of the agencies. The problem of development lies not with the resource flow, but with the agencies which are entrusted to execute the development projects. The existing agencies largely controlled by the local state have failed while alternative agencies have not been tried for. We shall discuss about the alternative agencies in the concluding chapter.

Besides the issue of choice of alternative agency, the old strategy of development that stresses on the social sector also needs to be reviewed. It has already been pointed out in chapter 3 that state sponsored planned development in Manipur has created a wide gap between the real and social sectors. With the growth of the social sector coupled with underdeveloped real sector, educated unemployed youths get frustrated while they do not find opportunities of employment. Thus, the material base of the society creates push factors for them and motivates them to join the struggle for social justice.

Thus, the failure of state responses to liberate the people of Manipur from economic underdevelopment, to restore the honour and dignity of individual freedom and to expand their political, social and economic choices has allowed the 'circular causation', to use Myrdalian phraseology, of the negative forces to perpetuate in the state. Indian democracy as well as ethnic nationalist ideologues of Manipur has to find an alternative response to militancy in the state.

Crisis of Legitimacy

The development-social or economic-cannot take place in a political vacuum. In a way, mismanagement and ill-governance of the polity by the local power elites has been largely responsible for the mess that has grown in Manipur over time. Politics in Manipur is more guided by personal interests rather than ideology and commitments to the people. Social welfare has become the hostage of the race for personal aggrandizement. Defection of the elected representatives in the state legislature may be considered as an indicator of ethical standard of the local politicians.

With the attainment of statehood, a new hope has dawned upon the people. The assembly election to the 60 seat assembly was held in 1972 and a new coalition government under the banner of United Legislators' Party (ULP) was formed under the leadership of Md. Alimuddin of Manipur Peoples' Party (MPP) (Singh, 1981: 174). It may be noted here that MPP was formed by a group of Congress dissidents after the 1967 elections and is purely a regional party. Initially MPP did provide an alternative to the Congress, who were facing popularity crisis at the height of statehood movement. But Congress still managed to secure 17 seats out of 60 and MPP secured 15. A major chunk of 19 seats went to independents. These independents are the parties representing their own ethnic groups and 13 of them were from hill districts (www.electioncommision.gov.in). The independents were, in fact, the deciding factor of forming a government as no party could secure majority. This indicates that mainstream political parties were unable to influence the ethnic groups in the hills. However, within a year and six days, the ULP was toppled up due to the game of defections and President Rule (PR) was imposed from March 23, 1973 (Singh, 1981: 178).

The PR lasted for about a year and a mid-term assembly election was held in 1974. The results were startling this time as MPP secured the maximum number of seats to the tune of 20 seats. Congress could secure only 13 and independents 5. A new party of the hills under the banner of Manipur Hills Union (MHU) secured 12 seats (www.electioncommision.gov.in). ULP led by Md. Alimuddin formed the ministry but survived only for about 4 months. A new government under the banner of Progressive Democratic Front led by Yangmaso Shaiza of MHU was installed on July 10, 1974. However, it was again toppled up and a new government under the banner of Democratic Legislature Party (DLP) led by R. K. Dorendra Singh of Congress was installed. At the wake of national emergency, DLP was replaced by a Congress government on July 23, 1975 led by Dorendra (Singh, 1981: 182-183). Thus we see that within a year Manipur had four different governments. Such a frequency of change in government only shows the gravity of the situation. In such a volatile democratic set up it is really difficult to address the needs of the people. As the politicians are after power, they hardly find any time to fulfill the aspirations of the people.

With Janata party coming to power at the centre after the emergency, a Janata led government led by Yangmaso Shaiza was installed in the state on June 28, 1977. It may be noted here that with the formation of a new government, after the emergency, by Janata Party at the centre, the members of the Congress defected to Janata, including Yangmaso. With the split of Janata party at the centre, the rule of Janata also ended in the state and PR was imposed with effect from November 14, 1979 (Singh, 1981: 184-185).

The next assembly election was held in 1980. This time a major chunk of 19 seats went to independents again. The Congress could secure 13 seats and Janata 10 (www.electioncommision.gov.in). A Congress-MPP led coalition government was formed with Dorendra as the Chief Minister (CM). Dorendra was replaced by Rishang Keishing in November, 1981. But due to defections and political instability, PR was imposed with effect from February 28, 1981. By June, 1981 a Congress led government under Rishang was installed and this time it could run the government till the next election in 1984 (Bhagat & Akoijam, 2002: 520).

The assembly election of 1984 was a turning point of the Congress party. It could secure a simple majority by wining 30 seats out of 60 (www.electioncommision.gov.in). A Congress led government under the leadership of Rishang was installed and it was in power till 1988. In 1988, Rishang was replaced by R. K. Joychandra as the CM. This Congress led government survived till the next election in 1990 without any break up (Bhagat & Akoijam, 2002: 520).

The assembly election of 1990, however, changed the whole political scenario in the state. Though Congress ruled in previous years, it could secure only 24 seats. Janata and MPP staged a comeback by wining 11 seats and 9 seats respectively (www.electioncommision.gov.in). In 1990, a MPP led coalition government was installed under the leadership of R. K. Ranbir. However, defection and party hopping led to the downfall of Ranbir's government and PR was imposed with effect from January 7, 1992. In April 1992, a Congress-MPP alliance government under the leadership of Dorendra was installed. It could not stay in power for a long time and the game of defections again led to its downfall. With no option left, PR was again imposed with effect from December 31, 1993 and this time it lasted for about a year. Just before the next election in 1995, Rishang staged a comeback and ruled for a brief period of about three months (Bhagat & Akoijam, 2002: 520).

In spite of frequent toppling of government, Congress still have a strong hold over majority of the people. In 1995 assembly election, Congress secured 22 seats out of 60. MPP staged a comeback and secured 18 seats (www.electioncommision.gov.in). A Congress coalition government under the banner of United Front Ministry led by Rishang was sworn in. Rishang, however, could stay in power for about two years. An internal cohesion within the Congress led to the formation of Manipur State Congress Party (MSCP) and downfall of Rishang ministry. A MSCP led government under the leadership of W. Nipamacha was installed in December 1997 and it lasted till the next election in 2000 (Bhagat & Akoijam, 2002: 520).

The 2000 assembly election gave an altogether different result. MSCP secured maximum number of seats to the tune of 23 seats out of 60. Congress managed to secure only 11 seats (www.electioncommision.gov.in). Nipamacha's MSCP ministry was installed again in 2000. It, however, could not last long as most of MSCP men defected again. A Samata-BJP coalition government under the banner of Manipur Democratic Front led by Radhabinod Koijam was installed in 2001 (Bhagat & Akoijam, 2002: 520). It may be noted here that BJP and Samata won only 6 seats and 1 seat respectively in 2000 election (www.electioncommision.gov.in). It is surprising as to how a minority party formed a government in the state. It appears that BJP-led National Democratic Alliance (NDA) government under the Prime Ministership of Atal Bihari Vajpayee which was ruling at the centre during this time has brought about this change.

With the outbreak of mass movement in the valley against the Indo-Naga cease-fire extension 'without territorial limits' in June, 2001 (for details chapter 2, Note 70), the whole administration in the state collapsed. PR was imposed with effect from June 2, 2001 and it continued for about a year till election was held in 2002.

Thus, for about 30 years since statehood Manipur passed through a volatile political environment. Self-interest had been the cardinal factor that led to frequent defection and shifting of political loyalty. This political instability, arising out of power mongering attitude of the local political elites, had weakened the functioning of the democratic institutions in the state. The development interest of the state had been bartered for personal gain and hence anarchy ruled the roost instead of rule based governance. Defection has become a tool not only garnering personal benefits but also for regime change. Whenever there is a change at the centre, politicians in Manipur were quick to change their colour and loyalty accordingly in order to be accommodated within the new. This pattern of pendular and role-reversing political behavior has only stabilized since 2002.

In 2002 assembly elections there is a change in the poll results. Congress captured 20 seats. A regional party under the banner of Federal Party of Manipur (FPM) [For more details on FPM, Singh (J), 2006] secured 13 seats (www.electioncommision.gov.in). But most of old leaders suffered a crushing defeat including three former CMs, viz., Rishang, Nipamacha and Radhabinod. A Congress led coalition government under the banner of Secular Progressive Front (SPF) was installed under the leadership of Okram Ibobi [Parratt (J), 2005: 196]. SPF government could rule without any break up even in the midst of long agitation against AFSPA in 2004 and a more than 50 days long economic blockade in both the national highways. In 2007 assembly election Congress once again showed its credence by capturing 30 seats, the single largest party which enjoys a simple majority (www.electioncommision.gov.in). The SPF government under the leadership of Ibobi again came back to power in 2007 and is still ruling at present. Political stability at the centre under the congress-led United Progressive Alliance (UPA) since 2004 might have indirect contribution towards the political stability in Manipur.

Thus, one can see that the political environment of the state in the post statehood period is marked by high instability. The state which once boasted of having installed an elected government through adult franchise, just after Independence and before merger, even before India, has collapsed over the years. The state has experienced PR no less than six times since statehood excluding the 1977 national emergency. She also witnessed a change of government at least 12 times since 1980 till 2002. Such unstable political environment only bears testimony to the level of defection and party hopping among the local political elites of the state. Their power hungry and self interest guided nature have robbed the state of her stability and development. Considering the situation in Manipur, Pakem has rightly commented that

'Manipur is perhaps the only state in north east India where political instability is the rule rather than the exception' [quoted from Parratt (J), 2005: 196]. Such unstable nature of government only breeds individual opportunism and corruption.

Manipur has been placed among the four most corrupt states of India according to a survey report of the Transparency International India. The survey judged the level of corruption in terms of payment of bribes (IFP, July 20, 2008). Though it is difficult to provide with proofs, it is a very well known fact that government jobs in Manipur are all purchased. Many cases have been reported in media about fake appointments in various government departments especially in education department. It is reported that about 200 teachers were appointed who reportedly paid a bribe of Rs. 1 lakh each [Parratt (J), 2005: 197]. It is only the tip of the iceberg and there are many such cases which are not reported or hushed up. However, corruption is not only limited to taking bribes for government jobs but it also extends to siphoning of development funds. The development funds earmarked for any purpose hardly reach the target group. The lion's share is leaked along the pipeline. These funds often find their way to fill the pockets of politicians, contractors, high ranked officials, businessmen and even the undergrounds. In March-April, 2008, the State Power Department was pulled up for misappropriation of a huge amount to the tune of Rs. 17.2 crores (*The Sangai Express*, April 1, 2008). Even the Police Department, a law enforcing department, was charged by the Comptroller and Auditor General for showing an amount of Rs. 8.67 crores as expenditure whereas the amount was not spent at all (IFP, August 28, 2008). A radio poll conducted by Regional News Unit of All India Radio (AIR), Imphal in November, 2005 showed that corruption was more serious a problem and a major cause of concern among the Manipuris than HIV/AIDS

(*The Shillong Times,* November 7, 2005). Thus, corruption at the public offices and involvement of the public officials has, to a large extent, robbed the legitimacy of governance. As the public servants including the ministers are neither transparent and nor accountable, they hardly command any respect from their respective constituencies. As a result, electoral politics is increasingly being rooted into money and muscle power rather than ideology and clan image of the contestants. As people are getting increasingly disillusioned with electoral politics, politicians have to bank on the non-state actors for getting them elected. This has led to the emergence of a symbiotic relationship between the power elites and the militant groups.

The unholy alliance between the politicians and the militants is also a major cause of concern. With the losing credibility of the politicians due to their indifferent attitude and corrupt practices, they have to bank on the undergrounds for capturing power in the electoral process. On the other side, the undergrounds also depend on the politicians for fund and other purposes like providing safe houses. On August 17, 2007 at least 12 militants were nabbed from MLA quarters of the ruling Congress government. The militants belonged to KYKL, KCP, PLA and PREPAK and were nabbed along with arms, ammunitions and demand letters. The three MLAs involved in this incident are W. Brajabidhu, Bijoy Koijam and N. Sovakiran (ex-MLA) (IFP, August 18, 2007). One may note here that these militants were nabbed along with arms and ammunitions from one of the most secured areas of the state. One can, thus, imagine the gravity of the situation. This is not the only case. Besides, there are many allegations and counter-allegations reported in media about the nexus between politicians and militants. The former CM Rishang was reported to have paid a sum of Rs. 3 million to the undivided NSCN. He had also reportedly supplied uniforms to NSCN (I-M). Phungzathang, a former Power Minister from

Zomi sub-tribe of Kuki, provided two vehicles and a sum of Rs. 2.6 laks to ZRA. In 2005 the present CM Ibobi was accused of paying a large sum to the tune of Rs. 10 million to PLA and Rs. 5 million to KYKL. The accusations were denied from both the sides. However, KYKL admitted to having received financial help from politicians (Routray, 2007).

It appears that there exists a strong symbiotic relationship between a section of the power elites and the underground groups. They protect each other in various ways that maximizes benefits of both the parties. These modules of interactions are designed solely based on give and take policy. It is difficult for an individual researcher to fathom out these relations in clear terms, nonetheless this aspect needs to be studied in order to understand as to what keeps insurgency going in Manipur. The political economy dimension of insurgency indicates that it is being used by the local power elites as the bargaining tool against the centre for getting more funds. If this problem is settled once for all, the local power elites will be loosing the bargaining power. As a result, for them, controlled militancy pays dividends than its elimination. The view that one-should-not-kill-the-goose-that-lays-golden-eggs, appears to explain, to a certain extent, the reasons for the perpetuation of militancy in the state. It is often said that the underground problem has come as 'halwa puri (sweetmeat)' for politicians something more than the 'dal roti (bread and butter)' issue (Dev, 2009: 111).

Interplay of Ethnicity and Development

Besides militancy and governance failure, tenuous inter-ethnic relationship is also another source of tension in the society and polity of Manipur. We have already discussed in detail the growth of ethno-nationalism among various ethnic groups in the state in chapter 2. We have also seen how the overlapping territorial interests have sown the seeds of hatred among the Meiteis, Nagas and Kukis. This overlapping interest coupled with losing credibility of the state and the feeling of deprivation have aggravated the problem of cementing inter-ethnic relations for the construction of territorial Manipuri identity.

Development efforts of the state are judged and interpreted through ethnic lenses. While the state as a whole is suffering from economic underdevelopment syndrome, there is a general feeling, perceived or real, among the tribals in the hills that they are being neglected by the people in the valley (read by the Meiteis). They feel that they are being deprived of the benefits of whatever development that is taking place in the state. The logic of market driven development, which is uneven in nature, is often forgotten and interpreted as the deliberate design of the majority who controls power and state resources. As the forces of market bypass the areas lacking infrastructural growth, having scattered human habitation, involving higher transportation costs, lagging in terms of private initiatives and deprived of resources and human skills, as the hills areas are often characterized, the intervention on the part of the state can only partly address the problems of market failure in these areas. The institution of state in Manipur being very weak, inefficient and insolvent could hardly play adequate role to redress the market failure and consequent relative underdevelopment of the hill areas inhabited mainly by the Nagas and Kukis. As the Meiteis are the dominant group in terms of the size of population and constitute the majority in the power structure, the failure of the state is often seen as the deliberate design of the Meiteis. Ethno-centric life-world, thus, often misinterprets the role of the 'others' without being critical about the role of the agency. These ethno-centric views are often constructed based on the feeling of perceived relative deprivation. Instead of looking from a vantage point beyond ethnic interest and mobilizing other collectivities in order to affect development for all, these ethno-centric ideologies often takes an insular view and mobilizes the members of a particular group against others creating a situation of ethnic tension and conflict. This has exactly happened in case of the ethnic communities in Manipur, be the Meiteis, Nagas or Kukis. All the ethno-national groups work for their respective identities at the cost of 'Manipuri identity' and in the process weaken the state which tries to forge a territorial nationhood rather than ethno-national identity. The divergence of nation-building goals between the state and the ethno-national groups on the one hand and among the various ethno-national groups on the other has, indeed, been a major source of tension in Manipur.

However, it is important to analyze the causes behind the growth of the feeling of deprivation among the people living in the hill areas of Manipur. It may be pointed out that the tribals in Manipur enjoy special treatment than their valley counterparts in the form of scholarships, seat reservations in government jobs and educational institutions, tax exemption[6] and other concessions. Moreover, about 40 per cent of the total outlay is usually spent for the development of hill region where about 40 per cent of the total population resides (Tarapot, 2005: 54). But the problem is that the funds meant for development hardly reach its target. It is often drained to fill the pockets of politicians, contractors, high officials, businessmen and the undergrounds. As a result, not only the hills but the state as a whole is lagging behind her counterparts in the country. Rooting out corruption from the Manipuri society, thus, should constitute a secular agenda and people needs to be mobilized across ethnic identities.

Land is another bone of contention in Manipur. In fact, articulation of ethno-national aspirations largely revolves around land. Besides being the prime resource, land is also viewed as homeland and, therefore, constitutes an integral part of the community identity. As the notion of identity is embedded in territoriality, territorial claim is viewed to be the core of identity claim. Thus, every ethno-national groups strives for political autonomy to be fructified within their respective traditional or imagined territorial spaces. As a result, maintaining the customary control over land is viewed to be *sine qua non* for the identity assertion.

This ethno-national position relating to land has led to the emergence of multi-layer complexities in inter-ethnic relationships in Manipur. Let us first explain the complexities involving in tribal-non-tribal relationships. While viewed from pan-Indian perspective, tribals are the minority and their interest as far as resource ownership is concerned needs to be protected. The experiences of land alienation of the tribals and their consequent economic deprivation have led the Indian state to devise a legal framework wherein non-tribals are prohibited to acquire the land of the tribals. This piece of regulatory measure has been largely successful in protecting the tribal interest in land all across the country. In case of Manipur, Meiteis are non-tribal and hence the Manipur Land Revenue (MLR) and Land Reforms (LR) Act, 1960[7], does not apply in the hills.

Land system in the hills is governed by tribal customary laws and customs. This again varies from tribe to tribe. Land is owned by the community in case of Nagas and by chiefs in case of Kukis. Even at sub-tribe and clan level, land is governed by their respective laws and customs (For more details on tribal land system, Devi, 2006; Singh, 2004). As a result, land market is coterminous with clan/sub-tribe/tribe boundaries. Not only the non-tribals are barred from buying and owning land in tribal areas, even the members of one tribe are not allowed to own land in the territory of another.

From economic point of view, customary laws, thus, regulate the forces of the market. The state is facing tremendous challenges in ensuring optimal use of its resources. While the valley districts are already overpopulated, with population density of 631 persons per square km., the hills are sparsely populated with 44 persons per square km. Being an agrarian state with little scope for industrialization, Manipur cannot afford to keep land in the hinterlands underutilized. If the pressure of population on land has to be reduced, given the fact that inter-sectoral transfer of population has limited scope, land in the hills needs to be opened up for those who can best utilize that resource. This commodity view (Das, 2005), thus, calls for disjoining land from identity.

Besides the economic logic for opening up and freeing the land from monopoly control of the tribal groups in the hills, the living space view (Das, 2005), which looks at land as habitat or homeland also calls for scaling down the ethnic control over land. While the Nagas and Kukis can buy and own land in the valley, it is unfair on their part to bar the Meiteis from acquiring the same in the hills. The ideologues of Meitei ethno-nationalism feel that every community should have the level plying field. The existing structure of land relations discriminates against the interest of the Meities.

Contrary to this Meitei-view, tribal communities see land as an inseparable element to their identity. The fear that once community control over land is bartered for market, the community itself will tend to disintegrate. The community control over land is thus at the core of tribal social formation. Moreover, apart from land, tribals do not have any other resources to fall back upon. The relative economically weak position of the tribals will lead to the fast growth of land alienation and thereby further marginalize the community.

These conflicting community interests in land have led to the articulation of demand for Sixth Schedule status for the hills. Both the Nagas and Kukis are pressing for this status as this will provide necessary framework in which community control over land will get constitutional recognition as has been done in case of the tribal groups in Assam,[8] Meghalaya,[9] Mizoram[10] and Tripura.[11] On the contrary, Meiteis are working through the state government to extend the MLR and LR Act, 1960 in the hills.

While the tribals feel that extension of MLR and LR Act will deprive them of their traditional rights over land, the Meiteis feel that the grant of Sixth Schedule status will be, in a way, equivalent to give in to the demands of Naga integration and Kuki homeland which will ultimately lead to the disintegration of the territorial boundary of the state. These conflicting territorial interests constitute the basic faultlines in the Manipuri society. Mobilization of the members of respective groups by both the state and non-state actors in favour of community interests has widened and hardened the inter-ethnic faultlines over the years. As the ethno-national goals are mutually exclusive, inter-ethnic distrust and animosity has almost precluded any negotiated settlement. There is no easy answer to this problem. The ethno-national groups have to strike a balance between the security of identity and accommodation of the interests of others within the poly-ethnic social space in Manipur.

With the demand for unification of Naga inhabited areas into a single administrative unit as professed by NSCN (I-M) gained momentum since 1988, whose implementation requires hill areas of Manipur to be added to Nagaland, the inter-ethnic relations in Manipur further deteriorated as the materialization of this demand would only be possible at the cost of the interests of both the Kukis and Meiteis. This demand for unification is not only supported tacitly by the Nagas of Manipur but even the Nagaland state assembly also supported the demand. As this demand is in direct conflict with the demand for Kuki homeland, having overlapping territorial claim, and Meiteis' demand for territorial integrity of the existing boundary of the state, the inter-ethnic distrust and rivalry reached to its zenith. While the Nagas under the leadership of NSCN (I-M) are trying to realize this goal through negotiations with India government, the Meiteis have all along resisted such move, as has happened in 2001 peace agreement between Indian Government and NSCN (I-M), where ceasefire was extended 'without territorial limits' first and then reverted back in the face of stiff opposition from the Meiteis. It may also be noted that this Naga aspiration for unification has also triggered the NSCN (I-M) drive towards ethnic cleansing of the Kukis in the hills of Manipur.

Thus, incongruity of different ethno-national goals not only stands on the way of development of territorial Manipuri identity, but also pulls the institution of state in different directions. As a result, conflict management has become the primary function of the state rather than promoting economic development. As the status quo minimizes inter-ethnic conflict, change is not politically desirable, even if important from economic point of view, on many occasions particularly in relation to development projects and schemes. In fact, the social and political segmentation holds on economic integration of the hills and plains in Manipur.

Degeneration of Militancy

The militant movements of the Nagas and Meiteis have lost much of their political relevance with the grant of statehood to Nagaland in 1963 and Manipur in 1972. There has not been any compelling argument as to why the provincial level autonomy is not sufficient for these ethno-national groups in maintaining their respective identities. Like any other Indian nationalities, these two communities also enjoy the highest level autonomy permissible within the Indian federal structure. With electoral democracy in place, people only elect their representatives and governed by them.

As such, the argument of internal colonialism, often cited by the militant groups as the basic cause of conflict, hardly cuts any ice. Devoid of any strong and sound political ideology, these movements relapse into ethnocentric irredentism. As a result, clan, tribe, race, language and religion have crept in surreptitiously only to split them in different directions. With political ideology taking the backseat; power, authority and economic gains have become the drivers that keep these movements going. As already discussed that the race for leadership has caused vertical disintegration of almost all the militant groups operating in Manipur. Most of these small groups act more like extortion rackets, of course, under the garb of patriotic struggle. It is, in fact, hard to distinguish them, of course, except patriotic garb, from the innumerable underground crime gangs that operate in the metropolitan cities across the world. A strong nexus between the power elites and these underground groups often provide them necessary immunity against the law of the land. Extortion, kidnapping and killing have been made a regular phenomena in order to mime the sane voices in the society. We shall discuss the social and economic costs of this degenerated insurgency in detail in the next chapter. Meghen, chairman of UNLF has rightly remarked, "Once people supported the revolutionaries by fondly calling them *Naharol* (youths) but today revolutionaries are called *miyam da akal-aring singba khutpu* (groups who show their power)" (IFP, July, 21, 2008).

Field Survey Observations

A primary survey has been conducted in the state of Manipur. A sample of 300 has been taken cutting across various sections of the people. A multi-stage purposive sampling technique has been followed while choosing the elements of the sample. In the first stage the whole sample is divided equally among the following categories.

Table 4.1
Sample Distribution

Category	*Size*
General	50
Surrenderree	50
Farmer	50
Businessmen	50
Service holder	50
Manufacturer	50
Total	300

The general category is further distributed among the following heads.

Table 4.2
General Category

Different Heads	*Size*
Teachers	10
Students	10
Police	5
Journalist	5
Government Employee	5
Self-employed	5
Unemployed	5
Housewife	5
Total	50

Except the categories of the surrenderee, which has been drawn exclusively from the valley districts due to accessibility, and general, drawn from Imphal West due to the concentration of the white collar employees, the other categories, viz., farmers, businessmen, service holder and manufacturer are distributed equally in five districts in the state. The districts are Imphal East, Imphal West, Bishnupur, Thoubal and Churachandpur. As the Naga insurgency in Manipur is the extension of the Naga movement developed in Nagaland, Naga inhabited districts are not considered in this sample. Thus, a sample of 10 each has been drawn from every district for these 4 categories (Table 4.3).

Table 4.3

District-wise distribution of the sample by category

Districts	*Farmer*	*Businessmen*	*Service holder*	*Manufacturer*
Imphal East	10	10	10	10
Imphal West	10	10	10	10
Bishnupur	10	10	10	10
Thoubal	10	10	10	10
Churachandpur	10	10	10	10
Total	50	50	50	50

A questionnaire has been designed to generate data on individual's perception on the cause of underground movement in the state and its subsequent proliferation into various rag-tag groups, the impact of underground activities on the different sectors of the economy, individual freedom, people's aspirations, law and order situation and the role of politicians behind the growth of militancy in the state. The surrendered militants have been interviewed to assess their perceptions on the justification of the movement.

All the respondents have been given the freedom to choose more than one option against a particular query. The responses have not been ranked and have been given equal weightage in our analysis.

Table 4.4
Causes of Underground Movement

Cause	*Responses*				*Total*	
	Yes	*Percent*	*No*	*Percent*	*Respondents*	*Percentage*
Economic Under-development	35	11.7	265	88.3	300	100
Growing Unemployment	50	16.7	250	83.3	300	100
Neglect of the state and people by the Indian state	160	53.3	140	46.7	300	100
Army operation	3	1.0	297	99.0	300	100
Aspiration of the nationality for freedom	227	75.7	73	24.3	300	100
Earning easy money	4	1.3	296	98.7	300	100
Poor governance and corruption	87	29.0	213	71.0	300	100
Large scale immigration of the people	2	0.7	298	99.3	300	100

Source: Field Survey.

Regarding the cause of underground movement in the state 75.7 per cent of the respondents feel that it is the aspiration of the nationality for freedom. 53.3 per cent feel that it is the neglect of the state and people by the Indian state. Poor governance and corruption is another cause for underground movement and 29 per cent of the respondents opted for this option. Another 16.7 per cent opted for growing unemployment and 11.7 per cent for economic underdevelopment as the cause of underground movement in the state. It may be noted that ethno-national aspirations, economic underdevelopment and consequent problem of unemployment coupled with the poor governance have been viewed to be the roots of insurgency in Manipur. Our study also corroborates this people's perception.

Table 4.5
Do you think UG movement is the result of social frustration?

Response	*Frequency*	*Percent*
Yes	32	10.7
No	236	78.7
Don't know	32	10.6
Total	300	100

Source: Field Survey.

While asked as to whether militancy is the result of social frustration, majority of the respondents replied in negative (Table 4.5). This implies that people perceive militant political activism is the result of deliberate choice on the part of the actors to affect change rather than an alternative mode of action of the refused.

Two major factors have been identified by the respondents that are responsible for the proliferation of insurgency in Manipur. About 76 per cent (table 4.6) of the respondents believe that ideological difference among the militant leadership is the cause behind the factionalism and proliferation of insurgent groups in the state. However, 65 per cent (Table 4.6) of the respondents believe that greed for power also plays a major ole behind factionalism and proliferation.

Table 4.6
Reason behind the proliferation of the underground groups

Reasons behind proliferation	*Response*				*Total*	
	Yes	*Percent*	*No*	*Percent*	*Respon-dents*	*Percen-tage*
Difference in ideology	227	75.7	73	24.3	300	100
Greed for power	195	65.0	105	35.0	300	100
Quarrel among the leaders	11	3.7	289	96.3	300	100

Source: Field Survey.

Majority of the respondents do not agree with the idea of secession from the Indian Union. 48 per cent of them feel that independence of the state will not provide better future to the people. 25.3 per cent of them feel that independence will provide better future to the people while the rest 26.7 per cent did not give any opinion regarding this issue.

Table 4.7
Do you think independence will provide better future to the people?

Response	*Frequency*	*Percent*
Yes	76	25.3
No	144	48.0
Don't know	80	26.7
Total	300	100

Source: Field Survey.

While canvassing the interview schedule, informal discussions have been held with the respondents. It appears that the respondents neither repose faith on the power elites who govern the state, nor do they repose faith on the leadership of the insurgent groups. While corruption and inefficiency being the prime causes for not trusting the over ground political elites; extortion, killing and lack of transparency about the political agenda of the under grounds have been cited as reasons for lack of trust on them.

Table 4.8
Do you think UG groups represent the aspirations of the people?

Response	*Frequency*	*Percent*
Yes	92	30.7
No	176	58.7
Don't know	32	10.6
Total	300	100

Source: Field Survey

While asked as to whether the insurgent groups represent the aspirations of the people in the state, majority of the respondents (58.7 per cent) replied in negative. This perhaps indicates the divergence of perceptions between the people and the militants. Majority of the people of the state do not subscribe to the political views of the militant groups.

On further query as to how do the militant groups represent the aspirations of the people of the state, out of 92 respondents, who feel that insurgent groups represent the aspirations of the people, majority feels that they fight against the injustice done to the people of this state by the Indian Government, corruption and to restore the pride of the people (Table 4.9).

Table 4.9
How do underground groups represent the aspirations of the people?

Underground groups represent the aspiration of the people by	*Response*				*Total*	
	Yes	*Percent*	*No*	*Percent*	*Respondents*	*Percentage*
Fighting against corruption	57	61.96	35	38.04	92	100
Fighting against injustice	64	69.57	28	30.43	92	100
Fighting for the pride of the people	57	61.96	35	38.04	92	100
Fighting for the socio-economic development	7	7.61	85	92.39	92	100
Fighting against immigrant communities	0	0	92	100	92	100

Source: Field Survey.

A very interesting observation is that 90 per cent of the respondents feel that it is our own politicians who are responsible for the overall messy situation in the state (table 4.10). As has been pointed out earlier, the rent seeking behavior of the local power elites; their clandestine connection with the underground activists, and their failure to provide clean and transparent governance have weakened the legitimacy of the state significantly.

Table 4.10
Do you think local politicians are responsible for the mess in the state?

Response	*Frequency*	*Percent*
Yes	270	90.0
No	8	2.7
Don't know	22	7.3
Total	300	100

Source: Field Survey.

Majority of the respondents (79 per cent) believe that there exists a nexus among the local power elites, bureaucrats, businessmen, contractors and the underground activists in the state (Table 4.11).

Table 4.11
Do you think that there exists a nexus among politicians/bureaucrats/businessmen/contractors and the UG?

Response	*Frequency*	*Percent*
Yes	237	79.0
No	21	7.0
Don't know	42	14.0
Total	300	100

Source: Field Survey.

Thus, the general framework for the exposition of the problem of militancy in Manipur, as has been outlined in this and the preceding chapter, has been validated by the field observations. The impact of the militant movement on the economy and society will be taken up in the next chapter while the options for conflict resolution will be discussed in the concluding chapter.

NOTES

1. There is a confusion regarding the year of formation of the MSC*. While Sanajaoba (2006) gave 1960 as the year of its formation, Singh (N) (2005) and Constantine (1981) gave 1967.

2. Meitei Pangal form about 8 per cent of the total population in Manipur according to 2001 Census. The present day Meitei Pangal community is, in fact, the result of the expansion of Meitei identity in the beginning of 17th century. As already been mentioned in chapter 2, following the Kachari-Muslim invasion of 1606 A.D. many Muslim war captives were brought in the Imphal valley. They were not only allowed to stay in the valley but they were also allowed to inter marry with the Meiteis and hence the present day Meitei Pangal community came into existence.

3. On May 28, 1989, the new military junta (State Law and Order Restoration Council - SLORC) seized power in Burma. Since then Burma has been known as Myanmar (Egreteau, 2003: xi).

4. *Shanti Bahini*, a Chakma community underground organization was set up with the help of RAW in 1976 to take up arms against the Dhaka government (Egreteau, 2006).

5. 'Disturbed Area' means an area which is for the time being declared by notification under Section 3 of AFSPA, 1958, to be a disturbed area (GoI, 2005).

6. All the people under the category of Scheduled Tribes are exempted from income tax.

7. In MLR and LR Act, 1960, it is expressly mentioned that 'the Act extends to the whole of the state of Manipur except the hill areas thereof: provided that the State Government may, by notification in the official Gazette, extend the whole or any part of any section of this Act to any of the hill areas of Manipur also as may be specified in any such notification'. Again, in Section 158 of the Act, it is also mentioned that transfer of land from tribal to non-tribal is prohibited without the permission of the Deputy Commissioner and previous consent of the District Council within whose jurisdiction the land lies (www.manipur.nic.in).

8. In Assam, there are three district councils under the Sixth Schedule one each for the Karbis, Dimasas and Bodos.

9. In Meghalaya, three district councils under the Sixth Schedule are operating one each for the Khasis in Khasi hills, Garos in Garo hills and the Jaintias in Jaintia hills.
10. In Mizoram, one district council under the Sixth Schedule is working for Chakmas in Shaiha district.
11. In Tripura, one district council for the Tripuris and other tribal groups is working in the hill areas.

5

Security and Development: Is there any trade off?

Economic development requires a socio-political environment which guarantees the security of investment, encourages entrepreneurs to undertake risk, ensures a decent rate of return on investment and facilitates the expansion of choices and opportunities which people value for themselves, reduces the unfreedoms where people enjoy full freedoms in the sphere of politics, culture and initiatives at personal as well as collective sphere. A democratic political environment encourages public debates, discussion and criticism and through frank deliberations on issues that matter to the lives of the people, alternative options are articulated and the regime is chosen who opts for the best course of action for the well-being of the society. There is hardly any space for violence in a democratic process. No group imposes its ideology on the gun points. Knowledge is the power in the hands of the opponents and not the gun which is used to silence the political rivals. Social policy debates are deeply informed and adequately reflected from all corners before they are put into practice. Where discourses on public issues are charted by the use of brawn and not the brain, options become jaundiced and brutality is used as means instead of consciousness. The lack of security—personal or collective—adds to the unfreedoms and negatively impacts upon development par se. Thus, the issues of security and development are intertwined. The lack of the former leads to the deterioration of the latter.

In this chapter we shall make an attempt to examine the processes as to how the growth of militancy in Manipur has negatively impacted upon the development and well-being of the people of Manipur

Insurgency and Insecurity

The underground movement in the state which started with the formation of UNLF in 1964 with a justified cause to restore the lost sovereignty has degenerated and proliferated into a number of rag-tag groups. These groups have now become a primarily extortion rackets, which have spread like a cancer into all facets of politics, administration and the social life of the state (Rammohan, 2002: 1). Frequent bandhs, strikes, blockades, extortions, kidnappings and murders have become a way of life in the state.

In the name of counter insurgency, large numbers of security personnel deployed in the state are involved in various atrocities often leading to human rights violation. Not a single day goes without reports of violence. The whole security scenario in the state has deteriorated. Today the state of Manipur is known for its underground activities, rampant corruption, deteriorating law and order, human rights violation, economic underdevelopment, high unemployment rate, drug addicts, HIV/AIDS cases, etc.

The insecure environment negatively impact upon the local economy. Economic decisions like production, investment, saving and capital formation are worst affected by the precarious position of the state. Extortion, kidnapping for ransom, murder for non-compliance, etc. by the underground groups have become the order of the day. The counter insurgency operations are, also, no less dreadful than those committed by the underground groups. The innocent civilians often fall victims to the activities of both the undergrounds and security personnel.

What could be the outcome of such insecure environment? For an underdeveloped state like Manipur, instead of moving ahead along with the era of globalization and look east policy the state is moving backwards. The situation has become rather worse off after the entire state was declared as 'disturbed area' under the provisions of the Armed Forces (Assam and Manipur) Special Powers Act 1958 (AFSPA) on September 8, 1980. It can be remembered here that during the late 1970s and early 1980s the situation was very tense and the authorities were worried by the unlawful violent activities unleashed by the ultras. The number of persons killed increased from 2 in 1978 to 14 in 1979 and 36 in 1980 to 50 in 1981. Incidents of robbery, dacoity, and ambush of security personnel by armed extremists also recorded an increase in 1981 at 118 against 77 in 1980 (Tarapot, 1996: 82). With no other alternative left than to deploy army personnel, the authorities made a last effort before deployment by asking the 'revolutionary youths' to lay down arms and gave a 15-day ultimatum on June 11, 1980. Failure on the part of the underground groups to meet the ultimatum led to the imposition AFSPA, despite various protests against its imposition by the elderly people and the students including the womenfolk led by *Manipur Nupi Kanglup* (Manipur women's organization). According to a government notification, the AFSPA had been promulgated in Manipur because of the "unprecedented increase in the commission of crimes, such as killing of innocent persons and police and para military personnel, robbery, dacoity, arson, sedition, offences under the Arms Act, harbouring and rescuing of criminals, terrorizing peaceful and law-abiding citizens, disturbing the normalcy of life and public tranquility, endangering the lives of civil authorities and attempts and incitement to commit the above offences and also violation of the Unlawful Activities (Prevention) Act, 1967 together with secessionist activities by unlawful elements" (Tarapot,1996: 82-86). Even 28 years after the enforcement of the Act, the violent activities have not shown any sign of abatement. One can rather see a contrasting picture where the violent activities are increasing day by day. Today Manipur has been placed as the second most violent state in the northeastern region after Assam (Routray, 2007a) and third most violent theatre of conflict in the country behind Jammu and Kashmir and Assam (Routray, 2007b).

The deteriorating security environment can be seen from table 5.1-5.4 showing the various activities of both underground groups and security personnel.

The indicators like number of violent incidents committed by the insurgent groups, number of arrest of the insurgent activists, number of surrender, number of insurgent activists killed, number of persons killed by the insurgents etc., which inter alia, are generally used to measure the intensity are not out of doubt. As statistics relating to these indices are recorded by various security agencies and classification of these events under various heads is very often done on the basis of intuition and pro-state bias, there remains enough room for subjective judgment. Moreover, these statistics without details hardly lend themselves to researcher's verifications. Besides their limitations, these statistics are not easily available, even while available, they very often lack in continuity and comparability. Nonetheless one can form an idea of the intensity of insurgent activities in the region over the years.

Table 5.1
Incidence of Insurgency Activities in Manipur 1992-06

Activities	*1992*	*1995*	*1998*	*2002*	*2003*	*2004*	*2005*	*2006 (upto 30/6/06)*	*Total*
Extremists Arrested	151	363	1008	898	881	685	1019	370	5375
Extremists Surrendered	15	-	39	11	5	7	25	21	123
Arms Recovered	97	68	278	126	131	140	179	96	1115
Ammunitions Recovered	229	647	6526	1727	1907	1992	5508	1044	17588
Money Recovered(Rs.)	106705	-	163193	1260086	334875	106103	1708220	273195	3952377

Source: Manipur Today, Various Issues.

Table 5.2
Incidence of Crimes in Manipur

Name of Crimes	*Year*														
	1991	*1992*	*1993*	*1994*	*1995*	*1996*	*1997*	*1998*	*1999*	*2000*	*2001*	*2002*	*2003*	*2004*	*2005*
Dacoity	7	23	12	41	27	22	18	8	23	20	10	18	3	1	2
Robbery	37	37	60	51	44	37	31	25	18	24	26	13	5	9	4
Murder	102	114	141	297	264	291	250	315	192	185	226	197	155	143	200
Riot	119	166	128	91	45	41	101	57	59	107	42	159	63	59	100
Burglary	145	137	100	103	94	111	106	110	91	74	70	66	49	79	69
Culpable Homicide	-	-	-	-	-	-	-	2	5	7	3	4	5	11	14
Kidnapping &Abduction	102	126	156	123	105	112	105	186	89	80	97	117	159	128	154
Counter-fieting	-	-	-	-	-	-	-	4	15	9	12	19	11	6	3
Misc. (IPC)	856	1040	1438	1704	1559	1585	2758	2597	2130	1843	1710	1779	1854	1816	1937
Other Theft	266	314	352	251	277	320	260	281	245	280	208	223	247	242	270
Total	1634	1957	2387	2661	2415	2519	3629	3885	2867	2629	2404	2595	2551	2494	2753

Source: Statistical Abstract Manipur 2005.

Table 5.1 shows the various insurgency related activities from the period 1992 to 2006. The number of extremists arrested totaled to 5375 in this period of 14 years whereas the number of extremists surrendered totaled to 123 in the same period. Arms and ammunitions recovered totaled to 1115 and 17588 respectively and total money recovered was Rs. 39, 52,377.

The incidence of various crimes in Manipur is shown in Table 5.2. Among the various crimes, murder, riot and kidnapping and abduction registered a high rate in the period from 1991 to 2005. Total murder committed during this period was 3072 which accounted for 8 per cent of the total crimes in the state in the referred period. Riots and kidnapping and abduction totaled to 1337 and 1839 respectively which accounted for 3 per cent and 5 per cent respectively to the total crimes in the state. The total crimes committed in the state also registered an increase from 1634 in 1991 to 3885 in 1998. It decreased to 2494 in 2004 but again increased to 2753 in 2005.

The security environment characterized by high rate of incidence of insurgency related activities and crimes in the state are further worsened by the high rate of insurgency related killings. Table 5.3 shows the insurgency related killings from the year 1992 to 2008. In this period of 16 years insurgency related killings totaled to 4857. Highest casualty is suffered by the civilians registering a total of 1995 deaths which account for 41.07 per cent of the total deaths in the state during the said period. This is followed by terrorists whose total death is 1951 accounting for 40.17 per cent of the total death. Security force suffered a total death of 911 which account for 18.76 per cent of the total death during the said period.

Table 5.3
Insurgency Related Killings

Year	*No. of Persons Killed*			
	Civilians	*Security Force*	*Terrorists*	*Total*
1992	84	30	51	165
1993	266	91	66	423
1994	189	98	63	350
1995	183	64	74	321
1996	117	65	93	275
1997	233	111	151	495
1998	87	62	95	244
1999	89	64	78	231
2000	93	51	102	246
2001	70	25	161	256
2002	36	53	101	190
2003	27	23	148	198
2004	50	41	127	218
2005	138	50	143	331
2006	107	37	141	285
2007	150	40	218	408
2008 *	76	6	139	221
Total	1995	911	1951	4857

Source: www.satp.org
* till June 16 2008

One can observe from Table 5.3 that on an average 125 civilians die per year due to insurgency related killings. While all types of recorded insurgency related deaths are taken into consideration, 304 persons died every year for last 16 years.

This implies 25 deaths every month, 6 deaths per week, 1 death in every 29 hours. In addition to the insurgency related killings, extra judicial killings are also a major area of concern. Extra judicial killings refer to the custodial deaths in the hands of the security personnel.

Table 5.4
Extra Judicial Killings

Year	*No. of Deceased*	*No. of Injured*
1995	19	15
1998	8	2
2000	8	-
2001	8	-
2002	23	1
2003	15	2
2004	13	27
Total	94	47

Source: Ranjit, 2004.

Table 5.4 showing the extra judicial killings portray the gravity of the situation. Total custodial deaths were 94 persons in the period between 1995 and 2004 whereas number of injured was 47. A total casualty of 94 persons in the hands of security personnel in a period of 9 years gives an average death of 10 persons in a year. If we combine insurgency related killings and extra judicial killings then, on an average, 1 person dies everyday in Manipur. Given this figure one can imagine the gravity of the security environment in the state. But these figures are only reported or recorded ones. There are several cases of persons missing and never found even if their cases are being registered.

Both insurgency and counter-insurgency operations have usurped the political space at the cost of civil society. The binary vision of these warring groups sees an entity either in one camp or the other. The independent voices are viewed with suspicion resulting into the elimination of any sane voice with considered and reflective opinion. Public media—print or electronic—are frequently threatened with dire consequences in case of any adverse publicity. The dictates of the gunrunners rule the roost in every nook and corner and the intense feeling of insecurity, as pervasive as it might be, has crippled the public life. In no single instance the perpetrators of crime—be it the militants or security forces—have ever brought to book and made accountable for their deeds. The legitimacy of the state has already withered away and to large extent militant groups administer the justice not only against social maladies but also in private arenas. In the killing field of Manipur, public law and order exists only for namesake and the militant groups have penetrated deep into the institutions of democracy and governance making the ordinary citizens helpless and dumbfounded.

Security and Development: The Economic costs of Insurgency

There are two-way linkages between economic underdevelopment and insurgency. An underdeveloped material base provides little opportunities to people for gainful employment. Unemployed youths then hardly find any viable alternative for their livelihood. They perceive that the 'failed state' is the prime cause for their misery. This perception encourages them to join the non-state actors who vouch for revolutionary change. Thus economic underdevelopment helps in sharpening anti-state political discourse and strengthens the ideology of the so called revolutionary groups.

Insurgent activities help in perpetuating economic underdevelopment. As has been described, militancy has created deep insecurity in the minds of the people in general and entrepreneurial class in particular. It has already been pointed out in chapter 3 that Meiteis lack entrepreneurial skill and majority of the entrepreneurs hail from outside—be it large business in goods or services. These 'others' are really vulnerable as they are often considered as outcast and pejoratively known as 'mayang' or 'outsider'. They often become the soft targets and easy source for extortion. The economic space held, hitherto, by these mayang is gradually being restored to the sons-of-the-soil through a strong nexus among the politicians, local contractors and insurgents. The 'nouveau riche' Meitei entrepreneurial class who emerged out of state patronage following the coming of the state of Manipur into existence since 1972 appears to have been acting as a cog in the wheel of the militancy machine. They appear to play the role of the interface between the power elites and the undergrounds particularly in siphoning the development fund earmarked for public works. Thus while private investments shy away with the rising risk factor, public investment is squandered away in the name of development leading to the perpetuation of economic underdevelopment making the socio-political space fertile for the growth of insurgency in Manipur. A Nurkesian type of vicious cycle between underdevelopment and insurgency has trapped the economy of the state at low level equilibrium which calls for an appropriate policy intervention and about which we shall refer to the concluding chapter. However, the economic costs of insurgency manifested in different forms are not easy to quantify. It is all the more difficult to establish empirical association between them. This, however, should not deter us to look into the economic costs of insurgency in terms of descriptive and consequential analysis.

Economics of Insurgency: Crippling effects of Rent Seeking (Extortion)

The militancy machine requires huge resource mobilization to wage war against the state. Besides the maintenance of the cadres and camps, they need huge amount of cash for procuring arms and ammunitions primarily from the arms markets abroad, arranging safe shelters for the leaders and cadres outside the state and abroad, arranging training for the cadres in hideouts of other insurgent groups, undertaking subversive operations, replenish the men and materials lost in operations and for other logistics. Unlike the civil war groups in African countries, Manipur does not have any natural resources of any significance on which the militant groups can fall back on for resource mobilization. Neither the state has large business operators to be milked, nor the communities have strong diasporas to bank on. As a result, the lion's share of the resources is primarily mobilized from within.

Moreover, as the constituency of the ethnic militant groups is primarily limited by the ethnic boundary, it is difficult for one ethnic militant group to compel people of other ethnic groups to pay for their struggle. As for illustration, a Meitei militant group keeps away from the Nagas or Kukis, and a Naga militant group keeps away from the Meiteis and Kukis. As the different ethnic militant groups often fight for overlapping interests, allowing the 'other-ethnic-militant groups' to operate within the domain of 'us-militant-group' will only rob the loyalty and weaken the social base of the latter. As a result, ethnic boundaries are jealously guarded by the respective ethnic militant groups. Of course, for operational purposes, homeland concept is generally used for resource mobilization. As ethnic boundaries and homeland boundaries, by and large, coincide, people in the valley pay to the Meitei insurgent groups, whereas people in Naga inhabited hills pay to Naga insurgent groups and people living in the Kuki inhabited areas fill the coffer of the Kuki insurgent groups. However, in isolated pockets and ethnic enclaves, the scenario may be different. Thus, the resource domains of the insurgent groups are largely limited by the territorial boundaries of the homelands of the different ethnic groups.

Furthermore, the existence of multiple militant groups within a particular ethnic community further reduces the resource domain of a group and leads to conflicting loyalty claims. The proliferation of ethnic armies and inter-group competition imposes heavy demand on the resources of the people. Today Manipur tops the Union Government's list of underground groups with five valley based groups being declared unlawful under the sub-section 1, section 3 of the Unlawful Activities (Prevention) Act, 1967 (*Imphal Free Press* (IFP), July 11, 2008).

Table 5.5
Terrorist/Insurgent Groups Operating in Manipur

Proscribed Terrorist/ Insurgent Groups	*Active Terrorist/ Insurgent Groups*	*Inactive Terrorist/ Insurgent Groups*
1	*2*	*3*
1. United National Liberation Front (UNLF)	1. Hmar People's Convention–Democracy (HPC-D)	1. Chin Kuki Revolutionary Front (CKRF)
2. People's Liberation Army (PLA)	2. Kuki Liberation Army (KLA)	2. Hmar People's Convention (HPC)
3. People's Revolutionary Party of Kangleipak (PREPAK)	3. Kuki National Army (KNA)	3. Hmar Revolutionary Front (HRF)
4. Kangleipak Communist Party (KCP)	4. Kuki National Front (KNF)	4. Indigenous People's Revolutionary Alliance (IRPA)
5. Kanglei Yawol Kanna Lup (KYKL)	5. Kuki Revolutionary Army	5. Iripak Kanba Lup (IKL)
6. Manipur People's Liberation Front (MPLF)		6. Islamic Revolutionary Front (IRF)
		7. Islamic National

(Contd...)

1	*2*	*3*
	(KRA) 6. National Socialist Council of Nagaland – Issac-Muivah (NSCN I-M) 7. People's United Liberation Front (PULF) 8. United Kuki Liberation Front (UKLF) 9. Zomi Revolutionary Army (ZRA)	Front (INF) 8. Kangleipak Kanba Kanglup (KKK) 9. Kangleipak Liberation Organisation (KLO) 10. Kom Rem People's Convention (KRPC) 11. Kuki Defence Force (KDF) 12. Kuki Independent Army (KIA) 13. Kuki International Force (KIF) 14. Kuki Liberation Front (KLF) 15. Kuki National Organisation (KNO) 16. Kuki National Volunteers (KNV) 17. Kuki Revolutionary Front (KRF) 18. Kuki Security Force (KSF) 19. Manipur Liberation Tiger Army (MLTA) 20. North East

(Contd...)

1	*2*	*3*
		Minority Front (NEMF)
		21. People's Republican Army (PRA)
		22. Revolutionary Joint Committee (RJC)
		23. United Islamic Liberation Army (UILA)
		24. United Islamic Revolutionary Army (UIRA)
		25. Zomi Revolutionary Volunteers (ZRV)

Source: www.satp.org

The instruments of resource mobilization adopted by the majority of the groups constitute extortion or often eulogize as 'protection tax' or 'monthly donation for freedom struggle', ransom or captive tax primarily collected through kidnapping, commission for public works and development projects, fines from the wrong doers collected from the corrupt officials, and 'beneficiary tax' mainly collected from the contractors and suppliers who act as the surrogate of the militant groups.

In absence of any alternative source for resource mobilization, the burden of extortion largely falls on the people in general and salaried, professional and business groups in particular. The multiplicity of extortion demands due to the existence of multiple groups has made it very difficult for the people to comply with. The level of extortion has indeed surpassed the level of tolerance. Informal discussions that we had with different people from different walks of life suggest the current extent of extortion to the tune of 10-12 per cent of the net pay of the salaried groups. What is more important is the question of compliance. It has been learnt that the dreaded the image of a group, the higher is the level of compliance. In order to have a dreaded image, different groups adopt different code of conduct for non-compliance. Some opt for kidnapping, some for shooting at the leg, some for outright killing, and some for creating panic by throwing hand grenades. Unlike the militant groups in Assam who extort bigger amount mainly from the limited number of large players, Meitei militant groups deal with innumerable small players to make up a large amount. Hence, they have to face a difficult task as far as the compliance is concerned.

Except the Army and the Central Paramilitary Forces who are engaged in counter insurgency activities (Routray, 2007b), the wide extortion network has affected every earning citizen of the state. As seen in table 5.5, there are 40 underground groups in the state out of which 15 are active. All these groups resort to extortion, kidnapping, murder, etc. The extortion racket of the underground groups works in a well channelised path. Almost all the active groups used to collect 'monthly donations' from thousands of government employees and other salaried groups. Apart from these they collect money from all the business houses including even the petty shopkeepers on regular basis. All the shopkeepers have to pay a sum regularly to the underground groups. This sum ranges between Rs. 300 to 500 to 1000 and even more per annum depending on the size of the business and negotiations. In their extortion racket they have not even spared petty shopkeepers and rickshaw pullers.

In January 2004 police shot an 'unidentified suspect' who was found not only having a hand grenade but also receipts of taxes collected the previous month. These included amounts of Rs. 10,000 from Education Department, Rs. 12,000 from the Public Health Department, Rs. 5,000 from minor irrigation projects, Rs. 7,000 from the Medical Department and Rs. 15,000 from the Public Works Department [Parratt (J), 2005: 170].

Apart from monthly and annual donations, the underground groups often resort to special drive for collection. They used to demand a huge sum amounting to lakhs of rupees from the well-to-do section as one time donation ostensively to meet the emergency need of the organizations.

Besides cash, sometimes tax is also collected in kinds. The militants ask for supplies like jackets, shoes, clothes, medicine, mobile sets, motorcycle, fuels, etc. In villages, although they do not demand cash, but tax in kinds like eatables, shelter and hospitality are demanded.

As far as the system of collection of extorted fund is concerned, the militant groups follow different methods for different groups of people. For salaried class of people, they follow exactly the pattern laid out by the income tax authority in the country. They collect the booty from the disbursement desk in one shot for all the employees in an office. The 'monthly donation' of the employees is deducted at source based on the agreed upon formula which ranges from 1.5 to 3 per cent depending upon the strength of a group. Thus public offices have been tamed to work as the back office of the insurgent groups. In order to buy peace, most of the public offices and institutions persuade their employees to comply with the dictates of the militant groups. As the state has utterly failed to protect the life and property of its citizens, denial to comply only invites death. In case of business, most of the groups settle for annual donation. Unlike the salaried group, there is no mechanism for collective payment. The militants, based on the perceived business turnover, negotiate an annual amount and get them collected either through agents or cadres.

As has already been mentioned, it is not only the amount of extortion which is a fear factor but the actions of the underground groups on the failure to accede to their demands. Evidences are plenty when the underground groups have resorted to severe actions when their demands are not met. In a press release by KCP on September 20, 2004, justified its extortion activities and said "the revolutionary movement could survive only on the goodwill of the people". It asked the people to honour the 'demand notes' and also warned of punitive actions in case anybody 'dares to defy'. On April 25, 2005, KYKL announced its 'new tax policy' where it was stated that the outfit will "stop serving donation letters for huge amounts and will collect extensive tax from the people". It was further stated that "money in bulk will continue to be collected from the corrupt officials, outsiders and from those who earn their money through dubious means" (www.satp.org). In 2002 KYKL (O) shot Dr. Bedikumar of Regional Institute of Medical Sciences (RIMS) in leg because, it alleged, he had refused to levy its tax of 1.5 per cent on RIMS employees. Again in 2004 the same group shot an officer of the state's Horticulture and Conservation Department in the thigh in pursuance of their demand for no less than Rs. 57 lakhs from the department [Parratt (J), 2005: 170-171]. Another incident which shocked everyone was the gunning down of three Catholic priests of the Don Bosco Training Centre at Ngariyan hill, about 10 kms south-east of Imphal on May 15, 2001. The police version was that KYKL (T) was behind the act for not paying the full amount of the huge monetary demand but the outfit denied the charges (Tarapot, 2005: 280). Again on November 10, 2005, KYKL exploded a bomb in Imphal city targeting a particular shop for refusing to pay the demand of tax. On October 21, 2005, PREPAK attacked the residence of Arambam Binodini,

Joint Director, Department of Tribal Development and Other Backward Classes for failure to meet the deadline for payment of extortion money. On November 27, 2006, the same group locked up main office of Manipur State Agriculture Department at Sanjengthong for refusal to pay money and again on December 12 of the same year the outfit hurled a bomb at the residence of the Director of Agriculture (www.satp.org).

These are only the tip of the iceberg of the various incidents relating to extortion and consequences of non-compliance. There are many more such incidents. Several senior officials including Chief Engineer (PWD), S. Binoykumar Singh, Chief Engineer (PHE), Thingom Ibochouba, Loktak Hydro Electric Project Chief Engineer, Subhas Chandra Ser, Director (Health services), Surchand Singh, a telecom department engineer, Ambe, Director (Tourism), Dasarath Prasad (IAS), executive engineer of Singda Dam project, A K Mathur, an assistant accounts officer of the project, T K Das, a contractor of the project, Phoni Bushan Verma, etc. fell to the bullets of the different underground groups for refusing to concede to their pressures (Tarapot, 2005: 279-280).

Highway extortion is another important source particularly for the groups operating in the hills through which the lifelines of Manipur run. The Naga and Kuki groups collect 'taxes' from all the vehicles plying through both the Imphal-Dimapur-Guwahati and Imphal-Jiribam-Silchar national highways since 1990. On August 6, 1996, the All Manipur Road Transport Drivers and Motor Workers' Union (AMRTDMWU) and Manipur Ttruck Owners Welfare Association submitted a memorandum to the Union Home Minister stating that the NSCN (I-M) cadres in the name of GPRN were collecting 'various taxes' ranging between Rs. 1,000 to Rs. 10,000 from every vehicle plying along these two highways. In another memorandum on March 12, 1999, the AMRTDMWU sought protection of road transporters and passengers on the highways alleging that the NSCN (I-M) members 'demanding and extorting with receipts in the name of GPRN 'from each and every truck as goods tax in the following rates: (1) from every gas cylinder truck, Rs. 2,000 per trip, (2) from every oil tanker, Rs. 3,000 per trip, (3) all the trucks carrying different goods: (a) truck carrying iron rods and scrap irons, Rs. 3,000 per trip, (b) trucks carrying cement, Rs. 1,000 per trip, (c) trucks carrying rice from FCI godown, Rs. 500 per trip, (d) trucks carrying essential commodities such as rice, pulses, edible oils and others, Rs. 700 to 800 per trip, (e) truck carrying sand, Rs. 300 per trip. The memorandum also pointed out that the NSCN (I-M) collected road taxes from the vehicles on the basis of Rs. 12,000 from every tourist bus, Rs. 7000 from every truck and Rs. 10,000 per annum per agent of gas cylinder (Tarapot, 2005: 57-58).

The most important source of rent seeking by the militant groups constitutes public works, development schemes and development projects. It is learnt that all the groups together collects 10-12 per cent of the project allocation from the implementing authorities and the booty is then divided among the groups based on certain agreed arrangement. This sum is collected through the public agencies at the district level. Very often, development projects are routed through a class of contractors either drawn from the close aids of the insurgent groups or from their commission agents (Das, 2002a). This intense rent seeking activities of the militant groups have a number of ramifications for the economy of the state.

First, insurgency legitimizes corruption. As the people working in public domain have to pay to the insurgents, they develop a tendency to get it compensated through corruption. Since the militant groups stand solidly behind these people, they get emboldened in their pursuit. Politicians, contractors, business class—all follow the footprints of the insurgent in sucking the development funds meant for the welfare of the ordinary citizens particularly the poor. It is learnt from discussion with the informed group of people that rent seeking by the people who control the state power is no less a menace than their insurgent counterparts. It is believed that around 45-50 per cent of a development project or public work is being siphoned off by both the state and non-state actors put together. The only difference is that while a part of the ill-earned money is ploughed back in the local economy by the state actors, the lion's share of the booty in the hands of the militant groups finds its way out of the state and very often out of the country to buy arms and other logistics. A conservative guesswork suggest that multilayer modes of rent seeking by the militants involves at least 15-20 per cent of the budgetary allocation of the state which stands to the tune of Rs. 633 crores as per the 2007-08 budgetary expenditure of the state. Thus, at least one-fifth of the budget of the state goes to oil the militancy machine of the state. Assuming half of this amount going for counter-insurgency operations, rent seeking by the state actors and the intermediary agents like the contractors and suppliers, another Rs. 317 crores is withdrawn from the productive services. Thus the actual size of the economy gets reduced to one-third due to the combined rent seeking from all quarters. This has a pernicious impact on the growth and development of the state.

Second, rent seeking by the insurgents acts as disincentive against entrepreneurial initiatives and capital formation particularly in non-farm urban sector, as the farm sector is not heavily targeted, of the economy. It penalizes the entrepreneurs for undertaking wealth and income creating pursuits. Any signs of accumulation, asset formation and wealth creation are immediately greeted with extortion notes. As a result, very often the idea dies before it fructifies and the baby is thrown away with the bath water. Only the entrepreneurships of violence thrive only to extend the horizon of despair and destitution for the ordinary citizen in the state.

A cross-section study conducted by the NSSO on the average fixed capital expenditure by the households during 2002-03, while taken as proxy for private investment, reveals the precarious situation of the urban non-farm sector in Manipur. As has been mentioned earlier, the impact of insurgency on the rural sector is felt only marginally. The average fixed capital expenditure per household in case of rural farm business in Manipur stands at Rs. 389, the second highest among the north eastern states. As the people in the valley of Manipur suffer from intense food insecurity, particularly during the blockades of the life lines of the state in the wake of inter-ethnic clash of interests, there is a consensus; it appears, across the shades of political ideology, about the need to protect the farm sector for the survival of the Meitei nation. Any contrary position taken by any entity will be at the cost of an erosion of public support for it.

Table 5.6
Average Amount (Rs.) of Fixed Capital Expenditure of Particular Type per Household during 1.7.2002 to 30.6.2003 in North Eastern States (Farm)

States	*Farm Business*					
	Rural			*Urban*		
	Cultivator	*Non-cultivator*	*All*	*Self-employed*	*Other*	*All*
Arunachal Pradesh	144	548	231	0	0	0
Assam	139	47	105	1	7	4
Manipur	389	119	336	17	80	52
Meghalaya	253	57	204	137	47	68
Mizoram	47	0	41	0	0	0
Nagaland	563	126	479	91	62	71
Tripura	13	0	5	32	0	11
All -India	942	74	593	296	72	154

Source: NSSO, 2006.

Table 5.7
Average Amount (Rs.) of Fixed Capital Expenditure of Particular Type per Household during 1.7.2002 to 30.6.2003 in North Eastern States (Non-Farm)

States	*Farm Business*					
	Rural			*Urban*		
	Cultivator	*Non-cultivator*	*All*	*Self-employed*	*Other*	*All*
Arunachal Pradesh	110	38	94	0	16	15
Assam	23	68	40	1566	78	780
Manipur	158	187	164	202	104	147
Meghalaya	8	447	118	654	3291	2672
Mizoram	16	696	113	346	330	337
Nagaland	544	232	484	1331	25	435
Tripura	75	20	40	9	14	12
All -India	372	403	384	1749	332	850

Source: NSSO, 2006.

As we have already mentioned, urban non-farm sector is the major target for extortion, the average fixed capital expenditure per household in urban non-farm business in Manipur stands at Rs. 147, third from the bottom (table 5.7). Thus, the average fixed capital expenditure per household in the rural sector is far better than the urban sector indicating the deleterious effects of insurgency in terms of heightened insecurity and rent seeking.

Third, rent seeking behavior of the insurgent groups and their collaborators leads to the low quality of public works. As has already been mentioned, 45-50 per cent of all project allocation, in general, is leaked in the pipeline and hence the quality of the project suffer and the high maintenance cost that follow make most of them economically unviable. This causes poor quality of infrastructure which in turn retards economic and social development.

Fourth, besides the actual economy, the rent seeking activities of the militant groups have tremendous effects on the potential economy. Insurgency directly affects business confidence and investment climates. Due to the high risk factor, private investment is hard to come by. Rather the business enterprises owned particularly by the 'mayangs' including the Marwaris, Punjabis, Sindhis and Bengalis are investing a part of their profit outside Manipur as a long term strategy so that if they are to wind up their business in the state so that they can fall back upon the alternative business opening elsewhere. This is leading to a large scale flight of capital from the state through non-institutional channels. The extent of flight of capital through institutional channels will be discussed next. While the private sector investment is shying off, public sector investment just melted down following its utter failure in the past, as already discussed in chapter 3, as well as adoption of market driven strategy of development adopted in the country following the economic reforms since early 1990s. Thus insurgent activities have shut the doors of investment only to cause the economy to languish in the morass of underdevelopment.

Flight of Institutional Capital

It has already been mentioned in the previous section that deteriorating security environment has led to flight of capital through both institutional and non-institutional channels. Besides the business sector and insurgent groups, a significant amount of fund also goes out of the state by way of transfer income. A sizeable segment of the student population from the state migrate every year to other pats of the country particularly to places like Delhi, Bangalore, Pune, Shillong and Guwahati for acquiring formal education. As the parents want to keep their wards from the war theatre, those who can support send their children out of the region. Safety of the child is, in fact, paramount in the minds of the parents. This causes a huge transfer of income from the state which is required for the up keeping of the children. Moreover, as Manipur is neither self-sufficient in food production nor has any industrial base of its own, a huge amount of fund moves out of the state in order to procure goods and services. It is, thus, not possible even to arrive at any reasonable conjecture as to what is the size of the transfer of fund through the non-institutional channel.

The flight of capital through the institutional mechanism can be partially captured through the trend in credit-deposit ratio of the scheduled commercial banks in the state.

Table 5.8
Deposits and Credit of Scheduled Commercial Banks of Manipur

(as on 31st March)

Year	*No. of Banks*	*Deposit (Rs. In Lakhs)*	*Credit (Rs. In Lakhs)*	*Credit-Deposit Ratio (percent)*
1992	84	10916	7925	72.60
1993	85	10511	8865	84.34
1994	85	14576	9524	65.34
1995	85	17742	9865	55.60
1996	85	23093	12406	53.72
1997	85	26421	15195	57.51
1998	85	28343	16657	58.77
1999	86	40622	16923	41.66
2000	87	46100	16800	36.44
2001	80	42300	16500	39.01
2002	79	61100	15500	25.37
2003	79	63900	18000	28.17
2004	77	81900	23800	29.06
2005	78	97200	39800	40.95
2006	78	121400	61500	50.66
2007	77	144000	76900	53.40

Source: Economic Survey Manipur 2006-07 & 2007-08.

It may be noted from table 5.8 that the number of bank branches has increased from 84 in 1992 to 87 in 2000. But this expansion of banking area could not be sustained primarily due to the problem of security. The number has gone down to 77 in 2004. Ten branches in the interior areas had to be closed down due to poor security environment. As far as the C-D ratio is concerned, it has declined from 84 per cent in 1993 to 25 per cent in 2002, a hopping 59 percentage point fall in 10 years. This fact indicates the tumultuous condition through which the banking system in the state had passed. A complete loss of confidence either on the part of the banking system on the prospect of loan recovery or the low business prospect perceived by the entrepreneurial class might have contributed to this great fall. After touching the bottom line in 2002, C-D ratio for the state started looking up and reached at 53 per cent in 2007.

Table 5.9

Credit-Deposit Ratio of Scheduled Commercial Banks in the North Eastern States (as on 31st March)

State	*1996*	*1998*	*2001*	*2002*	*2004*	*2005*	*2006*	*2007*
Arunachal Pradesh	10.4	13.1	17.2	15.8	17.2	24.4	25.07	26.81
Assam	39.3	32.9	32.4	31.4	30.8	34.4	41.97	43.30
Manipur	53.7	58.8	39.0	25.4	29.1	41.0	50.66	53.40
Meghalaya	14.4	15.2	16.8	18.0	36.9	45.3	39.36	35.84
Mizoram	16.2	23.2	25.6	25.9	38.3	51.0	51.52	53.89
Nagaland	27.4	18.3	14.0	12.6	16.9	22.9	22.32	28.90
Tripura	42.1	34.0	23.0	22.3	25.4	29.7	31.63	33.98
All India	61.9	55.5	58.5	62.3	58.7	66.0	72.50	75.02

Source: Basic Statistics of NER 2006, Economic Survey Manipur 2002-03, 2006-07 & 2007-08.

However, the C-D ratio of Manipur rather looks moderately good while compared with the same in other North Eastern states (table 5.9). In fact, Manipur is only marginally trailing behind Mizoram while the other North Eastern states are lagging far behind. One probable reason for a relatively higher C-D ration in Manipur might be traced to the system of determination of extortion amount from many small players by the insurgent groups of Manipur. The extortion/donation is based on the net pay of the salaried segment of the population as has already been pointed out. This fact encourages the salaried groups to borrow from the banks for buying the durable consumer goods, house sites, house construction, etc. As the repayment is made through equal monthly installment (EMI) which is deducted from the monthly salary, the quantum of net salary gets reduced and hence one has to pay less to the coffer of the insurgent groups. This hypothesis, however, needs to be verified. No studies have yet been undertaken to find the impact of the extortion demand on the consumer behavior. As a result future studies on this aspect might be revealing for the stakeholders of market economy.

Low Economic Growth

It has already been demonstrated in chapter 3 that the decennial compound growth of NSDP is declining over the years. It has declined from 7.37 per cent in 1961-70 to 6.84 per cent and 4.80 per cent in 1971-80 and 1981-90 respectively. It further declined to 4.68 per cent in 1991-2000 (table 3.29).

Similar trend is also found in case of per capita income. The decennial compound growth rate of per capita income declined from 4.16 per cent in 1961-70 to 3.81 per cent and 2.14 per cent in 1971-80 and 1981-90 respectively (table 3.29).

What is important to note is that the 7.37 per cent decennial compound growth rate of NSDP for the decade 1961-

70, which may be called as pre-insurgency period, was quite high. In fact the growth rate of Manipur was more than double to that of the national average (3.16 per cent, table 3.30). It has come down slightly during the early years of insurgency in the state during the 1971-80. Even then growth rate of NSDP in Manipur remained far higher than the national average (3.23 per cent, table 3.30). However, with northeastern region becoming the flashpoint of ethnic war during the 1980s particularly following the formation of NSCN (I-M) in Nagaland, ULFA in Assam, TNV in Tripura and PLA, KCP and PREPAK in Manipur, NSDP of Manipur has dipped down by more than two percentage points and fell below the national average (5.11 per cent, table 3.30). The intensity of militant activities remained very high althrough the 1990s in spite of peace initiatives like Assam Accord in 1985 and Mizo Accord in 1986. With the outbreak of Naga-Kuki conflict in 1992 and emergence of KYKL, the security environment in Manipur deteriorated to all time low and the NSDP had also touched to its all time low. However, following the adoption of 'new initiative for North East' in 1996 by the central government and subsequent creation of the central pool of resources for the development of North East as well as ceasefire agreement between the NSCN (I-M) and Government of India in 1997 that the economy of Manipur started looking up during 2001- 07 (table 3.29).

Thus, although it is difficult to establish inverse statistical association between the NSDP and insurgency, nonetheless qualitative evidences suggest that insurgent activities have severely affected the growth of the economy of Manipur.

Low Tax Base and Economic Dependency

Low economic growth has a significant bearing on resource mobilizing capacity of the state. As the size of the wealth creating population is small, the tax base has become very small. Moreover, since a significant size of the working population belongs to the scheduled tribes, who are out of the purview of taxation, tax revenue forms only an insignificant proportion of the total budgetary expenses of the state of Manipur. The size of the non-tax revenue largely depends on the resource endowments as well as the entrepreneurial skill of the state manifested particularly in the success of the public sector, as Manipur is neither resource rich nor has succeeded in creating a vibrant public sector enterprises, the non-tax revenue is also awfully insignificant. As a result, the state has failed to attain economic viability. The obvious outcome is the rise in fiscal dependency on the centre. While economic logic calls for gradual reduction of the dependency, which, in turn, necessitates creation of a competitive business environment, insurgent activities keep on pulling the economy in opposite direction. As no nation affords to live long on doles without compromising with pride and relative autonomy, insurgents, by waging political war and undermining the economic strength of the state, are standing on the way of consolidation of the Manipuri nationalism.

In case of Manipur we find that the share of tax revenue to total revenue receipts is very low. Althrough the years since 1980s, the share remained below 5 per cent. The same is the case with non-tax revenue whose share remained below 5 per cent althrough the years (table 5.10). This has led to economic dependency and the state is surviving on funds from the centre. The share of grants-in-aid from the centre account for more than 70 per cent of the total revenue receipts of the state. It may be recalled that the state also enjoys a liberal funding, being a part of SCS, and receives 90 per cent plan assistance as grant and 10 per cent as loan, whereas states other than SCS get 30 per cent plan assistance as grant and remaining 70 per cent as loan.

Table 5.10
Revenue Receipts of the Government of Manipur (% share)

Year	*State's Own Tax Revenue (a)*	*State's Own Non-Tax Revenue (b)*	*Share of Central Taxes (c)*	*State Own Revenue (a+b+c)*	*Grants-in-aid from centre*
1981	2.30	27.24	6.79	36.33	63.67
1985	3.53	3.04	7.45	14.02	85.98
1990	3.59	6.15	25.02	34.76	65.24
1995	4.02	8.45	30.64	43.11	56.89
2000	3.73	3.99	29.71	37.43	62.57
2001	4.70	3.99	15.65	24.34	75.66
2002	4.33	2.44	12.08	18.85	81.15
2003	4.91	4.25	14.17	23.33	76.67
2004	4.87	3.47	16.91	25.25	74.75
2005	4.67	4.01	16.47	25.15	74.85
2006	3.93	3.18	14.21	21.32	78.68
2007 (RE)	3.71	5.52	13.76	22.99	77.01
2008 (BE)	4.61	5.30	18.70	28.61	71.39

Source: Economic Review Manipur 1994-95 & Economic Survey Manipur 2006-07

RE – Revised Estimate; BE – Budget Estimate

Table 5.10 shows that a major part of the revenue comes from the centre. The state's own revenue which comprise of state's own tax revenue, state's own non-tax revenue and share of central taxes was 36.33 per cent in 1981. Since then it has declined to 34.76 per cent in 1990. It increased to 43.11 per cent due to increase in the share of central taxes in 1995 but it has declined to 37.43 per cent in 2000. Since 2000 the state's own revenue has declined due to decline in state non-tax revenue and share of central taxes. The state's own share in the total revenue receipts of the state is below 30 per cent althrough the years since 2000. In 2001 state's own share was 24.34 per cent of the total revenue receipts of the state. Its share had increased to 25.25 per cent in 2004 which came down to 21.32 per cent in 2006. It has increased marginally to 22.99 per cent in 2007 and to 28.61 per cent in 2008. One interesting feature is that the share of non-tax revenue is continuously declining over the years. Only recently in 2007 and 2008 the share of non-tax revenue has increased to 5.52 per cent and 5.30 per cent respectively. Even the share of central taxes kept on fluctuating althrough the years. With low tax revenue the state has become totally dependent on the centre for its functioning. The grants-in-aid from the centre account for more than 70 per cent of the total revenue of the state throughout the year since 2001. It implies that out of every rupee spent in Manipur more than 70 paisa comes from the centre in the form of dole. Manipur cannot earn even one-third of the expenses it incurs annually.

Be that as it may, the issue of economic viability might have nothing to do with insurgency in the state. Besides Manipur, there are states like Meghalaya, Mizoram and Arunachal Pradesh, where insurgency is not posing any serious challenge, which also lack economic viability. The argument that we intend to put forward is that it is all the more difficult for a state to reduce the dependency while the dictates of economic growth run in contradistinction with the dictates of militancy.

Increase in the share of Non-Development Expenditure

Looking from the point of view of the state management, increased investment in income generating economic activities can only address the issue of economic viability in the long run. This necessitates higher expenditure in development projects. This implies higher allocation for development expenditure, to use fiscal jargon.

Table 5.11
Revenue Expenditure of Manipur State Government
(% share)

Year	*Development Expenditure*	*Non-Development Expenditure*
1981	73.08	26.92
1985	66.55	33.45
1990	71.52	28.48
1995	63.18	36.82
2000	58.60	41.40
2001	54.17	45.83
2002	57.97	42.03
2003	54.03	45.97
2004	57.21	42.79
2005	57.35	42.65
2006	64.12	35.88
2007 (RE)	62.69	37.31
2008 (BE)	64.23	35.77

Source: Economic Review Manipur 1994-95, Statistical Abstract Manipur 1998, Statistical Handbook Manipur 2002 & Economic Survey Manipur 2006-07.

The revenue expenditure of Manipur (table 5.11) shows that the share of non-development expenditure is increasing over the years. This is expected in any conflict zone. Its share has increased from 26.92 per cent in 1981 to 28.48 per cent in 1990 and further to 41.40 per cent in 2000. In 2003 its share reached 45.97 per cent of the total revenue expenditure but subsequently decreased 35.88 per cent in 2006 and since then more or less remained constant till 2008.

A further look at the components of the non-development expenditure gives us a picture as to how the revenue has been spent by the government. Table 5.12 shows the components of the non-development expenditure out of the total revenue receipts of the state.

Table 5.12
Non-Development Expenditure and its components (% share)

Year	*Organs of State*	*Fiscal Services*	*Interest Payments & Servicing of Debts*	*Administrative Services*	*Pension & Misc. General Services*
1991	4.90	3.95	31.07	50.82	9.26
1992	5.15	3.79	24.82	46.04	20.20
1993	4.06	3.85	33.60	44.78	13.71
1994	4.70	3.74	31.51	46.14	13.91
1995	7.36	3.44	27.66	47.73	13.81
1996	5.55	3.55	27.48	47.85	15.57
1997	6.42	3.62	27.09	43.51	19.36
1998	5.15	3.93	28.69	42.54	19.69
1999	3.97	3.24	31.21	43.13	18.45
2000	4.72	3.36	23.65	42.16	26.11
2001	3.85	2.64	34.41	34.34	24.76
2002	3.28	2.72	34.05	34.96	24.99
2003	2.48	2.27	39.15	30.32	25.78
2004	3.69	2.43	34.39	32.91	26.58
2005	2.73	2.29	37.83	31.18	25.97
2006	3.11	2.86	33.02	37.48	23.53
2007 (RE)	3.54	2.34	33.28	35.21	25.63
2008 (BE)	3.45	2.04	34.91	35.60	24.00

Source: Statistical Abstract Manipur 1998 & Economic Survey Manipur 2006-07.

It may be noted that a major share of the non-development expenditure is spent on administrative services. Administrative services account for 50.82 per cent in 1991 but it came down in the succeeding years. Its share declined to 42.16 per cent in 2000 which further declined to 31.18 per cent in 2005. It again increased to 35.21 per cent and 35.60 per cent in 2007 and 2008 respectively. Higher expenditure in Administrative Services might be interpreted as due to the higher cost for the maintenance of law and order. With the rise of militancy, the network of counter-militancy activities has to be expanded, the size of the state security personnel has to expanded and armed, network of security blanket around the important installations, facilities, lifelines, public utilities and public figures has to be strengthened, casualty compensations have to be made—all these appear to have contributed to the higher expenditure under Administrative services. Besides Administrative Services, interest payment and servicing of debts also account for considerable non-development expenditure. In fact, as has already been discussed, with limited resource, the state has to borrow frequently in order to tie over with any emergency in order to ensure uninterrupted supply of public utility services in the wake of continuous efforts to sabotage them by the militant activists. Taking together, Administrative Services, and Interest Payments & Servicing of Debts explain, on an average, more than 70 per cent of the non-development expenditure.

Thus, the higher allocation for non-development expenditure necessitated due to the operation of militant groups ultimately reduces the fund allocation for development which has a strong bearing for the perpetuation of economic underdevelopment and ever rising fiscal dependence of the state on the centre. Further, as has already been pointed out, the lion's share of the development expenditure is incurred in social sector leaving the real sector of the economy deprived of resources. The consequent widening gap between these two has resulted in mounting pressure of unemployment in the state which has direct bearing on the growth of militancy. A further discussion on the nexus between unemployment and insurgency is in order.

Unemployment-Insurgency Nexus

Manipur is one of the highly literate states in India. But the high literacy rate is overshadowed by the higher unemployment rate. Manipur is suffering from a chronic unemployment problem. The avenues for employment are very extremely limited due to very weak industrial base of the state. There is a mismatch between educational level and employment opportunities.

Table 5.13
Literacy Rate (percentage)

Year		*Manipur*	*India*
	M	64.15	56.38
1981	F	34.67	29.76
	P	49.66	43.57
	M	71.63	64.13
1991	F	47.60	39.29
	P	59.89	52.21
	M	80.30	75.30
2001	F	60.50	53.70
	P	70.50	64.80

Source: National HDR 2001 & Statistical Abstract Manipur 2004.

Table 5.13 shows the literacy rate of Manipur vis-à-vis India in the census years. In the census year 1981 the literacy rate was 49.66 per cent in Manipur compared to all India level of 43.57 per cent. This increased to 59.89 per cent in

Manipur compared to all India level of 52.21 per cent in 1991 and further to 70.50 per cent in Manipur against all India level of 64.80 per cent in 2001. In both cases of male and female literacy rate Manipur performed well above the national average. Male literacy rate was 64.15 per cent in Manipur against the all India level of 56.38 per cent in 1981. It increased to 80.30 per cent in 2001 in Manipur against the national average of 75.30 per cent. Similarly female literacy rate in Manipur increased from 34.67 per cent in 1981 to 60.50 per cent in 2001 against the national average of 29.76 per cent and 53.70 per cent in respective years.

Table 5.14
Adult Literacy Rate in 1995-96 (percentage)

Particulars	*Manipur*	*India*
M	76.03	67.25
F	52.29	40.67
P	64.49	54.32

Source: National HDR 2001.

In case of adult literacy rate also Manipur is above the national average. In the year 1995-96 the adult literacy rate was 64.49 per cent against the national average of 54.32 per cent. Both male and female adult literacy rates were also above the national average. Male adult literacy rate in Manipur was 76.03 per cent against the national average of 67.25 per cent and female adult literacy rate was 52.29 per cent against the national average of 40.67 per cent (table 5.14).

The fact that Manipur is performing well in case of education above the national average is overshadowed by the lack of employment opportunities in the state. The state is suffering from chronic unemployment problem especially among the educated youths.

Table 5.15
Growth in Employment (Percent per Annum)

State/ Country	1983 to 1993-94			1993-94 to 1999-2000		
	Male	*Female*	*Persons*	*Male*	*Female*	*Persons*
Manipur	3.6	2.9	3.3	3.2	-0.3	2.0
India	2.2	1.7	2.1	1.9	0.9	1.6

Source: National HDR 2001.

Growth in employment is estimated as compound annual growth in the persons employed in the age group 15 years and above on the usual principal and subsidiary status. There is a decline in the growth in employment from 3.3 per cent per annum in 1983 to 1993-94 to 2 per cent per annum in 1993-94 to 1999-2000. The all India average was 2.1 per cent per annum and 1.6 per cent per annum in 1983 to 1993-94 and 1993-94 to 1999-2000 respectively (table 5.15). The condition is worse in case of female as their growth in employment declined from 2.9 per cent per annum in 1983 to 1993-94 to -0.3 per cent per annum in 1993-94 to 1999-2000 in Manipur. The national average was 1.7 per cent per annum in 1983 to 1993-94 which declined to 0.9 per cent in 1993-94 to 1999-2000. Growth in male employment declined marginally from 3.6 per cent per annum in 1983 to 1993-94 to 3.2 per cent in 1993-94 to 1999-2000. The national average was 2.2 per cent in 1983 to 1993-94 which declined to 1.9 per cent per annum 1993-94 to 1999-2000 (table 5.15).

The incidence of unemployment is defined as the percentage of persons unemployed in the age group 15 years and above on the usual principal and subsidiary status to the total number of persons in the labour force. The incidence of unemployment is very high in case of Manipur compared to the national average. It increased from 0.4 per cent in 1983 to 1.8 per cent and 3.5 per cent in 1993-94 and 1999-

Table 5.16

Incidence of Unemployment (as a percentage of labour force)

State/ Country	*1983*			*1993-94*			*1999-2000*		
	Male	*Female*	*Persons*	*Male*	*Female*	*Persons*	*Male*	*Female*	*Persons*
Manipur	0.6	0.0	0.4	2.2	1.0	1.8	3.7	3.1	3.5
India	2.3	1.3	2.0	2.1	1.7	2.0	2.5	1.8	2.3

Source: National HDR 2001.

2000 respectively. The all India figure was 2 per cent in 1983 and 1993-94 which increased to 2.3 per cent in 1999-2000 (table 5.16).

The low growth in employment and high incidence of unemployment show the chronic unemployment problem in the state indicating a severe mismatch between the literacy rate and employment opportunities in the state.

The sense of deprivation among the unemployed youths encourages them to join the bandwagon of the militancy. Many of them consider militancy as an alternative means of livelihood. Joining the struggle for social justice is often considered far better than sitting idle at home and confronting social slur. Out of sheer desperation, many start acting as the conduits before joining the militant groups as full timer. Even those who do not chart the path of militancy feel that the state is responsible for their apathetic condition and nurtures a soft corner for the so called revolutionary movements which indict the Indian state for the miseries of the people of Manipur. They become the passive supporter of militancy and at times play an active role in mobilizing social and political support for the undergrounds. Many of the educated youths become the victims of widespread corruption. In spite of being one among the equals they are often denied state privileges as they are not in a position to meet the demand for bribes. Being dejected, deprived and depressed, they turn into harsh critic of the existing political order. They fantasize about the role of the underground revolutionaries and at times fall back on them for getting justice. In the process, a symbiotic relation is established between the militant groups and the members of civil society which provides sustenance to the militancy machine.

It may also be pointed out that the 'surrender policy', as one of the anti-insurgency measures, in a way encourages the unemployed youths to join militancy. The surrender policy has been devised in order to persuade the militants to give up the so called revolutionary agenda and to join back the 'mainstream' where they can play a vital role by participating in the process of social reconstruction through democratic means. As a result the policy is laden with only carrots and no sticks. Insurgents who return back to the 'mainstream' receive hero's welcome, often painted as the success story scripted by the ruling power elites, financial allowances, state security, state accommodation, free skill oriented training, job assurances and above all the support and backing from the politicians particularly of the ruling elites. These heroes are then often used by the power-elites for electoral gains and, in turn, they also gain from their proximity to power in terms of licence, permits, contracts, and other state privileges. For the unemployed youths this path to become someone from no one is often tantalizing.

A study (Kshetri, 2006) on the emergence of Meitei nationalism has clearly established the unemployment-insurgency linkage in Manipur. Although the sample in the study is drawn from the early insurgent activists and hence does not reflect the changes taken that have taken place in the later years, particularly during the 1980s and 1990s, nonetheless the findings are no less important. Table 5.17 adopted from the study reveals that the majority of the activists joined the militancy in their youths (20-25 age). It is important to note that in a sample of 100, 36 activists joined even before attaining the age of 20, while youths are guided more by emotion than reason.

It may be noted that the study found that 87 per cent of the respondents had educational qualifications below graduation (table 5.18). Maximum participants were under matriculate (33 per cent), another 30 per cent of the participants were matriculate, and another 22 per cent were undergraduate. Out of 100, only 1 was found to have done post-graduation and another 12 had graduated. Although the formal academic degree as such has nothing to do with the perception of revolutionary callings, there is, perhaps, no scope for debate that understanding of the social reality and guiding the social change call for deep realization of social complexity and philosophical aptitude to translate the theoretical paradigms of social change into practice.

Table 5.17
Year of Joining and Activists' Age at the Time of Joining

Joining Year	*Age at the Time of Joining (Years)*				*Total*
	14-19	*20-25*	*26-31*	*32-37*	
1964	5	06	2	0	13
1965	7	14	0	0	21
1966	3	04	0	0	07
1967	5	10	1	1	17
1968	6	09	2	0	17
1969	7	09	2	0	18
1970	0	01	0	0	01
1978	1	00	0	0	01
1979	1	00	0	0	01
1980	1	02	0	0	03
1981	0	01	0	0	01
Total	36	56	7	1	100

Source: Kshetri, 2006: 101.

Table 5.18
Education of Participants at the time of Joining

Education	*No. of Persons*
Illiterate	01
Primary	01
High School	33
Matriculate	30
Undergraduate	22
Graduate	12
Post-Graduate	01
Total	100

Source: Kshetri, 2006: 103.

The sample of the study indicates that the militancy in Manipur is characterized by more brawn than brain. The predominance of the student participants in militancy might be taken as an indication of the strong role of ideology in the early phase of the movement. Ideology plays a very important role in motivating people in their tender age. Students are more than willing to sacrifice their career for a cause which they consider to be noble. As it is easy to mould a tender mind than to convince a matured person who develop a deep stake in the family, they become the easy target for the recruiters. The appeal of the ideology is perceived differently by different people depending on their socio-economic condition. The influence of the revolutionary ideology is expected to be more on a person who intensely feel the need for a social change rather than a contended person. Here comes the role of economic status of a person. Unemployed persons and would-be-unemployed youths are generally more sensitive and quickly respond to the revolutionary callings.

Table 5.19 adopted from the study (Kshetri, 2006) shows the unemployment-insurgency nexus. Out of 100 respondents, 97 were unemployed, taking the students and unemployed together. Furthermore, 84 per cent of the respondents had come from the low income brackets. Only 3 persons from high income group chose to join the militancy.

Table 5.19

Parents' Income and Participants' Occupation at the time of Joining

Income (Rs. Per month)	*Student*	*Unemployed*	*Govt. Service*	*Ex-service-man*	*Total*
I. 100-350	30	17	1	0	48
II. 350-600	35	04	0	1	40
III.600-850	07	01	1	0	09
IV. 850	02	01	0	0	03
Total	74	23	02	1	100

Source: Kshetri, 2006: 102.

Thus, economic and employment status of persons greatly influence their decision on the mode of political struggle. A desperate man seeks to bring about social change through actively participating in movements for social justice as perceived by him.

The trends found in the micro study (Kshetri, 2006) have, by and large, been corroborated by our sample consisting of 50 surrendered militants. Responses received against the question, "At what age do you join the underground movement?" are displayed in table 5.20.

Table 5.20

At what age did you join the underground movement?

Age group	*Frequency*	*Percent*
below 15	5	10.0
15-20	25	50.0
21-25	20	40.0
25+	0	0
Total	50	100.0

Source: Field Survey.

It is observed that all the activists joined the movement in their youths. This strengthens our hypothesis mentioned earlier that the militant ideology has very strong influence over the young generation of the population and the militant organizations also target them for fresh recruits.

As far as the educational background of the activists is concerned, the dominance of the undergraduate continues to prevail with 76 per cent of the total respondents. What is important to note is that the general level of the education of the activists has gone up over the years. Although there is no post graduate in our sample, but the fact that 22 per cent of the respondents have graduate degrees in various disciplines only indicates that joining militancy might have been a considered choice during the 1980s and 1990s (table 5.21).

Table 5.21
Educational background of the surrendered militants

Educational qualification	*Frequency*	*Percent*
Below Matric	03	6
Matriculate	17	34
Undergraduate	18	36
Graduate	11	22
Post Graduate	0	0
Others	1	2
Total	50	100

Source: Field Survey.

The hypothesis that the revolutionary ideology has a strong influence over the youths having weak economic background is further strengthened from the observations made in our sample. It may be noted most of the respondents have come from low income families (Table 5.22). However, neither the people having very weak family economic background (less than Rs. 2000 per month) nor the people having better family economic background (Rs. 10,000 and above) have joined the militancy in a big way.

Table 5.22
Monthly Family income of the surrendered militants

	Frequency	*Percent*
Less than 2000	5	10
2000-4000	23	46
4001-6000	16	32
10000 and above	6	12
Total	50	100

Source: Field Survey.

As far as the unemployment-insurgency nexus is concerned, the positive relation between these two may once again be observed from our sample as well. Unemployed youths and students together constitute 80 per cent of the respondents (Table 5.23).

Table 5.23
What did you do before joining the underground movement?

Occupation	*Frequency*	*Percent*
Unemployed	15	30.0
Farming	5	10.0
Students	25	50.0
Others	5	10.0
Total	50	100.0

Source: Field Survey.

Thus, weak family background and wide spread unemployment are the two major drivers that feed the militant movement in Manipur.

Sample Observations

We have conducted an opinion survey on the effect of militancy on the economic development of Manipur. The result of the survey is displayed in tables 5.24-5.25.

Table 5.24
Do you think UG activities negatively affect the economic development of the state?

Response	*Frequency*	*Percent*
Yes	224	74.7
No	67	22.3
Don't know	9	3.0
Total	300	100

Source: Field Survey.

Out of the total 300 respondents, 74.7 per cent feel that underground activities negatively affect the economic development of the state. Of course, many of them are of the opinion that the present mess is the result of poor governance and long deprivation of the people of the state. Another 22.3 per cent of the respondents said that the underground activities do not affect the economic development of the state. Some of them have suggested that whatever the enhanced central assistance the state is receiving is only due to the strong protest from the militant groups. The remaining 3.3 per cent of the respondent did not give any opinion on the issue apparently due to their inability to judge the situation.

When asked as to in what way the militant movements affect the economy of the state, the responses were varied. As many have mentioned of multiple causes, we have registered all the responses and counted them giving the equal weightage irrespective of the ordering in which they have been mentioned. Table 5.25 exhibits the responses.

It may be discerned that majority of the respondents believe that militancy negatively affects investment through siphoning of development funds and extortions. Besides these, political commotions that result from the operation of the insurgents and counter-insurgency operations by the security forces and manifest in the form of bandhs or blockades also negatively affect the economic development of the state. A significant size of the respondents feels that flight of capital from the state owing to insecurity also deters the development process in the state.

The conformity between our analysis based on the study of the processes supported by secondary data and the analysis of the observations based on the primary data strengthens the hypothesis that security environment and economic development are positively correlated. A better security environment ensures the protection of life and property, enables to enforce búsiness contracts, ensures business freedom, allows investment decisions to be governed by the forces of market and makes the business competitive. Thus a secure environment is development friendly. It allows the entrepreneurs and businesses to thrive. An insecure environment raises the risk premium and makes investment unattractive, shakes business confidence and penalizes entrepreneurial initiatives, and distorts the market signals only to push the economy to operate at low level equilibrium.

Table 5.25

How do underground activities affect the economic development of the state?

Economic development of the state is affected due to	*Response*				*Total*	
	Yes	*Percent*	*No*	*Percent*	*Respondents*	*Percentage*
Low investment	47	20.98	177	79.02	224	100
Rural to urban migration	1	0.45	223	99.55	224	100
Siphoning of development fund	136	60.71	88	39.29	224	100
Extortion/ donation/ subscription	150	66.96	74	33.04	224	100
Bandhs/ blockades	112	50	112	50	224	100
Flight of capital	11	4.91	213	95.09	224	100

Source: Field Survey.

Social costs of Insurgency

Besides economic costs, insurgent activities directly or indirectly affect the social norms and values. In most cases, insurgent groups try to acquire the image of the social reformers. They play the role of self-styled guardian of society and culture primarily to establish their credibility in the larger society. They often issue dictates against the social evils and assume the role of moral guardians. Although they proclaim for revolutionary social change, their actions very often strengthen the orthodoxy. The impact of militancy on education, health, individual freedom, democratic values, social institutions, governance, and culture is enormous. In the following paragraphs we shall make an attempt to capture these aspects.

Insurgency and Suppression of Freedom of Speech

Militancy and democracy do not go together. While democracy encourages public debate, discussion and analysis in order to choose the best options out of the alternatives for implementation of the greater-good of the society, militant organizations do not put themselves for public scrutiny. The authoritative structures of these organizations run along command and control procedure. They adopt top-down approach. Decisions are taken by the handful of top office bearers and instructions are passed down the line for execution. The decisions and judgments of the top leadership are not open to scrutiny and criticism. The regimentation of thoughts is considered to be extremely important for maintaining loyalty of the followers. As a result, freedom of speech and freedom of press are viewed as anti-revolutionary. The leaderships of insurgent groups are neither accountable to people, for whom they claim to have been waging the war, nor are they accountable to the lower rung members of their respective groups. Neither they lend themselves to public criticism, nor do they tolerate the same. Their only interest is to use the press for publicity in their favour and in this bid they flex their muscle to tame them sending overt or covert signals of threat to the life of the media people.

As an illustration, mention may be made of a recent incident of threat to the office bearers of the All Manipur Working Journalists' Union (AMWJU) from KCP led by Kokai of the KCP (Lamphel) group in June, 2008, demanding that the president and general secretary to meet the underground at a place outside the state or with its cadres at a place in a hill district and in case of failure they will not be allowed publication of newspapers or broadcast of news on the local cable network and will 'gift' bullets to each and every media house (IFP, June 23, 2008).

In similar vain, mention may be made of ban on the publication of 'Poknapham', a vernacular daily, published from Imphal, imposed by a group of the KCP (MC), L. Khuman faction, on August 3, 2008, on the pretext that it has failed to carry a statement of the group in the front page as per their demand. This has created lot of panic among the media in Manipur (IFP, August 7, 2008).

In fact the media is caught in cross-fire. On the one hand, if they carry the stories the way the insurgent groups want them to be, they are under threat from the state actors who accuse them of hobnobbing with the militants and initiates legal proceedings for the cancellation of their licenses, and on the other, if they do not fall in line with the demands of the militant groups, they risk their lives. It is, indeed, a Hobson's choice. Threats, intimidation, bans, attacks on the journalists are in fact an every day phenomenon in Manipur. As life is dearer than anything else; it is only natural that media-print or electronic-do accommodate the interest of the insurgent groups.

Nonetheless, under the banner of the AMWJU, the media persons are being increasingly organized and negotiating a space for the freedom of press. In fact with the evaporation of the space for civil society, media people are waging the lone battle to protect the right to freedom of speech and the freedom of press. Pradip Phanjoubam, the editor of IFP, once lamented, "In this age of democracy, few will ever doubt that the pen is mightier than the sword. That this truism has ceased to have any meaning in Manipur today only can mean one thing—the obituary for democracy and democratic values has long been written" (www.thestatesman.net).

Thus, the democracy and democratic values like individual freedom, freedom of speech and freedom of press—all are at stake. The insurgency machine has gagged the voice of freedom. As Sen (2006) viewed, lack of freedom leads to lack of development. Insurgency has really hit hard the democratic values and development in Manipur.

Insurgency and Cultural Regimentation

The militant ideologies are often camouflaged with the value systems of their respective societies. Militant organizations often attempt to protect the traditional community values. The ethnic symbols which are fast disappearing under the influence of cultural liberalism are often protected through dictates. Some of the Meitei militant groups favour the continuation of traditional culture and languages which they think are the markers of uniqueness of Meitei society. In August 29, 2001, KYKL issued an warning that Meitei women should wear traditional dress—i.e, phaneks or sarongs—and any violation of this dictate will be met with death penalty (www.satp.org). The same organization issued another dictates on January 6, 2005, asking the school authorities in the valley to adopt a dress code for the girl student of class IX and X who should wear only "eeyongphi", a traditional local women wear (www.satp.org). As the militant movement is overwhelmingly led by the men, who consider the women to be the torch bearer of Meitei culture, such dictates are often seen as patriotic rather than male chauvinist.

RPF had issued a dictate calling for a ban on the screening of Hindi movies in the 1990s. Most of the major militant groups like UNLF, KYKL and PREPAK have, overtly or covertly, supported the ban. It had been done with the intention to weaken the emotional integration of the Meitei people with the mainland India which will ultimately work in favour of the militancy.

Most of the militant groups favour the use of 'Meitei Mayek' scripts for Manipuri language instead of Bengali language. This issue has gained considerable support from some quarters of Meitei intelligentsia and student community. School text books written in Bengali scripts have been burnt down and immediate replacement was sought. A public committee under the banner of *Meetei Erol Eyek Loinshillon Apunba Lup* (MEELAL) (or the United Forum for Safeguarding Manipuri Script and Language) was formed to spearhead the movement. The activists of MEELAL have destroyed 1, 45,000 books at the Manipur State Central Library on April 13, 2005 (Phanjoubam, 2005). They overhauled the distribution channels of the vernacular dailies and compelled them to script switchover overnight. Very few could resist the pressure. MEELAL had the backing from KCP and KYKL. Thus a 300 years old script in use was sought to be replaced instantly with a script fallen out of use without the slightest understanding of the process of linguistic development.

It appears that under the patronage of the insurgent groups a cultural revivalist agenda is in action that seeks cultural regimentation rather than cross cultural fertilization of the Meitei ethnic culture. It may be pointed out that while a liberal culture could have accommodated the different ethno-cultural aspirations including that of the Nagas and

Kukis, the attempts towards Meiteiaisation of Manipuri culture is rather leading to the widening of the inter-ethnic cultural gaps. Insurgent groups and the ambassadors of Meitei orthodoxy are, in fact, working for the talibanization of Meitei culture and further balkanization of the ethnic cauldron of Manipur.

Be that as it may, different insurgent groups often undertake programmes of actions against social evils like imposition of ban on consumption of liquor and drugs, prohibition of malpractice in examinations by the students, crimes against women, chewing of tobacco, punishment against corruption, prohibition against the shooting of obscene video films, surfing pornography sites, screening of blue films, etc. Evil doers are often threatened with dire consequences including death penalty. Needless to mention that anybody who stands against corruption and social evils is certain to receive public support as the society in Manipur is reeling under deep neck corruption and degenerated values. It has already been pointed out that while on the one hand the rent seeking behavior of the insurgent groups encourages corruption at all level, association of some groups with drug trade has helped in spreading drug use among the youths of Manipur, on the other they declare crusade against these evils only to obfuscate their evil designs and to garner public support in their endeavour.

Insurgency and Brain Drain

The most pernicious effect of insurgency that involves a huge social cost is reflected by the mass migration of the talent from Manipur to other parts of the country. We do not have any systematic records on the migration of entrepreneurs, professionals, and other capable persons. However, out migration of students from Manipur may be taken as an indicator of talent loss. Out-migration of students may be approximated from the decline of student enrolment in the

Table 5.26

Educational Institutions, Teacher strength and Student Enrolment in Manipur

Types of Institutions	*1991*				*2001*			
	No. of Institutions	*No. of Teachers*	*No. of Students*	*Teacher Pupil Ratio*	*No. of Institutions*	*No. of Teachers*	*No. of Students*	*Teacher Pupil Ratio*
Pre-Primary/ Primary/JB/UJB	3190	11010	189238	1:17	2572	9811	207317	1:21
Middle/Jr. High/ Sr. Basic	687	6723	74932	1:11	784	7935	145288	1:18
High/Higher Secondary	430	7770	129262	1:17	614	12097	236470	1:20
School for Professional & other education	2494	2832	70544	1:25	78	383	5933	1:15
College for general education	29	1127	39124	1:35	61	1411	20536	1:15
College for Professional & other education	33	249	3010	1:12	13	29	830	1:29
Universities	1	148	1272	1:9	2	189	877	1:5

Source: Statistical Abstract Manipur 2005.

educational institutions in the state. Table 5.26 provides a detail situation prevailing in the formal education sector of the state.

It may be noted that technical, vocational and higher education segments have been largely affected in the state. As has already been mentioned, parents prefer to send their wards outside the state when they finish school education in order to keep them away from the theatre of wars. When the students pass out higher secondary, they attain the age of 18+ which is considered to be the vulnerable age during which they are targeted and drawn into militancy. The student enrolment in general college education has declined from 39124 in 1991 to 20536 in 2001, registering a fall in enrolment by about 48 per cent in just 10 years (Table 5.26) although the number of colleges has gone up from 29 to 61 during this period. Student enrolment in professional college education has declined from 3010 in 1991 to 830 in 2001, registering an even higher decline by 72 per cent. This might have caused primarily due to the closure of a number of professional institutions which has gone down from 33 to 13 during this period. Besides professional colleges, number of professional schools has also sharply declined from 2494 in 1991 to only 78 in 2001. At the post-graduate level, student enrolment has declined from 1272 in 1991 to 877 in 2001, registering a decline by 31 per cent.

Students from Manipur are increasingly moving to Indian metros like Delhi, Bangalore, Pune and Chennai in order to pursue higher education. Those who succeed in making a good career hardly come back to the land of Labyrinth. Thus, the general sense of insecurity has created a tremendous push factor for the energetic youths and in the minds of their parents who no longer consider Manipur to be the safe place for their future attainments. Due to this mass out migration of creative, energetic and vibrant minds, the social space is increasingly being filled by the left outs, residuals, and below average performers only to join in the bandwagons of militancy soaking their mind with brutality and ethnic hatred. A further study in this aspect will be more revealing.

Insurgency and the Collapse of Health Care Services

Like education, health care services also have collapsed in the state. It is not possible to construct a credible picture based on the secondary data dished out by the health department of the Government of Manipur. Ground reality is hardly reflected in government statistics. While the conventional parameters, used in measuring the quality and access to health care services, like number of hospitals, number dispensaries, hospital/dispensary per thousand population, population per doctor, bed per thousand population, population per nurse, midwives and dais, population per bed, etc, project a rosy picture of the health care services in the state, as shown in table 5.27, the ground experiences are completely different. It is learnt that health care services particularly in rural areas in the hills do exist only in paper. Primary Health Centres have been constructed, doctors were appointed, para medics are appointed, but only on paper. In reality, doctors hardly visit those rural primary health care centres where they have been appointed, para medics, if they are from local area, sometimes work, if from outside hardly visit the work place, they stay either in Imphal or in other district towns and draw their salary without any work. They cite insecurity being the reason for their absence. As the state cannot ensure the security of its employees, it does not assert accountability.

Thus, rural health care services largely depend on the traditional tribal medicine men. As the ethno-medicine practitioners among the Kukis and Nagas play a pivotal role in the far flung villages, the morbidity and mortality rates among them do not pose any serious concern. Moreover, the healthy food habits of the rural tribals, as they consume very less oil and spices, harsh topography that requires heavy physical exercise in conducting day to day business, pollution free natural environment, cool climate, higher sense of general hygiene due to Christianity—all these contribute to the higher standards of general health. Thus, poor conditions of health care services get neutralized by the higher health standards. As a result reflections of the poor health care services are not felt in morbidity and mortality statistics.

Table 5.27
Health Care Services in Manipur

Item	*1971*	*1981**	*1991*	*2001*	*2006*
No. of Hospitals— (including PHCs)	25	44	90	103	101
No. of Dispensaries (including PHSCs)	99	190	472	440	440
Population in '000 per Hospital/ Dispensary	8.65	6.07	3.27	4.22	4.66
No. of Doctors	115	242	681	909	888
Population in '000 per Doctor	9.33	5.87	2.70	2.52	2.84
No. of Nurses, Midwives & Dias	340	454	611(*)	1064	1055
Population in '000 per Nurse, Midwives & Dias	3.16	3.13	3.01	2.16	2.39
No. of Beds	832	653	1873	2286	2290
Population per bed	1289	2176	980	1003	1100

Source: Statistical Handbook of Manipur 1992; Economic Survey Manipur 2007-08.
* Excludes RIMS
(*) Nurses only

Although the situation in rural plains is not as grim as the rural hills, primarily due their proximity to the state capital, nonetheless health care services even in Imphal are under duress. Medical institutions, professional and drug store business in Imphal city—all are under severe threats. Incidents in RIMS may be cited as a pointer in this regard.

In July 2008, KCP(MC) hurled bombs at the residential quarter of the chief accountant of RIMS, Mr. E. Debendro Singh, and its superintendent Dr. Y. Mohen (IFP July 5, 2008), the organization had also threatened to target top officials and employees of the RIMS for violating their diktat by the authority of the Institute. The KCP (Ibungo Ngangom) group has abducted 2 engineers of RIMS, Mr. Ng. Robindro Singh and Y. Surjit Singh, on December 10, 2008 and demanded Rs 3 crores as ransom (IFP, Dec. 11, 2008). The KCP (Ibungo Ngangom) also warned the director, deputy director, medical superintendent, chief account officer and the heads of department of RIMS who protested against the abduction activity.

As RIMS being at the apex institution in providing medical care in the state where more than 3 lakh patients per year are being treated, a continuous threat to its more than 1600 staffs had made the matter worse. Besides RIMS, other medical practitioners in Imphal are also facing the onslaughts of the militant groups.

While at RIMS professional bodies like Teachers' and Medical Officers' Association, Junior Association, Non-teaching Employees Association and Trained Nurses Association are actively building up resistances against the militant dictates and onslaughts, private practitioners are really helpless and have little options other than give in to the whims of the militants. Attacks on the health workers only reveal the brutal image of the militancy in the state.

Insurgency, Drugs Trade and Menace of HIV/AIDS

Insurgent groups in North East in general and Manipur in particular use the hills of Myanmar across the border as their springboard. A long 1643 km Indo-Myanmar border touches Manipur, Nagaland, Mizoram and Arunachal Pradesh. The ethnic war groups of Myanmar like the Kachins, Karens, Mons, Shans, Chins, Kayah, Rakhine and Wa, who have been fighting against the Burman dominance since Independence, have skillfully integrated insurgency with drug production and trade. In fact drug trade has been the driver of ethnic insurgency in Myanmar (For more details, Lintner, 1994). As the militants in Manipur are trained under one or other ethnic insurgent groups in Myanmar, some of them have adopted this model and found it viable and profitable enterprise to fund their war in the absence of any substantial local resource base. It is hard to identify their actual *modus operandi*. What can be ascertained is that they play the feeder role within the Golden Triangle drug trail. As they play the role of the career, the spillover effects are felt in Manipur. Youths are easily taken to drugs due to its easy availability in the surroundings The fact that the UNLF cadres including its chairman Meghen were captured and jailed in Burma in 2001 for drug trafficking (Egreteau, 2006) only establishes the linkage between insurgency and drug trade. Assam police had seized 27,000 capsules of spasmoproxyvon, a potent analgesic, used by intravenous drug users, from the activists of People's United Liberation Front (PULF), a Manipur based militant group, in Guwahati in April, 2008 (Hussain, 2008). However, the insurgent groups are not the only players involved, many people living in both sides of the Indo-Myanmar border, due to lack of opportunities, play either active, as drug peddlers and careers, or passive, as logistic provider, role in this trade. It is even alleged that a section of the border security forces also work in tandem with the drug barons across the border. Due to physical, ethnic, and linguistic affinities between people of the both sides of the border, it has become all the more difficult to identify and control of drug smuggling along the border. In fact, heroin and other synthetic pharmaceuticals illegally trafficked from Myanmar into India's North East has led to a rise in drug abuse and HIV epidemic in the region particularly in the bordering states of Manipur, Mizoram and Nagaland.

Since 1986 upto October, 2007, the number of blood samples screened is 156490 samples, out of which 22053 is reported HIV positive giving us sero-positivity rate of 14.09 percent. This shows that out of every 100 sample 14 are reported HIV positive. Again out of the same sample, 4154 cases of AIDS have been reported giving a rate of 2.65 per cent (table 5.28). In fact Manipur has the highest HIV prevalence in all the states in India. One can imagine the gravity of the situation given the state's high literacy rate and low per capita income.

Table 5.28
Yearly trends of HIV/AIDS Sero-Surveillance

Year	*No. of Blood Samples screened*	*No. of HIV Positive reported*	*No. of AIDS Cases reported*	*No. of Deaths due to AIDS*
1	*2*	*3*	*4*	*5*
1986	371	-	-	-
1987	970	-	-	-
1988	528	-	-	-
1989	828	-	-	-
1990	3147	961	4	4
1991	2223	422	0	0

(Contd...)

1	*2*	*3*	*4*	*5*
1992	3409	351	0	0
1993	4204	254	8	4
1994	16958	1137	56	11
1995	2926	429	36	11
1996	2021	557	114	35
1997	2117	757	83	29
1998	2779	984	61	6
1999	3436	1037	196	29
2000	4859	1242	203	18
2001	4329	1192	286	51
2002	6195	1389	632	73
2003	5423	1419	1187	133
2004	6854	2019	461	65
2005	13481	2394	297	48
2006	31811	2749	324	50
2007 (Oct.)	37621	2710	206	32
Total	156490	22053	4154	599

Source: Manipur State AIDS Control Society.

Thus, the social cost of militancy in Manipur is unimaginable. It is believed that there could be 1 lakh intravenous drug users in the state and majority of them are HIV positive (The Shillong Times, April 9, 2005). The drug epidemic has spread like a bonfire particularly among the young generations. When the situation is fast running out of control, some insurgent groups like KYKL and RPF issued dictates banning the use of drugs and vouched for capital punishment for both the drug peddlers and users. KYKL had gun downed a woman peddler in 2005 and shot another two peddlers at legs in 2004 as part of their ONK launched to free the state from the menace of drug addiction (The Shillong Times, April 9, 2005).

Insurgency and the stress on the Social Institutions

Besides drug addiction that has enormously increased the level of anxiety and stress of both the institutions of family and civil society, the recruitments of the children by the militant organizations has been another area of great concern. In July, 2008, several valley based militant groups like PREPAK (Vice President), PREPAK (General Secretary) and KCP (MC) undertook a special drive for new recruitments. Teenage boys and girls were targeted and kidnapped forcefully particularly either on their way to school or back home. Several children were reported missing and these incidents created a huge panic in the families and society at large. Many such incidents have been reported to media and there were outbursts of protests from the students, parents, civil bodies, and institutions in all the valley districts (IFP, July 16, 18, 20,21,25,26, and August 9, 2008, The Sangai Express, July 22, 25, 29, 2008). The anxiety level has gone up to such an extent that in several places cadres of various groups have been beaten by the local people for their alleged involvement with kidnapping of the school going teenagers. PREPAK owned up the responsibility and paraded a number of teens before the media who admitted that they have joined the organization on their own volition in order to serve the cause of the motherland (IFP, July 20, 2008).

Like Naosekpam Thoithoiba, 12 year old son of N. Tomba of Uripok Achom Leikai, Nongthombam Naoton, 14 year old son of N. Kumar of the same locality; 13-year old Ak. Ajoy, son of Ak. Ibungo, and Ak. Bipinchandra, 13 year old son of Ak. Ranjit, both residents of Thoubal Kiyam Siphai, Pebam Bishorjit, 13 year old son of P. Rojit of Kiyamgei Awang Leikai and 15-year old Ningombam Sarda, daughter of late

N. Ningthemjao of Pishum Ningombam Leirak—20 new children who recently joined the outfit were paraded before the media to convey the message that they have voluntarily joined the organization (IFP, July 20, 2008).

One can understand the truth when teenagers speak of the need for social revolution! There has been tremendous social anger against the insurgent groups and spontaneous public protest all over the valley districts. Many parents stopped sending their wards to school for the time being for fear of being kidnapped. This has led PREPAK to tender public apology for their misdeeds and UNLF to abrogate the policy of child recruitment (IFP, July 22, 2008). These incidents revealed only the tip of the iceberg of the malady of recruitment of the child soldiers by the insurgent groups. In their bid to carry on the struggle for so called social justice, the militant groups put the security of the children at stake, who needed the love and care of the elders most.

Insurgency and drug addiction have some other pernicious effects on the family. The numbers of unmarried girls, divorce, and widow-headed families in the societies of Manipur are on the rise. All these have put tremendous stress on the family and the society who find it hard to adjust with.

Besides the family, the functioning of other institutions like schools, colleges, medical institutions and public offices is also at stake due to the intense interference on the part of the militant groups in Manipur. Not only these institutions have to abide by the extortion notices served on them by the different underground organizations, as mentioned earlier, their day-to-day activities are also badly affected by the dictates of the militant groups. Their recruitment process, promotion decisions, the transfer decisions, work allotment decisions—all are under the surveillance of the insurgent groups. In case of a recruitment drive, different insurgent groups send their list of candidates and ask for compliance.

It creates a panic among the official higher ups as to who should be chosen for the job. As all cannot be accommodated, choosing one and rejecting others is interpreted as favouring one over the other group and the revenge from the rejected group will immediately follow.

Employees competing for promotion often use their underground connections to have mileage over others. Different underground organizations come up with different lists of people for promotion and ask the authority to comply with. Same thing happens with transfer posting. As everybody wants to be posted at the headquarters, in their bid to achieve the goal, they bring the undergrounds into the picture often only to maintain the status quo. For public works and government supply contracts, different groups come up with different lists and demand compliance.

Thus, the job of decision making is at stake. In order to avoid risk, often underground connections are given priority over efficiency parameter. As a result, it generates frustrating effects for them who compete on the strengths of efficiency and experience. At times, vital developmental decisions are kept in abeyance for indefinite period or are taken by the incompetent people having strong underground connections. Very often a person having low personal profile goes ahead of other having high personal profile due to the former's connections with the underground groups who wield their power for their client. Thus, the patron-client relationship between the insurgent groups and a section of the people has negatively affected the quality of decision making and the polity management in the state.

Militarization of the Society and Human Rights Violation

The security forces engaged in counter insurgency activities in the state are no less dreadful than the underground groups. While it is true that many innocent civilians have become the victims of the underground groups, it is also equally true in case of the security forces, who, in the name of counter insurgency activities, have been brazenly violating the basic human rights. Let us mention some of the cases before we assess the situation.

Heirangoithong Incident, 1984

The fateful day was March 14, 1984, when the CRPF jawans, while confronting the underground activists, killed 13 innocent civilians and injured 36 others. The CRPF jawans and some 3000 people were watching a volley ball match between the teams of Manipur Rifles and Border Security Force on that fateful day at Heirangoithong area in the outskirts of Imphal. During the course of the game some armed underground men fired upon the CRPF jawans killing one of them and injuring five and snatched away three self loading rifles, one grenade firing rifle and some other ammunitions. In retaliation the CRPF jawans started firing in all directions killing 13 innocent civilians and injuring 36 others. The government version said that the civilians were killed in the crossfire but the report of the enquiry commission headed by the then District and Sessions Judge of Manipur, Justice Y. Ibotombi Singh; found that the civilians were killed by the CRPF jawans who started firing indiscriminately in order to avenge the death of their colleague (Tarapot, 2005: 256-258).

RIMS Incident, 1995

It was about 7 in the morning of January 7, 1995, when some armed underground activists opened fire at the CRPF jawans posted at the RIMS gate while they were inside the toilet complex attending the morning needs. A jawan was seriously injured. In retaliation the jawans fired at the suspected persons and in the course 9 innocent civilians including a student of the institute from Arunachal Pradesh were killed. The rest were an employee of the institute, a driver of the institute, five auto rickshaw drivers and a rickshaw puller. The enquiry commission of the incident headed by a retired judge of the Guwahati High Court, Justice D. M. Sen, found that the deaths of the civilians were purely due to the actions of the CRPF jawans who resorted to firing after the suspected persons had retreated (Tarapot, 2005: 260-262).

Tonsen Lamkhai Incident, 1999

On October 3, 1999, some underground activists ambushed a CRPF team at Tonsen Lamkhai area in Thoubal district at around 1.15 pm killing seven CRPF personnel on the spot. In retaliation, the CRPF personnel returned fire killing one underground activist and ten innocent civilians who happen to pass by the area. Among the civilians killed were some of the passengers of a bus carrying polling personnel which happened to pass that area during that hour. While the CRPF authorities denied the charge of opening fire at the civilians and maintained all were killed in the crossfire, the survivor of the incident maintained that the civilians were killed by the CRPF personnel at close range. It was later on learnt that the ambush was carried on by MPA, the armed wing of UNLF (Tarapot, 2005: 262-264).

Malom Incident, 2000

Not long after the Tonsen incident, a similar incident took place in Malom area near the Imphal airport. On November 2, 2000, a powerful bomb planted by some underground activists exploded at around 3.30 pm and injured some Assam Rifles personnel. The jawans in retaliation opened fire in all directions killing ten civilians including a woman and her two nephews. Assam Rifles denied the charges and the findings of the magisterial inquiry were also not made public (Tarapot, 2005: 266-267).

It may be noted that in all the four cases mentioned above, security forces were attacked first and the burnt of the fury fell on the civilians. The hit and run urban warfare strategy of the insurgent groups designed to draw the civilians into conflict appears to aim at intensifying the wrath of the people against the security forces. This simultaneously serves two purposes. First, to pull down the moral of the security forces by conducting surprise attack on them. Second, intensifying anti-Indian sentiments of the people as the security forces are seen as the representative of the Indian state. The more the anti-Indian sentiments grow, the more is the prospect of new recruits. The support base of the insurgent groups expands particularly among the victims of the security excesses. Some kith and kin of the victims join militancy in order to take revenge. As the insurgents project themselves as patriotic revolutionaries, their valour in fighting the security forces is often eulogized. The security excesses are looked as anti-national (in the sense of ethnic nationalism).

What angers people most is the fact that in spite of killing the innocents, security personnel go scot free. As they are shielded by AFSPA they cannot be made accountable for their misdeeds. The Act provides wild powers in the hands of the security agencies. Section 4 of the Act[1] empowers a commissioned officer, warrant officer, non-commissioned officer or any other person of equivalent rank to fire upon any body to the extent of causing death or use force against anybody in order to maintain the law and order. Besides blanket power to kill people, the concerned officer is also empowered to arrest anybody without any warrant even under suspicion, and enter any premises with out any search warrant.

Given these wide powers, security forces often assume the role of supra-state and in the name of counterinsurgency operations trample the basic human rights of the people. Since the imposition of the Act in 1980, innumerable cases of civilian deaths, harassment, torture, molestation and rape have been reported. There are also a number of persons whose whereabouts are not known till today after being arrested by the security forces. Tarapot (2005) listed a number of such cases.

There has been a growing resentment among the people in the region in general and Manipur in particular against AFSPA. Just after the Malom incident, a 32 year old woman, Irom Sharmila went on fast unto death from November 4, 2000 demanding immediate withdrawal of the Act. She was arrested and is kept under nose feeding till today in the judicial custody. Sharmila's long fight for social justice has inspired the people of this state to join the protest which took an altogether different dimension following the brutality against Manorama Devi.

Manorama's Case

In 2004 an incident took place which sparked wide public protests all over the state. A woman of about 30 years, Thangjam Manorama, was arrested on July 10, 2004, by 17th Assam Rifles battalion from her residence at Bamon Kampu area in Imphal East district after serving an 'arrest memo'. In the following day her bullet ridden body was found near her house. It was alleged that she was an activist of an underground organization. The discovery of human semen stains on her undergarments had proved beyond doubt that she was raped before her killing. The 'Apunba Lup', an apex body of 32 organizations spearheaded the movement and demanded immediate withdrawal of the AFSPA. On July 15, 2004, twelve brave women protested the Manorama's incident in naked by holding placards which read 'Indian Army Rape Us', 'Indian Army Take Our Flesh' in front of the Assam Rifles Office in Imphal, the present Kangla Fort. Perhaps this is the first incident in the world where women had to resort to such kind of protest to register their legitimate grievances against the men in uniform. A 28 year old student, Pebam Chittaranjan, self-immolated demanding withdrawal of the

Act. In the face of steep public protest, the government of India withdrew the Act from the Imphal municipality areas only (Tarapot, 2005: 14-15).

Thus, the misplaced territorial security perception of the armed forces and the Indian state has led to the collapse of human security in the state. Ordinary people live in a constant fear of bumping into the conflict between the insurgent groups and security forces. We have tried to capture people's feeling of insecurity in our field survey. The observations are given below.

Sample Observation

In response to the query: "Do you feel insecure?" more than 85 per cent of the respondents answered in affirmative. About 13 per cent of the respondents answered in negative (table 5.29). This shows that people in general live in fear psychosis.

Table 5.29

Do you feel insecure?

Response	*Frequency*	*Percent*
Yes	256	85.3
No	40	13.3
Don't know	4	1.3
Total	300	100

Source: Field Survey.

On being asked to reveal the causes of feeling insecure, many of the respondents opted for multiple reasons. However, we have taken all the responses into account and classified them against the category of response instead of working out the distribution of responses over the size of the sample. As a result every category of response is weighted against the size of the sample.

About 57 per cent of the respondents perceive underground activities by the militants as the source of insecurity. About 68 per cent of the respondents feel that army operations are the potential source of insecurity. Only 19 per cent of the respondents perceive police excess to be the source of insecurity. More than 49 per cent of the respondents find deteriorating law and order condition in the state as the source of insecurity. And only about 7 per cent of the respondents find limited economic opportunities as the source of insecurity (Table 5.30).

Table 5.30
Why do you feel insecure?

Reasons for insecurity	*Response*				*Total*	
	Yes	*Percent*	*No*	*Percent*	*Respondents*	*Percentage*
Underground activities	145	56.64	111	43.36	256	100
Army operation	173	67.58	83	32.42	256	100
Police excesses	48	18.75	208	81.25	256	100
Deteriorating law and order situation	127	49.61	129	50.39	256	100
Limited economic opportunity	17	6.64	239	93.36	256	100

Source: Field Survey.

If percentage response is taken as the measure of weight, then it is obvious that people of Manipur are more worried from the operation of the security forces than the actions of the insurgent groups. This pattern of responses might be the reflections of Meitei nationalism which has grown through opposition against the Indian state as has been discussed in chapter 2.

Very few respondents perceive that absence of economic opportunities as the cause of internal insecurity which only strengthens our hypothesis that economic underdevelopment is not the sole cause for internal insecurity.

Against the query: "Do you think your fundamental rights have been curtailed?" more than 75 per cent of the respondents answered in affirmative (table 5.31).

Table 5.31
Do you think your fundamental rights have been curtailed?

Response	*Frequency*	*Percent*
Yes	226	75.3
No	71	23.7
Don't know	3	1.0
Total	300	100

Source: Field Survey.

On further question as to in what way one feels that the fundamental rights have been curtailed, majority of the respondents (85 per cent) linked it to the lack of freedom of speech in the society. Another 73 per cent of the respondents reported the lack of freedom of movement being the cause that has curtailed the fundamental rights of the people in Manipur.

Table 5.32
How are your fundamental rights curtailed ?

Fundamental rights curtailed because	*Response*				*Total*	
	Yes	*Percent*	*No*	*Percent*	*Respondents*	*Percentage*
Cannot express freely	194	85.84	32	14.16	226	100
Cannot move freely	166	73.45	60	26.55	226	100

Source: Field Survey.

Thus, as has been discussed, rights and freedoms of the individuals in Manipur have been caught into the cross-fire. The democratic values and institutions, which people have reason to value, have become the proverbial sacrificial goat and the space for civil society has got sandwiched between the militant groups and security forces. Governmentality and the legitimacy of the state are at stake in Manipur.

The Conflict Trap

The economy and polity in Manipur have been caught into a conflict trap. The vicious cycle of insurgency, a product of historical neglect and consequent underdevelopment of the economy and polity, and counter-insurgency operations keep on generating seamless specter of violence that cripple all efforts towards social development. Perceived sense of neglect and deprivation, aided by the strategic location, has led a section of the youths to opt for arms struggle as means to achieve social justice. This movement, in due course of time, got entangled with the game of the foreign powers to give birth insurgency. Counter-insurgency measures crafted by the Indian state in order to contain insurgent activities have only added fuel to fire. The imposition of the draconian AFSPA that has given wide power in the hands of the security forces and its misuse has further widened the feeling of deprivation and mistrust. The victims (direct or indirect) of security excesses keep on joining the insurgent groups in order to take revenge against the Indian state. Thus the vicious cycle of insurgency and counter-insurgency keeps on going without any sign of abatement.

The economy of Manipur is caught into the vicious cycle of insurgency and underdevelopment. The brutal method of rent appropriation by the insurgent groups has made fresh private investment risky and insecure and caused flight of private capital from the state. Low investment, in turn, has led to low income generation and limited economic openings.

These have led to high unemployment in the state. A section of the unemployed youths, in absence of alternatives, join militancy. Thus, the vicious cycle of insurgency and underdevelopment continues to operate in Manipur.

In fact the vicious cycle of insurgency and underdevelopment operates at multiple levels. It has already been pointed out that a huge amount of fund is raised by the insurgent groups through extortion and the lion's share of that fund is used for unproductive purposes. A significant part of it goes out of the state to buy arms and ammunitions and other logistics. This drain of resources keeps the economy perpetually underdeveloped.

As has already been pointed out, development projects are heavily extorted. This has led to poor capital formation and perpetuation of underdevelopment in the state. Furthermore, it may be reminded that a significant size of students move out of the state particularly for higher education. The overall insecure environment acts as the push factor as the parents want to keep their wards out of the theatre of war. As a result, while the institutional resources in the state remains under utilized, a sizeable fund moves out of the state in the form of transfer income in order to support the children who study outside.

As we have already delineated the linkages between insurgency and development, it appears that there exists a trade off between these two. Both cannot be sustained at the same time. Insurgent activities have clear detrimental effects on the pursuits of development. Besides economic development, human development is also at stake. Democratic values, individual freedoms, public debate and criticism over social choices cannot flourish while the power of guns is counted more than wisdom. The appropriate policy intervention needed to break the multi-layer vicious cycles that sustain insurgency and underdevelopment will be taken up in the concluding chapter.

NOTES

1. The Section reads as follows:
"Special power of the armed forces – any commissioned officer, warrant officer, non-commissioned officer or any other person of equivalent rank in the armed forces may, in a disturbed area, - (a) if he is of the opinion that it is necessary so to do for the maintenance of public order, after giving such due warning as he may consider necessary fire upon or otherwise use force, even to the causing death, against any person who is acting in contravention of any law or order for the time being in force in disturbed area prohibiting the assembly of five or more persons or the carrying of weapons or of things capable of being used as weapons or of firearms, ammunition or explosive substances;

(b) if he is of opinion that it is necessary so to do, destroy any arms dump, prepared or fortified position or shelter from which armed attacks are made or likely to be made or are attempted to be made, or any structure used as training camp for armed volunteers or utilized as a hideout by armed gangs or absconders wanted for any offence;

(c) arrest, without warrant, any person who has committed a cognizable offence or against whom a reasonable suspicion exists that he has committed or is about to commit a cognizable offence and may use such force as may be necessary to effect the arrest;

(d) enter and search without warrant any premises to make any such arrest as aforesaid or to recover any person believed to be wrongfully restrained or confined or any property reasonably suspected to be stolen property or any arms, ammunition or explosive substances believed to be unlawfully kept in such premises, and may for that purpose use such force as may be necessary (GoI, 2005).

6
Conclusion

The perceived external security threat of the Indian state at her north eastern most borders, which had further aggravated since the Sino-Indian conflict in 1962, had played a very important role in formulating India's responses to the problems of the north eastern region in general and Manipur in particular. In fact, due to this state-centric security perception, Indian state has failed to appreciate the national sentiments of the Meiteis and hence denied the legitimate aspirations for statehood for a long time. The national pride of the Meiteis, who developed one of the ancient states in the Indian sub-continent, was terribly hurt when statehood had been granted to people even without having a history of state formation, for example to the Nagas, without paying any heed to their demand for the same.

An accumulated grievance of the people was further strengthened by the non-transparent process of integration of the hills of the north eastern region with the mainland India immediately after her attainment of Independence. The logic of political integration was criticized and questioned in the social discourse and challenged by the left-wing splinters who subsequently gave birth to militancy in the state. Militancy as a preferred mode of political protest was encouraged in the region in general and in Manipur in particular by Indian state's responses towards the accommodation of the Naga militancy. As taking to guns could bring the Nagas a state of their own in early 1960s, other ethno-national aspirants in the region followed the suits. With the Mizos and Meiteis started following the footprints of the Nagas, others like the Tripuris, Bodos, Kukis, Karbis, Dimasas and Hmars joined the fray later only to balkanize the whole region.

Once born, the dynamics of global power politics in general and regional politics in South Asia in particular (read politics of Indo-Pakistan rivalry), provides the necessary logistics for the sustenance of militancy often long after the corrective measures were put in place. Often the militant groups, arising out of the legitimate grievances of the people, are caught in the politics of inter-state rivalry and are played in the hands of the antagonistic foreign powers. Militancy in Manipur was directly supported by the anti-Indian powers during the 1970s and 1980s and is being supported indirectly since then through other militant intermediaries.

A full blown insurgency campaign in today's Manipur, thus, has a root in the state-centric security perception of the Indian state. In spite of the collapse of the cold war paradigm, end of bi-polarity, sea change in India's perspectives towards global strategic partnership, and acquiring the status of nuclear state, there has not been much appreciable change towards the state-centric security perception in relation to the north eastern region in general and Manipur in particular which has bartered human security in favour of territorial security. This archaic attitude of the Indian state is reflected in the denial to abrogate AFSPA in Manipur in spite of tremendous mass upsurge against this draconian Act and the recommendations of the Jeevan Reddy Commission in favour of abrogation. Thus, the first and foremost policy intervention to bring back normalcy in the state involves the complete abrogation of AFSPA and restore the dignity and honour of the people of Manipur. Indian state has to accommodate the national sentiments of the Meiteis and offer them a place of honour in the comity of Indian nationalities. Indian state has to consider out-of-the-box solutions and device alternative responses to deal with the internal security issues that will arise once AFSPA is withdrawn. We shall discuss some of the alternative policy options in this regard later.

As India needs to accommodate the aspirations of the Meitei nationalism, the Meiteis, in turn, need to accommodate the national aspirations of the Nagas and Kukis. An approach towards ethnic accommodation rather than ethnic exclusion, a multi-cultural approach towards polity management rather than mono-cultural singularity approach, an approach towards the inculcation of Manipuri identity rather than Meitei identity will only advance the cause of the peaceful co-existence of different ethno-national groups within the political boundary of the state of Manipur.

The political accommodation of the ethno-national interests may be done within the framework of the Sixth Schedule of the Indian Constitution. While the Sixth Schedule arrangement is working satisfactorily in other North Eastern states like Assam, Meghalaya, Mizoram and Tripura, there is hardly any room for apprehension on the part of the majority Meiteis that according the same status to the hills of Manipur inhabited by the Nagas and Kukis will sow the seeds of territorial disintegration of the state. Simultaneously, the Nagas and Kukis also need to accommodate the interest of the Meiteis in terms of approving the extension of the MLR and LR Act at least in the urban areas in the hills if not in the entire hill areas.

The economic accommodation may be affected through an agreed formula, preferably based on the size of the ethno-national groups, for sharing government jobs. Additional weightage should be given based on an index of backwardness while allocating development funds to the districts.

The cultural accommodation may be affected through the adoption of an agreed upon medium(s) of instruction. While territorial disintegration should not be considered as the best options, as the social spaces are increasingly becoming multi-cultural all across the globe and the nations need to learn to stay together, global experiences of accommodation may be weighed in order to make Manipur a multi-cultural habitat *a la* Malaysia or Canada.

These twin processes of accommodations, inter-regional and intra-regional, i.e., between the Indian state and Manipur as well as within Manipur, have to be supported by the process of overall economic growth and development. Stunted growth exacerbates inter-ethnic squabbles while growing economy tends to moderate them. The existence of militancy is often cited as the cause of underdevelopment. As has already been discussed, the underdeveloped economic base, in turn, contributes towards the intensification of militancy. It is, therefore, central to any policy intervention to break the vicious cycle of insurgency and underdevelopment.

At the theoretical level, the militancy can be defeated only through development. It is important to eliminate the material base of the militant ideology in the first place which acts as the motivator for joining the struggle for social justice. The issue is often confused by invoking the analogy of chicken-egg dilemma as to whether development can be affected without rooting out the menace of insurgency and hence instead of focusing on development, efforts should be made to eliminate insurgency first which will then create a congenial environment for development to thrive. We believe the debate whether development first or war on insurgency first is misplaced. As underdevelopment acts as the springboard for insurgency, a strategy of riding over insurgency devoid of development is sure to backfire. The right question is: what will be development delivery system in a conflict situation? What kind of development model will be more effective for a conflict ridden economy?

There is no ambiguity that development acts as the panacea for militancy. The central argument runs like this: creation of opportunities for the people will dry up the pipeline that feeds militancy. As more and more youths find avenues for decent living, less and less of them will be waiting on the wings to join the bandwagon of militancy. As multi-layer linkages provide a militant movement its own dynamics for sustenance, all the militant activists, it is hard to expect, will shun the path of violence at a time and then the social cost for waiting to affect development will be extremely high. Alternatively, cutting the roots of the militancy tree through the creation of opportunities for the people will cause it to dry up eventually. The roots can only be cut through affecting large scale development and ensuring that the benefits percolate down the line. Thus, economic development and growth should be the foundation and cardinal principle of anti-insurgency policy intervention in Manipur.

Let us now deal with the question of development model that we have already mentioned. As far as the experience of Manipur goes, the agency of state as an initiator and implementer has already failed. The nexus between the state and non-state actors and their high rent seeking behavior have made the present model of development ineffective. Moreover, the militancy has often become a strong bargaining tool in the hands of the local power elites to extract more funds from the centre. As a result, continuation of militancy and at times escalation of violence often become a part of the real politicking. This vicious cycle of nexus between the militant groups and local power politicking groups is also no less responsible for the perpetuation of the industry of militancy. This nexus needs to be broken in the first place. Once broken, local power elites will not have any stake in militancy and then only they can take on militancy head on. But, how we are to break it?

One of the politically viable alternative models of development which would be effective in conflict ridden Manipur is making the community based organizations (CBOs) as the agency of development. Here, the word "community" refers to village community. Wherever Panchayati Raj system is working, Gramsabha and the office of the Panchayat need to be delegated the power of implementation of the local development activities. Broad based people's committees may be organized according to the servicing areas of the development projects. At the grass root, people will decide the resource allocation and oversee the implementation of the projects. Executing agencies should be made accountable to these grass root people's committees. This will put the responsibilities for the success of the development schemes and projects directly on the people concerned who will be the beneficiaries of these development activities. This will shift the war from state versus militant groups to militant groups versus people. The target of the militants' gun would get multiplied and in the process would miss the object giving development a chance to survive.

In the hills this change in agency would rest the responsibility of development in the hands of the traditional tribal institutions, and insurgent groups then have to negotiate with them for resource mobilization. The deleterious effects of rent seeking by the militant groups on the welfare of the people would be countered by the people's bodies at the grass root instead of the state bureaucracy. Any excesses by the undergrounds will then turn them to people's enemy. The state paraphernalia will only provide the necessary logistics to these people's committees.

Coming to macro-economic strategy of development, sectoral allocation of resources needs to be done based on the criterion of job creation. The sector having higher employment elasticity should get the larger share of resources. Investment and entrepreneurial initiatives need to be promoted through the institutions of co-operatives. As the private entrepreneurial initiatives are more vulnerable in a conflict zone like Manipur, collectivized initiatives are likely to succeed. Institutional credit and government support need to be integrated with the cooperative initiatives. These cooperative organizations would act as an agency of transformation of the economy of Manipur from tradition to modernity.

People's committee of the stake holders may be formed and the management and development of common property resources may be entrusted to them. This will particularly boost the tourism sector in the economy. Management and development of social services and other public goods may be brought under the surveillance of such people's committees.

Besides the reorientation of the agency of development and restructuring the sectoral priorities which will bring the focus on the people's initiative and their gainful employment, a huge effort needs to be undertaken in order to improve the connectivity of the state with the rest of the region as well as mainland India. The real sector would not grow unless cost conditions are altered. The huge transportation cost and bottlenecks stand on the way of the growth of the real sector. The development of multi-modal connectivity calls for a huge investment which can come only from the centre.

As the centres of national market are far away, leverages from cross-border trade with Myanmar and other South East Asian countries may be utilized to the maximum extent possible. Present Indo-Myanmar trade that flows through Moreh-Tamu sector is essentially transit in nature. It is important to establish the organic link between the local economy and the cross-border trade. Production decisions at the local level need to be informed of the demand structure across the border. The integration of the planned development initiatives with the export enhancing measures needs to be chalked out.

The development model for the conflict ridden economy of Manipur outlined above should be implemented alongside a sound strategy of containment of insurgency activities in the state. A two-pronged strategy may be adopted—one dealing with the internal security situation and other dealing with the elimination of external support to the militant groups. The elements of that strategy of internal containment may be pinned down as follows.

First, at the policy level, the present military approach to the problem of insurgency should give way to political struggle and resolution. The ideology of insurgency needs to be thoroughly scrutinized, logically answered, and defeated politically. The local power elites should not shy away with conducting a polemic. They need to attain the true confidence of the masses whom they represent. Instead of sitting at the ivory tower with foolproof security and working for personal aggrandizement, they should work for and with the people and mobilize the grass root support against mode of violence to attain power.

Second, army and other paramilitary forces should not be pressed to service unless the situation relapses to a critical condition. Counter-insurgency operations should be the sole responsibility of the state police. The strength and the combat quality of the state police force may be revamped in order to enable them to discharge this responsibility. As the army is seen as the representative of the Indian state, any excesses in their operation invites backlash against the Indian state and as a consequent moral support of the people gravitates towards the militant groups. A prudent counter-insurgncy strategy should not miss this point and allow army to take care of the external security leaving the affairs of internal security in the hands of the sons of the soil.

Third, the present policy towards persuasion and surrender of the militant activists in Manipur needs to be reviewed. As has been pointed out, the policy itself motivates the unemployed youths to join the militancy as it is full of carrots and no sticks. If offenders of crimes are not punished, it sends a wrong signal to the would-be-offenders. In the name of surrender, activists can get away with any kind of offences they commit like killing and murder. Accountability has to be fixed for one's action otherwise the rule of law could not be upheld.

These internal counter-insurgency measures have to be backed up with a set of anti-corruption measures. In fact high level of corruption in public offices has been another major source of public grievances that drive many of the victims to join insurgent groups. High level of corruption also leads to acute social frustration and brings down the legitimacy of governance. In fact legitimacy of governmentality is at stake in Manipur. Poor quality of decision making, delayed state response, failure of the state organs to protect the fundamental rights and democratic values, nexus between the local power elites and the militants, failure of law and order, failure to provide basic amenities to the people, self-centric political vision of the local power elites—all have pushed legitimacy of governance to the bottom. The war against insurgency cannot be won without the resurrection of the state and legitimacy of governance. It may be reminded that the outcome of the war against militancy largely depends on the role the local power elites play in the whole containment policy. In spite of moral, financial, and military support from the centre, the counter-insurgency strategy is destined to fail if the state in Manipur, the agency, fails to chart an alternative path for its people. As the power elites at the centre neither have direct contact with nor enjoy the loyalty of the grass root people, they can only influence the governance through their local counterparts. Thus, federal mechanism has to be devised in order to assert the accountability of the local power elites as the success and failure of the war against militancy is largely determined on the role they play.

This internal counter-insurgency strategy needs to be complemented with a suitable external counter-insurgency strategy as the militant movements in the region in general and Manipur in particular draw sustenance from both the foreign state and non-state actors. Use of foreign territorial spaces particularly of Myanmar, Bangladesh and Bhutan by the forces of militancy is no secret. Aiding the insurgents in the region by the foreign agencies like Inter Service Intelligence (ISI) and ethno-national militant groups like Kachin Independence Army (KIA) and Karen National Union (KNU) are well known. These external actors provide training and safe sanctuary, and supply arms and ammunitions to the operators in the region. These links have to be broken. An active diplomacy, bilateral engagements and structured relationships with the neighbouring countries can only neutralize the foreign actors and dissect the umbilical chord that binds them.

Besides diplomatic activism to counter insurgency in the region in general and Manipur in particular, the development architecture of the region can also be designed in such a way so that the neighbouring states develop a stake in the progress of the region. As both Myanmar and Bangladesh have a long stretch of border with the north eastern region, cross-border synergies may be mobilized for inter-state development projects which will benefit people across the border. This type of initiatives would only benefit the people of the land-locked bordering areas; they also make the neighbouring states partners of development and create leverage for containing cross-border militancy.

Bibliography

Ahmed, Abu Nasar Saied, 2007, *National Security Issues: Northeast India Perspective,* Akansha Publishing House, New Delhi.

Aitchison, C. U., 1931, *A Collection of Treaties, Engagements and Sanads Relating to India and Neighbouring Countries*, Vol. XII, Government of India, Central Publication Branch, Calcutta.

Allen, B. C., 2002 (reproduced), *Gazetteer of Naga Hills and Manipur*, Mittal Publications, New Delhi.

Agricultural Census Division, Ministry of Agriculture, New Delhi, www.agcensus.nic.in.

Anand, V. K., 1980, *Conflict in Nagaland*, Chanakya Publications, Delhi.

Banerjee, A. C., 1934, *The Eastern Frontier of British India*, A. Mukherjee & Bros., Calcutta.

Barpujari, H. K., 1963, *Assam in the Days of the Company*, Lawyer's Book Stall, Gauhati.

Barpujari, H. K., 1998, *North East India: Problems, Policies and Prospects since Independence*, Spectrum Publications, Guwahati.

Bhagat, Oinam and A. Bimol Akoijam, 2002, Manipur Assembly Election: Trends and Issues, *Economic and Political Weekly*, Vol. 37, No. 6, February 9-15.

Bhattacharyya, M., 1963, *Gazetteer of Manipur*, Government of India, Calcutta.

Bhaumik, Subir, 1996, *Insurgent Crossfire: North-East India*, Lancer Publishers, New Delhi.

Bhaumik, Subir, 1997, The External Linkages in Insurgency in India's Northeast, in B. Pakem (ed.), *Insurgency in Northeast India*, Omsons Publications, New Delhi.

Bisheswar, Nameirakpam, 1986, *The Last Expression on My Death Bed*, Pax Publication, Imphal.

Brown, R., 2001 (reproduced), *Statistical Account of Manipur*, Mittal Publications, New Delhi.

Central Statistical Organisation, http://mospi.nic.in.

Chandrasekhar, Kh. and N. Sanajaoba, 1988, Ancient Meetei Written Constitution: 'Loiyamba Shinyen' (From Original Text), in N. Sanajaoba (ed.), *Manipur Past and Present*, Vol. 1, Mittal Publications, New Delhi.

Chaube, S. K., 1999 (reprint), *Hill Politics in Northeast India*, Orient Longman, New Delhi.

Collier, Paul, 2004, Development and Conflict, Centre for the Study of African Economies, Department of Economics, Oxford University, http://www.un.org/esa/documents/Development.and.Conflict2.pdf.

Commission on Human Security, 2003, *Human Security Now*, New York.

Constantine, R., 1981, *Manipur: Maid of the Mountains*, Lancer Publishers, New Delhi.

Das, Gurudas, 1997, Understanding the Insurgency Phenomenon in India's Northeast: An Analytical Framework, in B. Pakem (ed.), *Insurgency in Northeast India*, Omsons Publications, New Delhi.

Das, Gurudas, 1998, Limits to Economic Development of North Eastern Region: An Analysis of Contradictions between Economic goals and Social choices, in B. Datta Ray and Prabin Baishyaa (ed.), *Sociological Constraints to Industrial Development in North East India*, Concept Publishing Company, New Delhi.

Das, Gurudas, 2002, India's North-East Soft Underbelly: Strategic Vulnerability and Security, *Strategic Analysis*, Vol. 26 No. 4, Institute for Defence Studies and Analyses, New Delhi.

Das, Gurudas, 2002a, Armed Struggle in Nagaland: Tactics, Strategies and its Ramifications for Economic Development, in C. J. Thomas and Gurudas Das (ed.), *Dimensions of Development in Nagaland*, Regency Publications, New Delhi.

Das, Gurudas, 2005, Land in the Hills of North East India: Factor Immobility Vs Market-led Growth, in C. J. Thomas (ed.), *Polity and Economy: Agenda for Contemporary North East India*, Regency Publications, New Delhi.

Datt, Ruddar and K. P. M. Sundharam, 1996 (35th Rev. ed.), *Indian Economy*, S. Chand & Company Ltd., New Delhi.

Datta, Sreeradha, 2004, *The Northeast Complexities and its Determinants*, Shripa Publications, New Delhi.

Dev, Nirendra, 2009, *The Talking Guns: North East India*, Manas Publications, New Delhi.

Devi, Ksh. Bimola, 1988, Manipuri Women – A Study, in N. Sanajaoba (ed.), *Manipur Past and Present*, Vol. 1, Mittal Publications, New Delhi.

Devi, Ksh. Bimola, 2000, Administrative Changes in the Hill Areas of Manipur, in M. Horam (ed.), *The Rising Manipur*, Manas Publications, New Delhi.

Devi, Ksh. Bimola, 2001, The Role of Women in Manipur Politics, in C. J. Thomas, *et al.* (ed.), *Constraints in*

Development of Manipur, Regency Publications, New Delhi.

Devi, P. Binodini, 2006, *Tribal Land System of Manipur*, Centre for Manipur Studies, Manipur University and Akansha Publishing House, New Delhi.

Dun, E. W., 1981 (reproduced), *Gazetteer of Manipur*, Vivek Publishing Company, New Delhi.

Dutta, B. B., 1994, Insurgency and Economic Development in North East, in R. K. Samanta (ed.), *India's North East: The Process of Change and Development*, B. R. Publishing Corporation, Delhi.

Economic and Political Weekly Research Foundation, 2003, *Domestic Product of States of India 1960-61 to 2000-01*, Mumbai.

Egreteau, Renaud, 2003, *Wooing the Generals: India's New Burma Policy*, Authorspress, Delhi.

Egreteau, Renaud, 2006, Instability at the Gate: India's Troubled Northeast and its External Connections, CSH Occasional Paper, No. 16, www.csh-delhi.com/publications/downloads/cps/OP16.pdf.

Gangte, T. S., 1993, *The Kukis of Manipur: A Historical Analysis*, Gyan Publishing House, New Delhi.

Ghosh, B. B., 1982, *History of Nagaland*, S. Chand & Company Ltd., New Delhi.

Gopal, Krishan, 2007 (reprinted), Islamic Fundamentalism in Bangladesh and Its Role in the North-East Insurgency, in Dipankar Sengupta and Sudhir Kumar Singh (ed.), *Insurgency in North-East India: The Role of Bangladesh*, Authorspress, Delhi.

Gopalakrishnan, R. and C. J. Thomas, 2005, *Conflict to Reconstruction: Some Observations on Nagaland and Manipur*, Regency Publications, New Delhi.

Government of India, 2002, *National Human Development Report 2001*, Planning Commission, New Delhi.

Government of India, 2005, *Report of the Committee to Review the Armed Forces (Special Powers) Act, 1958*, Ministry of Home Affairs, New Delhi, www.thehindu.com.

Government of India, 2006, *Basis Statistics of North Eastern Region 2006*, Ministry of Development of NE Region, North Eastern Council, Shillong.

Government of India, 2006, *Economic Survey 2005-2006*, Ministry of Finance, Economic Division, New Delhi.

Government of India, 2006, *Household Capital Expenditure in India during 1.7.2002 to 30.6.2003: All India Debt and Investment Survey*, National Sample Survey Organisation, Ministry of Statistics and Programme Implementation, New Delhi.

Government of Manipur, 1993, *Statistical Handbook of Manipur 1992*, Directorate of Economics and Statistics, Imphal.

Government of Manipur, 1994, *An Analysis of the Performance of the State Public Sector Undertakings 1988-1993*, Planning Department, Imphal.

Government of Manipur, 1998, *Economic Review 1994-95*, Directorate of Economics and Statistics, Imphal.

Government of Manipur, 1999, *Statistical Abstract of Manipur 1998*, Directorate of Economics and Statistics, Imphal.

Government of Manipur, 2001, *Fourth Economic Census 1998 Manipur*, Directorate of Economics and Statistics, Imphal.

Government of Manipur, 2002, *Statistical Handbook of Manipur 2002*, Directorate of Economics and Statistics, Imphal.

Government of Manipur, 2004, *Economic Survey Manipur 2002-2003*, Directorate of Economics and Statistics, Imphal.

Government of Manipur, 2005, *Statistical Abstract Manipur 2004*, Directorate of Economics and Statistics, Imphal.

Government of Manipur, 2006, *Statistical Abstract Manipur 2005*, Directorate of Economics and Statistics, Imphal.

Government of Manipur, 2007, *Economic Survey Manipur 2006-07*, Directorate of Economics and Statistics, Imphal.

Government of Manipur, 2008, *Economic Survey Manipur 2007-08*, Directorate of Economics and Statistics, Imphal.

Government of Manipur, 2009, *Annual Administrative Report 2008-2009*, Directorate of Commerce and Industries, Imphal.

Government of Manipur, *Industrial Policy of Manipur 1982, 1989, 1990 and 1996*, Directorate of Commerce and Industries, Imphal.

Government of Manipur, *Manipur Today*, Various Issues, Directorate of Information and Public Relations, Imphal.

Grimwood, Ethel St. Clair, 2003 (reproduced), *My Three Years in Manipur*, Gyan Publishing House, New Delhi.

Haokip, M. Thongkhosei, 2008, Towards Overcoming Church Division in Manipur: A Perspective drawn from the Kuki people experience, www.kukiforum.com.

Haokip, P. S., 2008 (Rev. ed.), *Zale'n-gam:The Kuki Nation*, Kuki National Organisation, Zale'n-gam.

Hazarika, Sanjoy, 1995 (Rev. ed.), *Strangers of the Mist: Tales of War and Peace from India's Northeast*, Penguin Books India, New Delhi.

Hazarika, Sanjoy, 1997, Insurgency in Northeast India, in B. Pakem (ed.), *Insurgency in Northeast India*, Omsons Publications, New Delhi.

Hemanta, Sagolsem, 2007, *Khengjoi Chingsangda*, Sagolsem Hemanta, Imphal.

Hettne, Bjorn, 1988, Three Models of Peace and Development with special reference to India and Sweden, in Narindar Singh (ed.), *Peace and Development*, Lancer India and Indian Council of Social Science Research, New Delhi.

Hodson, T. C., 2007 (reproduced), *The Meitheis*, Akansha Publishing House, New Delhi.

Hodson, T. C., 2007 (reproduced), *The Naga Tribes of Manipur*, Low Price Publications, Delhi.

Horam, M., 1988, *Naga Insurgency*, Cosmo Publications, New Delhi.

Hussain, Syed Zarir, 2008, Militants in North East using Drug Money to buy Arms, *South Asia Mirrior*, April 29.

Industrial Development Bank of India, 1972, *Industrial Potential Survey Manipur*, Bombay.

Johnstone, James, 2002 (reproduced), *Manipur and the Naga Hills*, Gyan Publishing House, New Delhi.

Joshi, S. C., 2002, *Manipur: Jewel of India*, Akansha Publishing House, New Delhi.

Kabui, Gangmumei, 1988, A Note on 'Loiyamba Shinyen' (1110 A.D.) (The First Written Constitution of Manipur), in N. Sanajaoba (ed.), *Manipur Past and Present*, Vol. 1, Mittal Publications, New Delhi.

Kabui, Gangmumei, 1990, Leftist Movement and Hijam Irabot Singh, in Lal Dena (ed.), *History of Modern Manipur (1826-1949)*, Orbit Publishers & Distributors, New Delhi.

Kabui, Gangmumei, 1990, Socio-Religious Reform Movement, in Lal Dena (ed.), *History of Modern Manipur (1826-1949)*, Orbit Publishers & Distributors, New Delhi.

Kabui, Gangmumei, 1990, The Anglo-Manipur War of 1891, in Lal Dena (ed.), *History of Modern Manipur (1826-1949)*, Orbit Publishers & Distributors, New Delhi.

Kabui, Gangmumei, 1990, Zeliangrong Movement under Jadonang and Rani Gaidinliu 1930-1949, in Lal Dena (ed.), *History of Modern Manipur (1826-1949)*, Orbit Publishers & Distributors, New Delhi.

Kabui, Gangmumei, 1991, *History of Manipur*, Vol. 1, Pre-colonial period, National Publishing House, New Delhi.

Kabui, Gangmumei, 1995, Genesis of the Ethnoses of Manipur, in N. Sanajaoba (ed.), *Manipur Past and Present*, Vol. 3, Mittal Publications, New Delhi.

Kamei, Gangmumei, 2008 (2nd ed.), *Ethnicity and Social Change*, Akansha Publishing House, New Delhi.

Kamei, Gangmumei, 2006, *On History and Historiography of Manipur*, Akansha Publishing House, New Delhi.

Kipgen, Donn Morgan, 2006, The Great Betrayal: Brief Notes on Kuki Insurgency Movement, http://manipuronline.com.

Kshetri, Rajendra, 2006, *The Emergence of Meitei Nationalism*, Mittal Publication, New Delhi.

Lal Dena, 1990, Christian Proselytism 1894-1949, in Lal Dena (ed.), *History of Modern Manipur (1826-1949)*, Orbit Publishers & Distributors, New Delhi.

Lal Dena, 1990, Kuki Rebellion, 1917-1920, in Lal Dena (ed.), *History of Modern Manipur (1826-1949)*, Orbit Publishers & Distributors, New Delhi.

Lal Dena, 1990, Some Anomalies of Colonial Rule, 1891-1919, in Lal Dena (ed.), *History of Modern Manipur (1826-1949)*, Orbit Publishers & Distributors, New Delhi.

Lhungdim, Ngulkhohao, 1995, The Kuki Economy Since 1780 A.D., in N. Sanajaoba (ed.), *Manipur Past and Present*, Vol. 3, Mittal Publications, New Delhi.

Lintner, Bertil, 1994, *Burma in Revolt: Opium and Insurgency since 1948*, White Lotus, Bangkok.

Mackenzie, Alexander, 1999 (reproduced), *The North East Frontier of India*, Mittal Publications, New Delhi.

Mahendra, N., 2000, Manipurda Economic Ehou – 2, *Poknapham*, December 6, Imphal.

Manikchand, K., 1988, The Evolution of the Meitei State (A Confederacy through the Last Two Millennia), in N. Sanajaoba (ed.), *Manipur Past and Present*, Vol. 1, Mittal Publications, New Delhi.

Manipur AIDS Control Society, 2008, *Epidemiological Analysis of HIV/AIDS in Manipur*, Imphal.

McCulloch, W., 1980 (reproduced), *Valley of Manipur*, Gian Publications, New Delhi.

Misao, P., 1995, The Early Life of Kuki-Chins, in N. Sanajaoba (ed.), *Manipur Past and Present*, Vol. 3, Mittal Publications, New Delhi.

Mishra, R. C., 2000, *Security in South Asia: Cross Border Analysis*, Authorspress, Delhi.

Nag, Sajal, 2002, Naga Identity: Formation, Construction and Expansion, in C. J. Thomas and Gurudas Das (ed.), *Dimensions of Development in Nagaland*, Regency Publications, New Delhi.

Nepram, Binalakshmi, 2002, *South Asia's Fractured Frontier: Armed Conflict, Narcotics and Small Arms Proliferation in India's North East*, Mittal Publications, New Delhi.

Nepram, Binalakshmi, 2004, North East India's Long Marches: Weapon Routes and Small Arms Proliferation in India's North East, *Borderlines*, Vol. 1 No. 1.

Nibedon, Nirmal, 1981, *North East India: The Ethnic Explosion*, Lancer Publishers, New Delhi.

Nuh, V. K. and W. Lasuh, 2002, *The Naga Chronicle*, Regency Publications, New Delhi.

Pan Manipuri Youth League, *Resistance* (a weekly newspaper), Various Issues, Imphal.

Parratt, John, 2005, *Wounded Land: Politics and Identity in Modern Manipur*, Mittal Publications, New Delhi.

Parratt, Saroj Nalini Arambam, 2005, *The Court Chronicle of the Kings of Manipur: The Cheitharon Kumpapa*, Routledge, London.

Pemberton, R. B., 1966 (2nd impression), *Report on the Eastern Frontier of British India*, Department of Historical and Antiquarian Studies in Assam, Guwahati.

Phanjoubam, Pradip, 2001, Insurgency and its Impact on the Development of Manipur, in C. J. Thomas, *et al.* (ed.), *Constraints in Development of Manipur*, Regency Publications, New Delhi.

Phanjoubam, Pradip, 2005, Manipur: 'Revivalist Wave', *South Asia Intelligence Review*, Weekly Assessments and Briefings, Volume 3, No. 41, April 25, www.satp.org.

Rajmani, A. and B. B. Pradan, 1998, Sociological Constraints in the Economic Development of Manipur, in B. Datta Ray and Prabin Baishyaa (ed.), *Sociological Constraints to Industrial Development in North East India*, Concept Publishing Company, New Delhi.

Ramana, P. V., 2002, 'Networking' the Northeast: Partners in Terror, *Faultlines: Writings on Conflict and*

Resolution, Volume 11, The Institute for Conflict Management, New Delhi.

Rammohan, E. N., 2002, Manipur: A Degenerated Insurgency, *Faultlines: Writings on Conflict and Resolution*, Volume 11, The Institute for Conflict Management, New Delhi.

Ranjit, Chirom, 2004, *Unrest in Manipur*, Chirom Ranjit, Imphal.

Ray, Asok Kumar, 1990, *Authority and Legitimacy: A Study of the Thadou-Kukis in Manipur*, Renaissance Publishing House, Delhi.

Reddy, Brig. G. B., 2001, *Nation in Crisis: Dimensions of National Security and Terrorism*, Vol. 3, Authorspress, Delhi.

Revolutionary People's Front, 1999, *Memorandum*, Department of Communication and Publicity, RPF, Manipur.

Routray, B. Prasad, 2007, Manipur: The Nexus Again, *South Asia Intelligence Review*, Weekly Assessments and Briefings, Volume 6, No. 21, December 3, www.satp.org.

Routray, B. Prasad, 2007a, Manipur: No End to Despair, *South Asia Intelligence Review*, Weekly Assessments and Briefings, Volume 6, No. 14, October 15, www.satp.org.

Routray, B. Prasad, 2007b, Manipur: Extortion Rules, *South Asia Intelligence Review*, Weekly Assessments and Briefings, Volume 5, No. 49, June 18, www.satp.org.

Sachdeva, Gulshan, 2001, *Economy of the North East: Policy, Present Conditions and Future Possibilities*, Konark Publishers, New Delhi.

Sahni, Ajai, 2001, The Terrorist Economy in India's Northeast: Preliminary Explorations, *Faultlines:*

Writings on Conflict and Resolution, Volume 8, The Institute for Conflict Management, New Delhi.

Sahni, Ajai and J. George, 2001, Security and Development in India's Northeast: An Alternative Perspective, in K. P. S. Gill and Ajai Sahni (ed.), *Terror and Containment: Perspectives on India's Internal Security*, Gyan Publishing House, New Delhi.

Sanajaoba, N. (ed.), 1988, *Manipur Past and Present*, Vol. 1, Mittal Publications, New Delhi.

Sanajaoba, N. (ed.), 1993, *Manipur Treaties and Documents (1110-1971)*, Vol. 1, Mittal Publications, New Delhi.

Sanajaoba, N, 2000, Revolutionary Nationalist Party and Buffer State Ultimatum, 1953 - I, II, III and IV, *Sangai Express*, December 4, 5, 6 and 7, Imphal.

Sanajaoba, N., 2006 (2nd ed.), *Manipur Puwari: Kunmathoisubha Chahicha*, National Research Centre, Imphal.

Sema, Hokishe, 1988 (4th impression), *Emergence of Nagaland: Socio-Economic and Political Transformation and the Future*, Vikas Publishing House, New Delhi.

Sen, Amartya, 2006 (10th impression), *Development as Freedom*, Oxford University Press, New Delhi.

Shimray, R. R., 1985, *Origin and Culture of the Nagas*, Mrs. Pamleiphi Shimray, New Delhi.

Shimray, R. R., 1995, Village Communes of the Nagas, in N. Sanajaoba (ed.), *Manipur Past and Present*, Vol. 3, Mittal Publications, New Delhi.

Singh, A. Koireng, 2008, *Ethnicity and Inter-Community Conflicts: A Case of Kuki-Naga in Manipur*, Akansha Publishing House, New Delhi.

Singh, Ch. Budhi, 1988, The Ethnonym "Meitei", in N. Sanajaoba (ed.), *Manipur Past and Present*, Vol. 1, Mittal Publications, New Delhi.

Singh, Ch. Priyoranjan, 2005, Manipur's Economy: Historical Roots and Structural Evolution, *Eastern Quarterly*, Vol. III Issue III, Manipur Research Forum, Delhi.

Singh, E. Bijoykumar, 2009, Nature of Unemployment in Manipur, in E. Bijoykumar Singh and Ksh. Jhaljit Singh (ed.), *Challenges of Economic Policy in Manipur*, Vol. II, Akansha Publishing House, New Delhi.

Singh, Justice R.K. Manisana, 2000, *A Short Constitutional History of Manipur (1891-1972)*, Smt. Usha Devi, Imphal.

Singh, K. Gyanendra, 2007, Human Resource Development in Manipur: A Disclaimer, in K. S. Chakraborty and Gurudas Das (ed.), *Human Development: Experiences of North East India*, Akansha Publishing House, New Delhi.

Singh, K. Gyanendra, 2007 (unpublished), Conflict and Development: Some Issues in Manipur, paper presented at a seminar on *Conflict Study in North East India* organized by Manipur University and sponsored by Indian Institute of Advanced Studies, Shimla at Manipur University, Imphal, March 28-30.

Singh, K. Gyanendra (with Gurudas Das), 2007, Unempolyment in Manipur: Some Policy Implications, in H. Sudhir and Jubita Hajarimayum (ed.), *Dimensions of Social Issues in India's North-East: Selections on Youth, Drugs, Education and Unemployment*, Akansha Publishing House, New Delhi.

Singh, K. Gyanendra, 2009, Role of Agriculture in the Economic Development in Manipur, in Ch. Priyoranjan Singh (ed.), *Tribalism and the Tragedy of the Commons*

– *Land, Identity and Development: The Manipur Experience*, Akansha Publishing House, New Delhi.

Singh, K. Manimohan, 1989, *Hijam Irabot Singh and Political Movements in Manipur*, B. R. Publishing Corporation, New Delhi.

Singh, K. Manimohan, 1991, *History of Christian Missions in Manipur and other Neighbouring States*, Mittal Publications, New Delhi.

Singh, K. Manimohan, 2006, *Nupi Lan (Women's War of Manipur)*, K. Premlata Devi, Imphal.

Singh, L. Iboongohal, 1987 (3rd ed.), *Introduction to Manipur*, S. Ibochaoba Singh, Imphal.

Singh, L. Iboongohal and N. Khelchandra Singh (ed.), 1989 (2nd ed.), *Cheitharol Kumbaba*, Manipuri Sahitya Parishad, Imphal.

Singh, M. Iboton, 2005, Political Economy of Manipur: Transformation within the Mixed Economy Paradigm, *Eastern Quarterly*, Vol. III Issue III, Manipur Research Forum, Delhi.

Singh, N. Bhupendro, 2007, *Capital Formation in Agriculture Sector of Manipur*, Akansha Publishing House, New Delhi.

Singh, N. Joykumar, 1990, 'The First Women's Agitation 1904', in Lal Dena (ed.), *History of Modern Manipur (1826-1949)*, Orbit Publishers & Distributors, New Delhi.

Singh, N. Joykumar, 1990, The Women's Agitation 1939, in Lal Dena (ed.), *History of Modern Manipur (1826-1949)*, Orbit Publishers & Distributors, New Delhi.

Singh, N. Joykumar, 1992, *Social Movements in Manipur*, Mittal Publications, New Delhi.

Singh, N. Joykumar, 1995, The Merger of Manipur into India and the Manipur State Congress, in *Annexation of Manipur 1949*, Peoples' Democratic Movement, Manipur.

Singh, N. Joykumar, 2002, *Colonialism to Democracy: A History of Modern Manipur*, Spectrum Publications, Guwahati.

Singh, N. Joykumar, 2005, *Revolutionary Movements in Manipur*, Akansha Publishing House, New Delhi.

Singh, N. Joykumar, 2006, *Federal Party of Manipur: 1993-2000 AD*, Akansha Publishing House, New Delhi.

Singh, N. Lokendra, 1998, *The Unquiet Valley*, Mittal Publications, New Delhi.

Singh, N. Lokendra (ed.), 2004, *Land Use System in Manipur Hills*, Rajesh Publications, New Delhi.

Singh, P. Bharat, 1997, *Elections in Manipur*, P. Mirabai Devi, Imphal.

Singh, Prakash, 1995 (4th ed.), *Nagaland*, National Book Trust, New Delhi.

Singh, R. K. Jhalajit, 1992 (2nd ed.), *A Short History of Manipur*, R.K. Jhalajit Singh, Imphal.

Singh, R. P., 1981, *Electoral Politics in Manipur: A Spatio-Temporal Study*, Concept Publishing Company, New Delhi.

Singh, S. Mangi, 2006, The Kuki-Paite Clash (1997-98) in Manipur, in N. Joykumar Singh (ed.), *Ethnic Relations Among the People of North-East India*, Centre for Manipur Studies, Manipur University and Akansha Publishing House, New Delhi.

Sinha, S. K., 2001, Violence and Hope in India's Northeast, *Faultlines: Writings on Conflict and Resolution*, Volume 10, The Institute for Conflict Management, New Delhi.

Singh, T. Hemo, 2009, *Manipur Imbroglio,* Akansha Publishing House, New Delhi.

Smith, Martin, 1999 (2nd ed.), *Burma: Insurgency and the Politics of Ethnicity*, The University Press, Dhaka.

Snahal, Rajkumar, 1988, Post-Merger Political History of Manipur, in N. Sanajaoba (ed.), *Manipur Past and Present,* Vol. 1, Mittal Publications, New Delhi.

Stewart, Francis, Development and Security, Working Paper 3, Centre for Research on Inequality, Human Security and Ethnicity, CRISE, Queen Elizabeth House, University of Oxford, www.crise.ox.ac.uk/pubs/workingpaper3.pdf.

Stracey, P. D., 1968, *Nagaland Nightmare*, Allied Publishers, New Delhi.

Tarapot, Phanjoubam, 1996 (Rev. ed.), *Insurgency Movement in North Eastern India*, Vikas Publishing House, New Delhi.

Tarapot, Phanjoubam, 2005 (2nd Rev. ed.), *Bleeding Manipur*, Har-Anand Publications, New Delhi.

The Shillong Times, 2005, *Radio poll indicates fear of Corruption rather than AIDS*, Monday, November 7, Shillong.

Vaiphei, S. Prim, 1995, 'The Kukis', in N. Sanajaoba (ed.), *Manipur: Past and Present*, Vol. 3, Mittal Publications, New Delhi.

Verghese, B. G., 2004 (2nd Rev. ed.), *India's Northeast Resurgent: Ethnicity, Insurgency, Governance, Development*, Konark Publishers, New Delhi.

World Bank, 2002, The Conflict Analysis Framework: Identifying Conflict-related Obstacles to Development, Conflict Prevention and Reconstruction Unit, http://siteresources.worldbank.org.

World Bank, 2003, *Breaking the Conflict Trap: Civil War and Development Policy*, World Bank and Oxford University Press.

World Bank, 2005, Conflict Analysis Framework, Conflict Prevention and Reconstruction Unit, http://siteresources.worldbank.org.

World Bank, 2006, Effective Conflict Analysis Exercises, http://web.worldbank.org.

Yumnam, Amar, 2005, Development Experience of Manipur: A Framework for Industrialization, in Gurudas Das (ed.), *Structural Change and Strategy of Development: Resource-Industry Linkages in North East India*, Akansha Publishing House, New Delhi.

ANNEXURE - I

Agreement between His Excellency the Governor of Assam and the Manipur State Durbar, July 1, 1947

1. It was agreed that the State should forthwith declare that it joins the Constituent Assembly (Hindusthan) and that Mr. Guha should be accepted forthwith as the representative of the State as it is not practicable to have a separate representative for the State. Mr. Guha should be assisted by advisers appointed by His Highness in Council representing both the Hill and Valley areas.

2. It was agreed that there ought to be the closest relationship on a reciprocal basis between Manipur and the Indian Union.

3. It was agreed that assistance both in external defence and in internal security by the Indian Government would be necessary and the Assam Rifles should be retained in Manipur State.

4. It was agreed that in principle that reciprocal arrangements based on similar arrangements with other Indian States should be entered into with regard to the Mao-Tamu Road.

5. It was agreed that the Union Government should retain the present Post and Telegraph facilities, and also continue the supply of controlled commodities, and that no discriminatory measures should be taken in regard to the export and import of goods. It was agreed that the present arrangements regarding Extradition, Currency and exemption from Provincial Taxation on goods passing through the Province of Assam in transit to Manipur should continue.

6. It was agreed that the Union Government should appoint an Officer to be stationed in Manipur to represent that Government in these matters.

7. It was agreed that there should be the minimum of interference in the internal affairs of the State.

8. It was agreed that the Union Government should retain their Treasury here as at present, and continue the existing facilities.

9. It was agreed that the retrocession of the British Reserve should be expedited, but until alternative arrangements were made the Cantonment area, the Residency and the Political Agents' Office Compounds and the area known as Babupara, should remain under the control of the Union Government.

10. It was agreed that it is desirable that an Interim Council be formed without delay, and that the members should be appointed under the new *Administrative Rules* and should comprise the present P.M.S.D. (President, Manipur State Durbar), as Chief Minister, two senior Manipuri Members of the existing Durbar, the present Muslim Member, two members of the public to be elected by the same system as was used for the elections to the Constitution-Making Committee, and one Hill representative to be nominated under the new rules.

11. It was agreed that the new Constitution should be inaugurated within a period of one year.

12. That the question of the future payment of the Kabaw Valley compensation should be taken up with the Union.

Agreement between His Highness the Maharaja of Manipur and His Excellency the Governor of Assam, July 2, 1947

Without prejudice to whatever agreement or treaty may in due course be arrived at between the Manipur State and the Union Government and till such time as an agreement or treaty is reached with the Union Government after the new State Constitution in introduced His Highness the Maharaja in Council agrees:

a. That the *Administration Rules* introduced on July 1st, 1947, and allied measures including the *Appointment Board Rules*, the *State Courts Act* and the *Account Rules* shall continue in force after August 15th, 1947, or such date as Paramountcy may lapse and shall not be the subject of amendment except by His Highness in Council, who shall inform His Excellency the Governor of such amendment.

b. That the controls provided in the Confidential Instruction to the *Administration Rules* shall continue saving that clause (a) shall lapse on the introduction of the *Hill Regulation* and that in clause (f) it shall be provided that the State Budget shall be submitted to His Excellency for his information and advice. Further that wherever the term 'Agent to the Crown Representative' and 'Political Agent' is used in the Instruction the terms 'Agent to the Government of the Indian Union' and 'Union Agent' shall be substituted.

In addition His Highness in Council shall accept any advice tendered by His Excellency the Governor of Assam as Agent to the Government of the Indian Union in any matter concerning the State, it being understood that there shall be the minimum of interference in the internal affairs of the State.

c. That the introduction of Constitutional Government shall be expedited and that His Highness in Council shall submit proposals in this regard as early as possible to His Excellency the Agent to the Union Government for his advice.

d. That His Highness in Council shall accept an officer appointed by the Union Government and residing in the State to act as agent to His Excellency in the exercise of functions vested in His Excellency by this agreement; further whatever facilities are required by this Officer and by whatever troops may be stationed in the State shall by mutual agreement be provided.

e. The Officer of the Union Government stationed in the State may call for any records connected with a matter concerning a member of the Hill Tribes at his discretion and may issue such advice as seems necessary. Further that facilities shall be given for the Union Officer to tour in the State and that no orders shall be issued under Section 77 or 78 of the *Hill Regulation* without the prior advice of the Union Agent. Should these actions be deleted in the course of discussions this last provision will not arise.

Further that in the application of the power vested in him under this Section the Union Agent shall avoid interference in the day to day administration of the Hills.

f. That the *Hill Regulation* shall be introduced simultaneously with the *State Courts Act* and that this shall be done before August 15th, 1947.

ANNEXURE - II

Standstill Agreement

Agreement between the State of ________________ and the Dominion of India

Whereas it is to the benefit and advantage of the Dominion of India as well as of the Indian states that existing agreements and administrative arrangements in the matters of common concern, should continue for the time being, between the Dominion of India or any part thereof and the Indian states:

Now therefore it is agreed between the ______________ State and the Dominion of India that:

1. (1) Until new agreements in this behalf are made, all agreements and administrative arrangements as to matters of common concern now existing between the Crown and any Indian State shall, in so far as may be appropriate, continue as between the Dominion of India or, as the case may be, the part thereof, and the State.

   (2) In particular, and without derogation from the generality of sub clause (1) of this clause the matters referred to above shall include the matters specified in the Schedule to this Agreement.

2. Any dispute arising out of this Agreement, or out of the agreements or arrangements hereby continued, shall unless any provision is made therein for arbitration by an authority other than the Governor-General or Governor, be settled by arbitration according, as far as may be to the procedure of the Indian Arbitration Act. 1899.

3. Nothing in this Agreement include the exercise of any paramountcy functions.

_______________ State.

____

Secretary to the Government of India.

Schedule

1. Air Communications
2. Arms and equipment
3. Control of commodities
4. Currency and coinage
5. Customs
6. Indian State Forces
7. External Affairs
8. Extradition
9. Import and Export control
10. Irrigation and Electric Power
11. Motor vehicles
12. National Highways
13. Opium
14. Posts, Telegraphs and Telephones
15. Railways (including police and other arrangements in Railway lands)
16. Salt
17. Central Excises, relief from double income-tax and other arrangements relating to taxation
18. Wireless

ANNEXURE - III

Form of Instrument of Accession of Semi-Jurisdictional and Jurisdictional States

Whereas the Indian Independence Act, 1947, provides that as from the fifteenth day of August, 1947, there shall be set up an independent Dominion known as INDIA, and that the Government of India Act, 1935, shall, with such omissions, additions, adaptations and modification as the Governor-General may by order specify be applicable to the Dominion of India:

And whereas the Government of India Act, 1935, as so adapted by the Governor-General provides that an Indian State may accede to the Dominion of India by an Instrument of Accession executed by the Ruler thereof:

I ____________________ Ruler of ____________________ in the exercise of my sovereignty in and over my said State so hereby execute this my Instrument of Accession and

1. I hereby declare that I accede to the Dominion of India with the intent that the Governor-General of India, the Dominion Legislature, the Federal Court and any other Dominion authority established for the purposes of the Dominion shall, by virtue of this my Instrument of Accession but subject always to the terms thereof, and for the purposes only of the Dominion, exercise in relation to the State of ____________ (hereinafter referred to as 'this State') such function as may be vested in them by or under the Government of India Act, 1935, as in force in the Dominion of India on the 15th day of August, 1947 (which Act asa so in force is hereinafter referred to as 'the Act'); and I further declare that the Dominion of India may, through such agency or agencies, and in such manner, as it thinks fit, exercise in relation to the administration of civil and criminal justice in this State

all such powers, authority and jurisdiction as were at any time exercisable by His Majesty's representative for the exercise of the functions of the Crown in its relations with the Indian States.

2. I herby assume the obligation of ensuring that sue effect is given to the provisions of the Act within this State so far as they are applicable therein by virtue of this my Instrument of Accession.

3. Without prejudice to the provisions of paragraph 1 I accept the matters specified in the schedule here to as the matters with respect to which the Dominion Legislature may make laws for this State.

4. I hereby declare that I accede to the Dominion of India on the assurance that if an agreement is made between the Governor-General and the Ruler of this State whereby any functions in relation to the administration in this State of any law of the Dominion Legislature shall be exercised by the Ruler of this State, then any such agreement shall be deemed to form part of this Instrument and shall be construed and have effect accordingly.

5. The terms of this my Instrument of Accession shall not be varied by any amendment of the Act or of the Indian Independence Act, 1947, unless such amendment is accepted by me by an Instrument supplementary to this Instrument.

6. Nothing in this Instrument shall empower the Dominion Legislature to make any law for this State authorizing the compulsory acquisition of land for any purpose, but I hereby undertake that should the Dominion for purposes of a Dominion law which apples in this State deem it necessary to acquire any land, I will at their request acquire the land at their expense or if the land belongs to me transfer it to them on such terms as may be agreed,

or, in default of agreement, determined by an arbitrator to be appointed by the Chief Justice of India.

7. Nothing in this Instrument shall be deemed to commit me in any way to acceptance of any future constitution of India or to fetter my discretion to enter into arrangements with the Government of India under any such future constitution.

8. Nothing in this Instrument affects the continuance of my sovereignty in and over this State, or, save as provided by or under this Instrument, the exercise of any powers, authority and rights now enjoyed by me as Ruler of this State or the validity of any law at present in force in this State.

9. I hereby declare that I execute this Instrument on behalf of this State and that any reference in this Instrument to me or to Ruler of the State is to be construed as including a reference to my heirs and successors.

Given under my hand this ________________ day of August, Nineteen Hundred and Forty seven.

____

I do hereby accept this Instrument of Accession dated this _______ day of August, Nineteen Hundred and Forty seven.

____

(Governor-General of India)

The matters with respect to which the Dominion Legislature may make laws for this State:

A. Defence:

1. The naval, military and air forces of the Dominion and any other armed forces raised or maintained by the Dominion; any armed forces, including forces raised or

maintained by an Acceding State, which are attached to, or operating with, any of the armed forces of the Dominion.

2. Naval, Military and Air Force works, administration of cantonment areaas.

3. Arms; fire-arms; ammunition.

4. Explosives.

B. External Affairs:

1. External Affairs; the implementing of treaties and agreements with other countries; extradition, including the surrender of criminals and accused persons to parts of His Majesty's dominions outside India.

2. Admission into, and emigration and expulsion from, India, including in relation thereto the regulation of the movements in India of persons who are not British subjects domiciled in India or subjects of any Acceding State; pilgrimages to places beyond India.

3. Naturalization.

C. Communications:

1. Post and telegraphs, including telephones, wireless, broadcasting and other like forms of communication.

2. Federal railway, the regulation of all railways other than minor railways in respect of safety, maximum and minimum rates and fares, station and service terminal charges, interchange of traffic and the responsibility of railway administrations as carriers of goods and passengers; the regulation of minor railways in respect of safety and the responsibility of the administration of such railways as carriers of goods and passengers.

3. Maritime shipping and navigation including shipping navigation on tidal waters, Admiralty jurisdiction.

4. Port quarantine.
5. Major ports, that is to say, the declaration and delimitation of such ports, and the constitution and powers of Port Authorities therein.
6. Aircraft and air navigation, the provision of aerodromes; regulation and organization of air traffic and of aerodromes.
7. Lighthouses, including lightships, beacons and other provisions for the safety of shipping and aircraft.
8. Carriage of passengers and goods by sea or by air.
9. Extension of powers and jurisdiction of members of the police force belonging to any unit to railway area outside that unit.

D. Ancillary:

1. Elections to the Dominion Legislature, subject to the provisions of the Act and of any Order made there under.
2. Offences against laws with respect to any of the aforesaid matters.
3. Inquiries and statistics for the purposes of any of the aforesaid matters.
4. Jurisdiction and powers of all courts with respect to any of the aforesaid matters but, except with the consent of the Ruler of the Acceding State, not so as to confer any jurisdiction or powers upon any courts other than courts ordinarily exercising jurisdiction in or in relation to that state.

ANNEXURE - IV

Merger Agreement

Whereas in the best interests of the State of Manipur as well as the Dominion of India it is desirable to provide for administration of the said state by or under the authority of the Dominion Government:

It is hereby agreed as follows:

Article I

His Highness the Maharaja of Manipur herby cedes to the Dominion Government full and exclusive authority, jurisdiction and powers for and in relation to the governance of the State and agrees to transfer the State to the Dominion Government on the fifteenth day of October 1949.

As from the said day the Dominion Government will be competent to exercise the said powers, authority and jurisdiction in such manner and through such agency as it may think fit.

Article II

His Highness the Maharaja shall continue to enjoy the same personal rights, privileges, dignities, titles, authority over religious observance, customs, usages, rites and ceremonies and institutions in charge of the same in the State, which he would have enjoyed had this agreement not been made.

Article III

His Highness the Maharaja shall with effect from the said day be entitled to receive for his lifetime from the revenues of the State annually for his Privy Purse the sum of rupees three lakhs free of taxes.

This amount is intended to cover all the expenses of the Ruler and his family, including expenses on account of his personal staff and armed guards, maintenance of his residences, marriages and other ceremonies, etc. and the allowances to the ruler's relations who on the date of execution of this agreement were in receipt of such allowances from the revenues of the State and will neither be increased nor reduced for any reason whatsoever.

The Government of India undertake that the said sum of rupees three lakhs shall be paid to His Highness the Maharaja in four equal installments in advance at the beginning of each quarter from the State treasury or at such other treasury as may be specified by the Government of India.

Article IV

His Highness the Maharaja shall be entitled to the full ownership, use and enjoyment of all private properties (as distinct from State properties) belonging to him on the date of agreement.

His Highness the Maharaja will furnish to the Dominion Government before the first January 1950 an inventory of all the immovable property, security and cash balance held by him as such private property:

If any dispute arises as to whether any item of property is the private property of His Highness the Maharaja or state property, it shall be referred to judicial officer qualified to be appointed as a High Court Judge, and the decision of that officer shall be final and binding on both parties:

Provided that His Highness the Maharaja's right to use of the residences known as 'Redlands' and "Les Chatalettes' in Shillong, and the property in the town of Gauhati known as 'Manipur Basti' shall not be questioned.

Article V

All the members of His Highness' family shall be entitled

to all the personal rights, privileges, dignities and titles enjoyed by them whether within or outside the territories of the State, immediately before the fifteenth August, 1947.

Article VI

The Dominion Government guarantees the succession, according to law and custom, to the gaddi of the State and to His Highness, the Maharaja's personal rights, privileges, dignities, titles, authority over religious observances, customs, usages, rites and ceremonies and institutions in charge of the same in the State.

Article VII

No enquiry shall be made by or under the authority of the Government of India, and no proceedings shall lie in any court in Manipur, against His Highness the Maharaja whether in a personal capacity or otherwise in respect of anything done or omitted to be done by him or under his authority during the period of his administration of that State.

Article VIII

The Government of India hereby guarantees either the continuance in service of the permanent members of the Public Services of Manipur on conditions which will be not less advantageous than those on which they are serving before the date on which the administration of Manipur is made over to the Government of India or the payment of reasonable compensation.

The Government of India further guarantees the continuance of pensions and leaves salaries sanctioned by His Highness the Maharaja to servants of the State who have retired or proceeded on leave preparatory to retirement; before the date on which the administration of Manipur is made over to the Government of India.

The Government of India also undertake to make suitable provisions for the employment of Manipuris in the various branches of Public services; and in every way encourage Manipuris to join them. They also undertake to preserve various laws, customs and conventions prevailing in the State pertaining to social, economic and religious life of the people.

Article IX

Except with the previous sanction of the Government of India no proceedings, civil or criminal, shall be instituted against any person in respect of any act done or purporting to be done in the execution of his duties as a servant of the State before the day on which the administration is made over to the Government of India.

ANNEXURE - V

Revenue Receipts of Manipur (Rs.)

Categories	1893	1901	1902	1903	1904
Land revenue	124382	249944	253967	220997	276573
Foreigner's tax		4429	4228	4281	5730
Hill house tax	30721	52609	63566	51294	45742
Fisheries	14522	27892	29072	28080	23794
Salt revenue	13265	6976	8539	6527	5829
Forests	4037	32427	25497	20093	26051
Others	27969	7279	4922	7660	5404
Total Revenue	214896	381556	389791	338932	389123

Source: Allen, 2002: 139.

ANNEXURE - VI

Five Year Plan Outlay and Expenditure in Manipur (1st – 4th Plan)

(Rs. in Lakhs)

Head of Development	*1st Plan (1951-56)*		*2nd Plan (1956-61)*		*3rd Plan (1961-66)*		*4th Plan (1969-74)*	
	Outlay	*Exp.*	*Outlay*	*Exp.*	*Outlay*	*Exp.*	*Outlay*	*Exp.*
Agriculture &	6.30	4.33	109.51	96.25	190.97	161.77	356.42	370.40
allied services	(4.07)	(4.22)	(17.52)	(16.12)	(14.83)	(12.63)	(11.78)	(11.95)
Co-operation	0.40	0.03	12.11	11.34	18.21	22.54	50.58	45.60
	(0.26)	(0.03)	(1.93)	(1.90)	(1.41)	(1.76)	(1.67)	(1.47)
Water & power	12.00	4.29	45.00	41.82	118.37	58.56	424.88	384.00
development	(7.75)	(4.18)	(7.20)	(7.01)	(9.19)	(4.57)	(14.05)	(12.39)
Industry &	0.60	0.68	13.06	12.08	49.39	35.28	117.22	215.00
mining	(0.38)	(0.66)	(2.09)	(2.02)	(3.84)	(2.75)	(3.88)	(6.93)
Transport &	91.89	74.17	215.46	208.90	441.00	503.23	1170.85	1260.00
communication	(59.33)	(72.33)	(34.47)	(34.99)	(34.25)	(39.28)	(38.71)	(40.65)
Social &	43.70	19.06	229.35	225.93	467.87	491.87	897.05	813.51
community ser	(28.21)	(18.58)	(36.69)	(37.85)	(36.34)	(38.39)	(29.65)	(26.24)
Economic services			0.62	0.61	1.75	8.03	8.00	11.49
			(0.10)	(0.11)	(0.14)	(0.62)	(0.26)	(0.37)
Total	154.89	102.56	625.11	596.93	1287.56	1281.28	3025.00	3100.00

Source: Statistical Handbook of Manipur 1992

Note: Value in parentheses shows the percentage share to total.

ANNEXURE - VII

Five Year Plan Outlay and Expenditure in Manipur (5th – 6th Plan)

(Rs. in Lakhs)

Head of Development	*5th Plan (1974-78)*		*6th Plan (1980-85)*	
	Outlay	*Exp.*	*Outlay*	*Exp.*
Agriculture &	1635.00	1069.81	4361.00	4550.83
allied services	(17.61)	(16.06)	(17.68)	(18.72)
Co-operation	126.00 (1.36)	84.69 (1.27)	178.00 (0.72)	192.00 (0.79)
Water & power development	2862.00 (30.82)	2056.78 (30.87)	6356.00 (25.77)	6210.12 (25.54)
Industry & mining	691.00 (7.44)	474.76 (7.13)	1498.00 (6.07)	1352.44 (5.56)
Transport & communication	1876.00 (20.20)	1480.60 (22.22)	3517.00 (14.25)	3706.51 (15.25)
Social & community ser.	1694.00 (18.24)	1230.92 (18.48)	7973.00 (32.33)	7410.26 (30.48)
Economic services	63.00 (0.68)	38.25 (0.57)	218.00 (0.88)	203.27 (0.84)
General services	339.00 (3.65)	226.10 (3.40)	564.00 (2.30)	686.89 (2.82)
Total	9286.00	6661.91	24665.00	24312.32

Source: Statistical Handbook of Manipur 1992
Note: Value in parentheses shows the percentage share to total.

ANNEXURE - VIII

Five Year Plan Outlay and Expenditure in Manipur (7th – 9th Plan)

(Rs. in Lakhs)

Head of Development	*7th Plan (1985-90)*		*8th Plan (1992-97)*		*9th Plan (1997-2002)*	
	Outlay	*Exp.*	*Outlay*	*Exp.*	*Outlay*	*Exp.*
1	*2*	*3*	*4*	*5*	*6*	*7*
Agri-culture & allied services	5660.00 (13.16)	6370.42 (12.62)	9149.00 (9.35)	11290.05 (9.22)	18317.00 (7.55)	9497.50 (5.14)
Rural development	1435.00 (3.34)	1562.20 (3.09)	1450.00 (1.48)	4525.19 (3.70)	6120.00 (2.52)	8146.78 (4.41)
Special area programme	-	-	-	-	-	675.78 (0.37)
Irrigation & flood control	7800.00 (18.14)	9157.69 (18.14)	17700.00 (18.08)	20550.21 (16.78)	32060.00 (13.21)	24153.96 (13.07)
Energy	3642.00 (8.47)	4974.66 (9.85)	18745.00 (19.15)	18437.49 (15.06)	33534.00 (13.82)	35893.96 (19.42)
Industry & mining	2410.00 (5.60)	2759.16 (5.47)	3980.00 (4.07)	5281.11 (4.31)	12651.00 (5.21)	9406.86 (5.09)
Transport	7150.00 (16.63)	7466.83 (14.79)	16060.00 (16.40)	20111.14 (16.42)	39968.00 (16.47)	25638.15 (13.87)
Comm-unication	-	-	-	-	-	-

(Contd...)

1	2	3	4	5	6	7
Science, tech. & environment	250.00 (0.58)	233.67 (0.46)	500.00 (0.51)	490.02 (0.40)	900.00 (0.37)	616.63 (0.30)
General economic serv.	916.00 (2.13)	838.72 (1.66)	1694.00 (1.73)	2129.59 (1.74)	13367.00 (5.51)	4575.68 (2.48)
Social services	12687.00 (29.50)	15019.50 (29.75)	26040.00 (26.60)	36269.64 (29.62)	56964.00 (23.47)	62278.33 (33.69)
General services	1050.00 (2.45)	2102.84 (4.17)	2582.00 (2.64)	3366.53 (2.75)	28788.00 (11.86)	3981.47 (2.15)
Total	43000.00	50485.69	97900.00	122450.97	242669.00	184865.10

Source: Statistical Handbook of Manipur 1992; Statistical Abstract Manipur 2005

Note: Value in parentheses shows the percentage share to total.

ANNEXURE - IX

Five Year Plan Outlay and Expenditure in Manipur (10th – 11th Plan)

(Rs. in Crores)

Head of Development	*10th Plan (2002-07)*		*11th Plan (2007-12)*
	Projected Outlay	*Actual Expenditure*	*Projected Outlay*
Agriculture & allied services	96.42 (3.44)	97.07 (3.47)	385.95 (4.73)
Rural development	81.98 (2.92)	142.06 (5.08)	192.79 (2.36)
Special area programme	22.88 (0.82)	95.10 (3.40)	347.24 (4.26)
Irrigation & flood control	368.54 (13.14)	465.82 (16.65)	772.38 (9.47)
Energy	236.22 (8.42)	187.19 (6.69)	1505.20 (18.46)
Industry & mining	332.94 (11.87)	164.84 (5.89)	656.14 (8.05)
Transport	223.48 (7.97)	263.32 (9.41)	403.16 (4.94)
Communication	-	-	-
Science, tech. & environment	34.65 (1.24)	48.55 (1.74)	180.91 (2.22)
General economic serv.	295.22 (10.53)	69.58 (2.49)	157.98 (1.94)
Social services	1015.22 (36.21)	1062.96 (37.99)	3229.27 (39.60)
General services	96.45 (3.44)	201.28 (7.19)	322.98 (3.97)
Total	2804.00	2797.77	8154.00

Source: Economic Survey Manipur 2007-08

Note: Value in parentheses shows the percentage share to total.

ANNEXURE - X

Percentage share of various components in Primary Sector in India

Year	*Agriculture*	*Forestry & Logging*	*Fishing*	*Mining & Quarrying*
1961	86.95	7.68	2.16	3.21
1970	85.10	8.31	2.47	4.12
1980	84.94	7.35	2.98	4.73
1990	85.42	4.83	3.28	6.47
2000	85.29	3.77	3.75	7.21
2005	84.08	3.74	3.63	8.55
2006	84.39	3.60	3.60	8.41
2007	84.38	3.53	3.55	8.54

Source: Calculated from CSO.

ANNEXURE - XI

Secondary Sector and its components in NDP in India (% share)

Year	Manufacturing			Construction	Electricity, Gas & Water Supply
	Regd.	Unregd.	Total		
1961	28.06	35.43	63.49	34.03	2.48
1970	29.69	30.39	60.08	36.45	3.47
1980	31.40	33.50	64.90	30.81	4.29
1990	39.25	26.10	65.35	28.98	5.55
2000	39.14	23.50	62.64	30.04	7.32
2005	39.75	20.71	60.46	33.30	6.24
2006	38.86	20.20	59.06	35.08	5.86
2007	38.91	20.25	59.16	35.26	5.58

Source: Calculated from CSO.

ANNEXURE - XII

Tertiary Sector and its components in NDP in India (% share)

Year	*Transport, Storage & Communication*	*Trade, Hotels & Restaurants*	*Banking & Insurance*	*Real Estate, Ownership & Business Services*	*Public Administration*	*Others*
1961	10.17	33.73	4.90	13.98	10.44	26.78
1970	11.90	33.48	5.52	11.67	12.87	24.57
1980	13.65	32.73	7.38	10.49	14.18	21.57
1990	12.97	30.32	10.34	13.81	14.39	18.17
2000	13.22	30.42	12.57	13.57	13.11	17.11
2005	17.68	30.97	11.62	12.96	10.60	16.17
2006	18.56	30.67	12.04	12.79	10.33	15.61
2007	19.72	29.89	12.99	12.55	9.77	15.08

Source: Calculated from CSO.

Index

■■■